Linux
Reversing
Disassembly
Reconstruction
Accelerated

Second Edition

Dmitry Vostokov
Software Diagnostics Services

Published by OpenTask, Republic of Ireland

OpenTask books and magazines are available through booksellers and distributors worldwide. For further information or comments, send requests to press@opentask.com.

A CIP catalog record for this book is available from the British Library.

ISBN-l3: 978-1-912636-74-7 (Paperback)

Revision 2.01 (March 2023)

Contents

About the Author

Dmitry Vostokov is an internationally recognized expert, speaker, educator, scientist, inventor, and author. He is the founder of the pattern-oriented software diagnostics, forensics, and prognostics discipline (Systematic Software Diagnostics), and Software Diagnostics Institute (DA+TA: DumpAnalysis.org + TraceAnalysis.org). Vostokov has also authored more than 50 books on software diagnostics, anomaly detection and analysis, software and memory forensics, root cause analysis and problem solving, memory dump analysis, debugging, software trace and log analysis, reverse engineering, and malware analysis. He has over 25 years of experience in software architecture, design, development, and maintenance in various industries, including leadership, technical, and people management roles. Dmitry also founded Syndromatix, Anolog.io, BriteTrace, DiaThings, Logtellect, OpenTask Iterative and Incremental Publishing (OpenTask.com), Software Diagnostics Technology and Services (former Memory Dump Analysis Services) PatternDiagnostics.com, and Software Prognostics. In his spare time, he presents various topics on Debugging.TV and explores Software Narratology, its further development as Narratology of Things and Diagnostics of Things (DoT), Software Pathology, and Quantum Software Diagnostics. His current interest areas are theoretical software diagnostics and its mathematical and computer science foundations, application of formal logic, artificial intelligence, machine learning and data mining to diagnostics and anomaly detection, software diagnostics engineering and diagnostics-driven development, diagnostics workflow and interaction. Recent interest areas also include cloud native computing, security, automation, functional programming, applications of category theory to software diagnostics, development and big data, and diagnostics of artificial intelligence.

Presentation Slides and Transcript

Linux
Reversing
Disassembly
Reconstruction

Accelerated

Second Edition

Dmitry Vostokov
Software Diagnostics Services

Hello, everyone, my name is Dmitry Vostokov, and I teach this training course. In the beginning, we go through a few introductory slides.

Prerequisites

- ⊙ Working C or classic C++ knowledge

- ⊙ Basic assembly language knowledge

To get most of this training, you are expected to have working C or C++ knowledge. Assembly language knowledge is not necessary as all constructs are explained, but if you can read assembly language, it helps. If you still have difficulty understanding, please refer to the **Foundations of Linux Debugging, Disassembling, and Reversing**[1] and **Foundations of ARM64 Linux Debugging, Disassembling, and Reversing**[2] books, which have many helpful diagrams.

---

[1] https://www.patterndiagnostics.com/practical-foundations-linux-debugging-disassembling-reversing
[2] https://www.patterndiagnostics.com/practical-foundations-arm64-linux-debugging-disassembling-reversing

Audience

- ⊚ **Novices**

  Improve x64 (x86_64, AMD64) and A64 (AArch64, ARM64) assembly language knowledge

- ⊚ **Experts**

  Learn the new pattern language approach

Novices learn a few bits of x64 and ARM64 assembly languages or refresh rusty old-time assembly language knowledge in the new 64-bit context. Experts learn the new pattern language approach. Both audiences also learn a new helper and teaching device called memory cell diagrams.

Pattern-Oriented RDR

- ⊙ Complex crashes and hangs (<u>victimware</u> analysis)

- ⊙ Malware analysis

- ⊙ Studying new products

Why does the course name include Reversing, Disassembly, and Reconstruction all at once? This is because all of these are necessary when analyzing complex software incidents that involve victimware[3] or malware analysis, or both, or studying new products. We introduce here a systematic pattern-oriented approach vs. traditional case-study-based reverse engineering teaching.

---

[3] https://www.patterndiagnostics.com/files/Victimware.pdf

Training Goals

- ⊚ Review fundamentals

- ⊚ Learn patterns and techniques

Our primary goal is to learn reversing, disassembly, and reconstruction in an accelerated fashion. So first, we review essential fundamental theory. Then we learn how to use the GDB debugger and, in the process, learn various patterns and techniques.

Training Principles

- ◉ Talk only about what I can show

- ◉ Lots of pictures

- ◉ Lots of examples

- ◉ Original content and examples

For me, there were many training formats to consider, and I decided that the best way is to concentrate on hands-on exercises. Specifically, for this training, I developed 12 of them (6 for each platform).

Course Idea

- Accelerated Linux Core Dump Analysis, Third Edition (x64 and A64)

- Accelerated Disassembly, Reconstruction and Reversing, Second Edition, Revised and Extended (Windows x64)

I took this course idea from an existing Windows course[4] that extended the corresponding Practical Foundations book. The Linux version of the course complements the Accelerated Linux Core Dump Analysis[5] training course.

---

[4] https://www.patterndiagnostics.com/accelerated-disassembly-reconstruction-reversing-book
[5] https://www.patterndiagnostics.com/accelerated-linux-core-dump-analysis

15

Part 1: Theory

Now I show a few theoretical slides to explain the pattern-oriented approach.

Computation

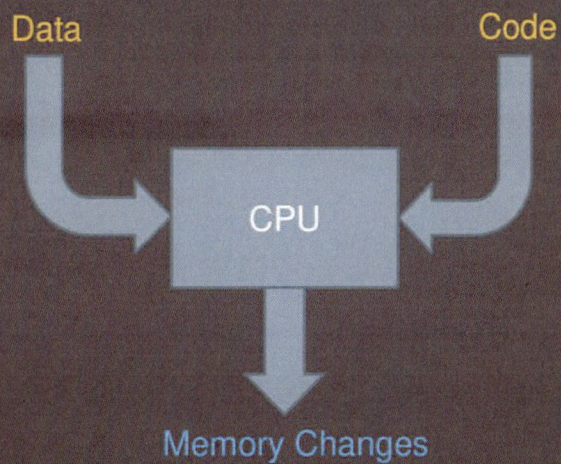

This diagram helps us to come up with a general reversing approach. Data and Code are processed in a CPU, resulting in memory changes.

Disassembly

Data/Code numbers

Data/Code symbolic

```
48 8d 05 a1 b4 07 00    lea    0x7b4a1(%rip),%rax       # 0x47d004
48 89 05 36 68 0a 00    mov    %rax,0xa6836(%rip)       # 0x4a83a0 <name>


                 e0 53 00 91    add    x0, sp, #0x14
                 e0 0f 00 f9    str    x0, [sp, #24]
```

Annotated Disassembly memory analysis pattern

Now a few words about disassembly. It is a process of converting code/data numbers into a symbolic representation. The latter can have various degrees of sophistication, depending on the tool. GDB disassembly output is simple, although it can annotate such code with additional comments that help in understanding (we originally introduced **Annotated Disassembly** memory analysis pattern for Windows with WinDbg SOS extension example[6]).

---

[6] https://www.dumpanalysis.org/blog/index.php/2011/10/13/crash-dump-analysis-patterns-part-151/

The Problem of Reversing

- Compilation to **M**achine Language$_M$

$$Language_1 \implies Language_M \impliedby Language_2$$

- Decompilation

$$Language_M \implies ?$$

Two different high-level programming languages or different code constructs in one language can be translated (compiled) into the same machine language code fragment. Therefore, the reverse process of decompilation (or reversing) is ambiguous or difficult to comprehend.

The Solution to Reversing

- **M**emory Language$_M$ Semantics

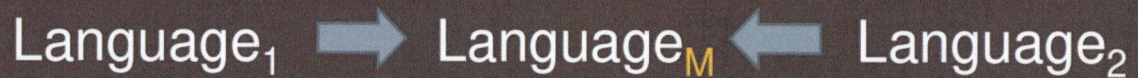

Language$_1$ ➡ Language$_M$ ⬅ Language$_2$

- Decompilation

Understanding of Language$_M$

The proposed solution is to think of memory. When coding in high-level languages, always think about the memory semantics of the underlying high-level language constructs and code. The reverse process then is to analyze low-level code with the same memory semantics.

The Reversing Tool

Memory Cell Diagrams

Idea when reading The Mathematical Structure of Classical and Relativistic Physics: A General Classification Diagram book

To facilitate memory thinking and to aid the complex reversing process (which complexity, of course, depends on the expertise and the length of practice), we introduce the teaching device called memory cell diagrams. They are gradually introduced in exercises, but for now, there is an example in this slide. As a side note, this idea arose when reading *The Mathematical Structure of Classical and Relativistic Physics: A General Classification Diagram* book.

Re(De)construction

⊙ Time dimension: sequence diagrams

⊙ Space dimension: component diagrams

How does it work temporally and structurally?

Deconstruction or Reconstruction helps in understanding how software products and operating systems work. An excellent example here is software internals, or when you support software but don't have much data from engineering. Here **Execution Residue** (see the corresponding section at the end of this book) and **Historical Information** memory analysis patterns help. Live debugging techniques such as tracing or Time Travel help with a time dimension, and memory dump analysis helps with a space dimension.

ADDR Patterns

- ⊙ **A**ccelerated

- ⊙ **D**isassembly patterns

- ⊙ **D**e(Re)construction patterns

- ⊙ **R**eversing patterns

Originally conceived as just patterns of disassembly such as function prolog and epilog and introduced in Windows Debugging: Practical Foundations book (now also available in Practical Foundations of Windows Debugging, Disassembling, Reversing training course). However, it is sometimes difficult to classify a particular pattern as a reversing or disassembly pattern, so we grouped them into one unified category called ADDR patterns. Notice a hint of memory addressing in this name.

Practical Foundations of Windows Debugging, Disassembling, Reversing, Second Edition:
https://www.patterndiagnostics.com/practical-foundations-windows-debugging-disassembling-reversing

ADDR Patterns (II)

- **A**ccelerated

- **D**isassembly patterns

- **D**ecompilation patterns

- **R**econstruction patterns

Here's another breakdown of the ADDR abbreviation.

ADDR Schemas

- Function Prologue → Function Epilogue

- Call Prologue → Function Call → Call Epilogue

- Potential Functionality → Call Skeleton → Call Path

- Call Parameter → Function Parameter → Local Variable

The so-called ADDR schemas combine various ADDR patterns to aid in reversing and reconstruction.

ADDR Implementations

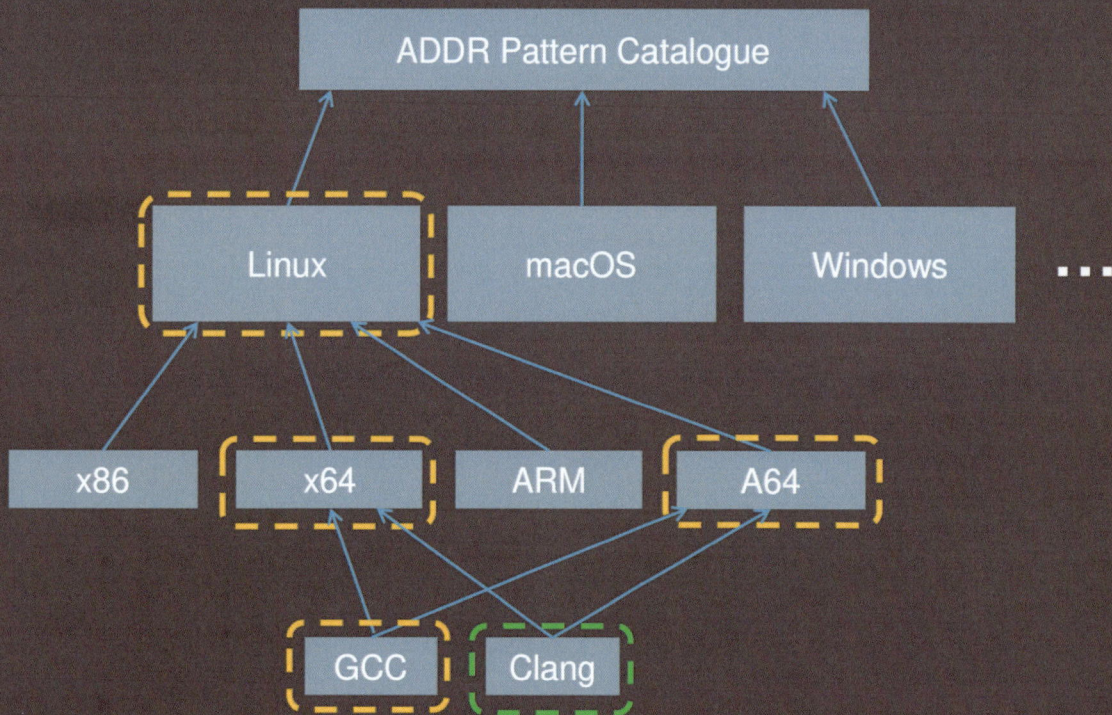

ADDR patterns are general due to the same underlying computation and compilation principles across diverse platforms and tools. However, different implementations (or descriptive pattern examples) are possible for each OS platform and associated compiler and debugging tools. In this training, we are concerned with Linux, GCC/G++, Clang/Clang++, and GDB. Of course, WinDbg and Visual C++ compiler examples would be different for Windows, but the underlying pattern-oriented principles would be the same.

Pattern Catalogues

- Elementary Software Diagnostics Patterns
- Memory Analysis Patterns
- Trace and Log Analysis Patterns
- Unified Debugging Patterns
- ADDR Patterns

© 2023 Software Diagnostics Services

In our past training courses, we introduced various pattern catalogs. So, in this training, we add an ADDR pattern catalog.

Elementary Software Diagnostics Patterns
https://www.dumpanalysis.org/elementary-diagnostics-patterns

Memory Analysis Patterns
https://www.patterndiagnostics.com/encyclopedia-crash-dump-analysis-patterns

Trace and Log Analysis Patterns
https://www.patterndiagnostics.com/trace-log-analysis-pattern-reference

Unified Debugging Patterns
https://www.dumpanalysis.org/pattern-oriented-debugging-process

Pattern Orientation

- Pattern-Driven ADDR

- Pattern-Based ADDR

In all our seminars, we split the pattern-oriented process into two main constituents. The pattern-driven part is about the actual software diagnostics and debugging process. The pattern-based part is about pattern catalog evolution because patterns are continuously refined, and new patterns are added.

x64 Disassembly

Part 2: x64 Disassembly

Now we come to a brief overview of relevant x64 disassembly. We only cover what we would see in the exercises.

CPU Registers (x64)

Illustrated in memory cell diagrams: \ADDR-Linux\MCD-R1-x64.xlsx

- ◉ **RAX ⊃ EAX ⊃ AX ⊇ {AH, AL}** | **RAX 64-bit** | **EAX 32-bit** |

- ◉ ALU: **RAX, RDX**

- ◉ Counter: **RCX**

- ◉ Memory copy: **RSI** (src), **RDI** (dst)

- ◉ Stack: **RSP, RBP**

- ◉ Next instruction: **RIP**

- ◉ New: **R8 – R15, Rx(D|W|L)**

© 2023 Software Diagnostics Services

There are familiar 32-bit CPU register names, such as **EAX,** that are extended to 64-bit names, such as **RAX**. Most of them are traditionally specialized, such as ALU, counter, and memory copy registers. Although, now they all can be used as general-purpose registers. There is, of course, a stack pointer, **RSP**, and, additionally, a frame pointer, **RBP**, that is used to address local variables and saved parameters. It can be used for backtrace reconstruction. In some compiler code generation implementations, **RBP** is also used as a general-purpose register, with **RSP** taking the role of a frame pointer. An instruction pointer RIP is saved in the stack memory region with every function call, then restored on return from the called function. In addition, the x64 platform features another eight general-purpose registers, from **R8** to **R15**.

Instructions: registers (x64)

- Opcode SRC, DST # default AT&T flavour

- Examples:

```
mov    $0x10, %rax          # 0x10 → RAX
mov    %rsp, %rbp           # RSP → RBP
add    $0x10, %r10          # R10 + 0x10 → R10
imul   %ecx, %edx           # ECX * EDX → EDX
callq  *%rdx                # RDX already contains
                            #    the address of func (&func)
                            # PUSH RIP; &func → RIP
sub    $0x30, %rsp          # RSP-0x30 → RSP
                            # make a room for local variables
```

This slide shows a few examples of CPU instructions involving operations with registers, such as moving a value and doing arithmetic. The direction of operands is opposite to the Intel x64 disassembly flavor if you are accustomed to WinDbg on Windows. It is possible to use the Intel disassembly flavor in GDB, but we opted for the default AT&T flavor in line with our **Accelerated Linux Core Dump Analysis** book.

Memory and Stack Addressing

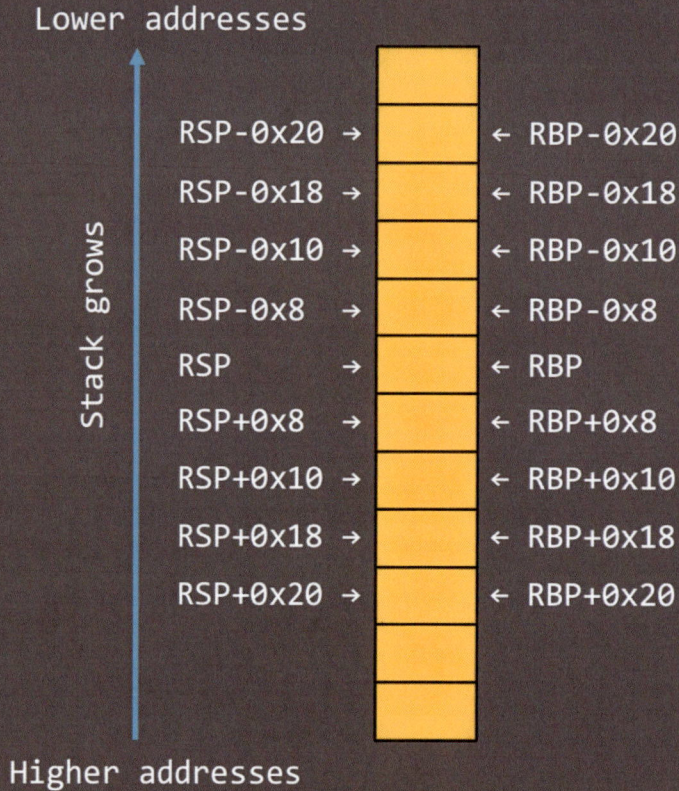

Lower addresses

Stack grows

RSP-0x20 →	← RBP-0x20
RSP-0x18 →	← RBP-0x18
RSP-0x10 →	← RBP-0x10
RSP-0x8 →	← RBP-0x8
RSP →	← RBP
RSP+0x8 →	← RBP+0x8
RSP+0x10 →	← RBP+0x10
RSP+0x18 →	← RBP+0x18
RSP+0x20 →	← RBP+0x20

Higher addresses

Before we look at operations with memory, let's look at a graphical representation of memory addressing. A thread stack is just any other memory region, so instead of **RSP** and **RBP,** any other register can be used. Please note that stack grows towards lower addresses, so to access the previously pushed values, you need to use positive offsets from **RSP**.

34

Instructions: memory load (x64)

- Opcode Offset(SRC), DST

- Opcode DST

- Examples:

```
mov    0x10(%rsp), %rax      # value at address RSP+0x10 → RAX
mov    -0x10(%rbp), %rcx     # value at address RBP-0x10 → RCX
add    (%rax), %rdx          # RDX + value at address RAX → RDX
pop    %rdi                  # value at address RSP → RDI
                            # RSP + 8 → RSP
lea    0x20(%rbp), %r8       # address RBP+0x20 → R8
```

Constants are encoded in instructions, but if we need arbitrary values, we must get them from memory. Round brackets show memory access relative to an address stored in some register.

Instructions: memory store (x64)

◉ Opcode SRC, Offset(DST)

◉ Opcode SRC|DST

◉ Examples:

```
mov    %rcx, -0x20(%rbp)        # RCX → value at address RBP-0x20
addl   $1, (%rax)               # 1 + 32-bit value at address RAX →
                                #      32-bit value at address RAX
push   %rsi                     # RSP - 8 → RSP
                                # RSI → value at address RSP
inc    (%rcx)                   # 1 + value at address RCX →
                                #      value at address RCX
```

Storing is similar to loading.

Instructions: flow (x64)

⊙ **Opcode** DST

⊙ Examples:

```
jmp     0x10493fc1c      # 0x10493fc1c → RIP
                         # (goto 0x10493fc1c)


call    0x10493ff74      # RSP – 8 → RSP
0x10493fc14:             # 0x10493fc14 → value at address RSP
                         # 0x10493ff74 → RIP
                         # (goto 0x10493ff74)
```

Goto (an unconditional jump) is implemented via the **JMP** instruction. Function calls are implemented via **CALL** instruction. For conditional branches, please look at the official Intel documentation. We don't use these instructions in our exercises.

Function Call and Prolog (x64)

```
# void proc(int p1, long p2);
mov  $0x1, %edi
mov  $0x2, %rsi
call proc
addr:

# void proc2();
# void proc(int p1, long p2) {
#    long local = 0;
#    proc2();
# }
proc:
push %rbp
mov  %rsp, %rbp
sub  $0x8, %rsp
mov  $0, -0x8(%rbp)
call proc2
adr2:
...
```

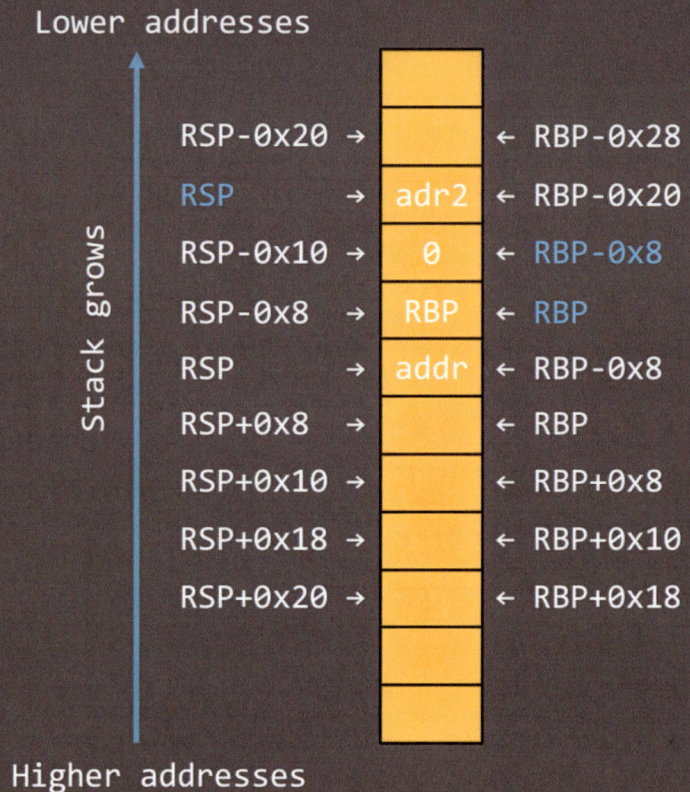

Lower addresses

Stack grows

RSP-0x20 →		← RBP-0x28
RSP	→ adr2	← RBP-0x20
RSP-0x10 →	0	← RBP-0x8
RSP-0x8 →	RBP	← RBP
RSP	→ addr	← RBP-0x8
RSP+0x8 →		← RBP
RSP+0x10 →		← RBP+0x8
RSP+0x18 →		← RBP+0x10
RSP+0x20 →		← RBP+0x18

Higher addresses

When a function is called from the caller, a callee needs to do certain operations to make room for local variables on the thread stack. There are different ways to do that, and the assembly language code on the left is one of them. I use a different color in the diagram on the right to highlight the updated **RSP** and **RBP** values from the start of the *proc* function up to the moment when the *proc2* function is called. For simplicity of illustration, I only use 64-bit values.

Function Epilog and Return (x64)

```
# void proc2();
# void proc(int p1, long p2) {
#   long local = 0;
#   proc2();
# }
proc:
push %rbp
mov  %rsp, %rbp
sub  $0x8, %rsp
mov  $0, -0x8(%rbp)
call proc2
adr2:
...
leaveq              # GCC
retq

adr2:
...
add  $0x8, %rsp     # Clang
pop  $rbp
retq
```

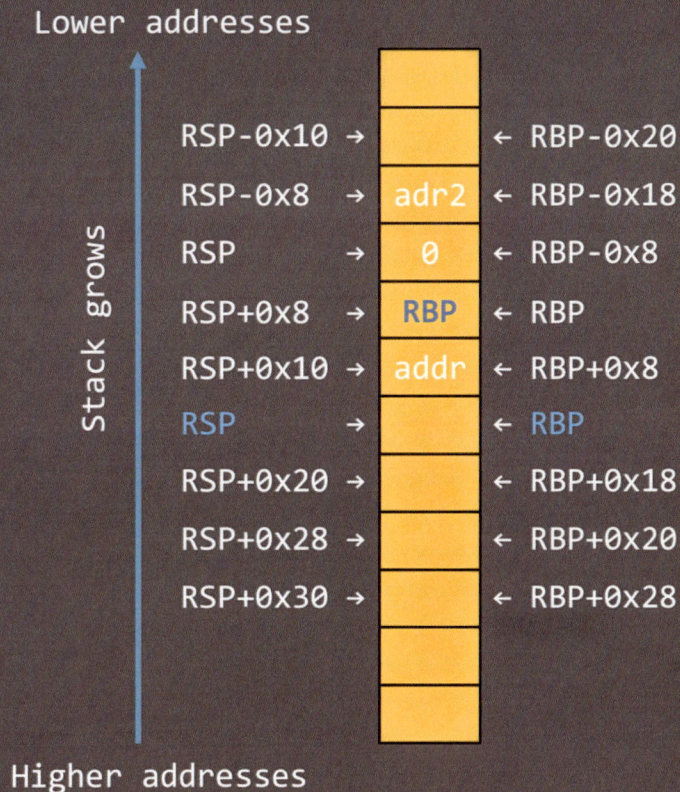

Lower addresses

Stack grows

RSP-0x10 →		← RBP-0x20
RSP-0x8 →	adr2	← RBP-0x18
RSP →	0	← RBP-0x8
RSP+0x8 →	RBP	← RBP
RSP+0x10 →	addr	← RBP+0x8
RSP →		← RBP
RSP+0x20 →		← RBP+0x18
RSP+0x28 →		← RBP+0x20
RSP+0x30 →		← RBP+0x28

Higher addresses

Before a function is returned back to the caller, a callee needs to do certain operations to on the thread stack, for example, to adjust **RSP** and restore saved **RBP**. There are different ways to do that (GCC and Clang use different instructions by default), and the assembly language code on the left is one of them. I use a different color in the diagram on the right to highlight the updated **RSP** and **RBP** values after the return from the *proc2* function up to the moment when we return from the *proc* function. For simplicity of illustration, I only use 64-bit values.

Stack Trace Reconstruction (x64)

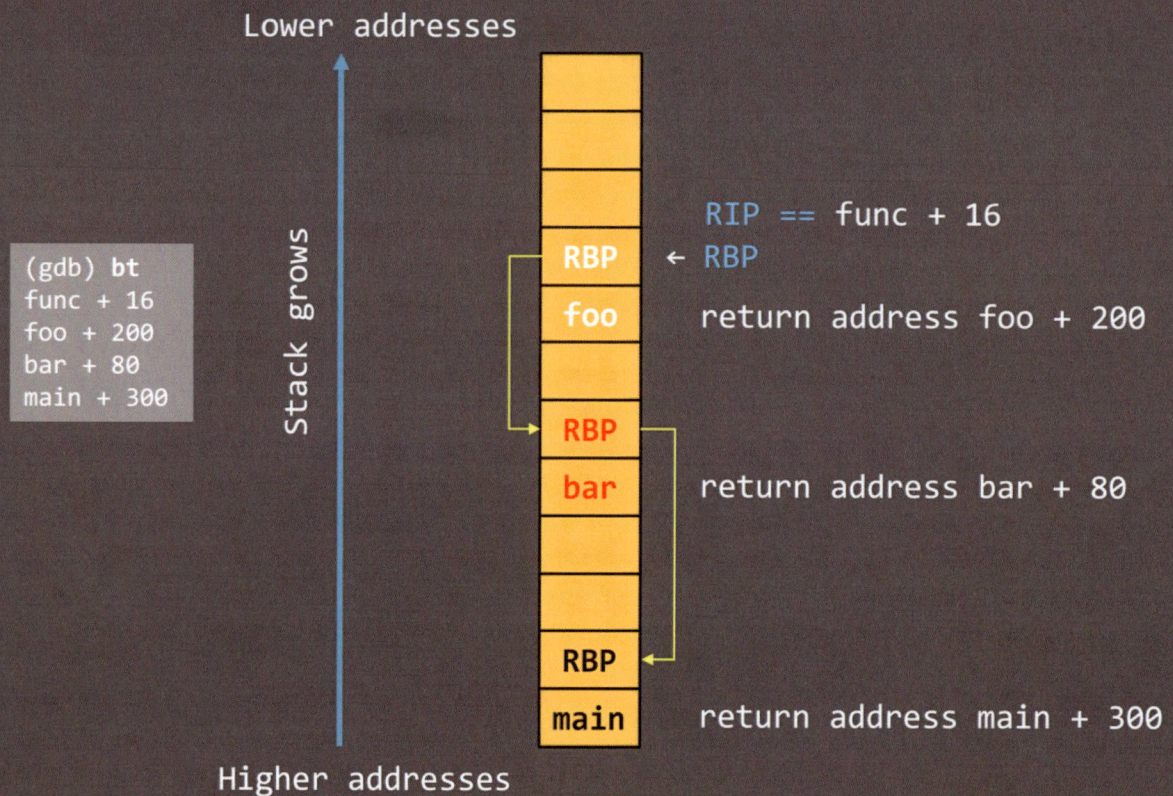

Lower addresses

↑

Stack grows

```
(gdb) bt
func + 16
foo + 200
bar + 80
main + 300
```

RIP == func + 16

RBP ← RBP

foo   return address foo + 200

RBP

bar   return address bar + 80

RBP

main   return address main + 300

Higher addresses

You may have noticed on the previous diagram that the new **RBP** points to the **RBP** of the caller, and below the previous **RBP** is the return address of the caller. So, if you know the **RBP** value, you can reconstruct the stack trace if the compiler follows the preceding function prolog convention.

A64 Disassembly

Part 3: A64 Disassembly

Now we come to a brief overview of relevant ARM64 disassembly. We only cover what we would see in the exercises.

CPU Registers (A64)

Illustrated in memory cell diagrams: \ADDR-Linux\MCD-R1-ARM64.xlsx

- **X0 – X28**, **W0 – W28**

X 64-bit	W 32-bit

- Stack: **SP**, **X29** (**FP**)

- Next instruction: **PC**

- Link register: **X30** (**LR**)

- Zero register: **XZR**, **WZR**

- 64-bit floating point registers **D0 – D31**

- 128-bit **Q0 – Q31**

There are 31 general registers from **X0** and **X30**, with some delegated to specific tasks such as addressing stack frames (Frame Pointer, **FP**, **X29**) and return addresses, the so-called Link Register (**LR**, **X30**). When you call a function, the return address of a caller is saved in **LR**, not on the stack as in Intel/AMD x64. The return instruction in a callee uses the address in **LR** to assign it to **PC** and resume execution. But if a callee calls other functions, the current **LR** needs to be manually saved somewhere, usually on the stack. There's Stack Pointer, **SP**, of course. To get zero values, there's the so-called Zero Register, **XZR**. All **X** registers are 64-bit, and 32-bit lower parts are addressed via the **W** prefix. There are also 128-bit SIMD registers. The References slide provides links to the ARM64 instruction set architecture. Next, we briefly look at some aspects related to our exercises.

Instructions: registers (A64)

- Opcode DST, SRC, SRC$_2$

- Examples:

```
mov    x0, #16          // X0 ← 16 (0x10)
mov    x29, sp          // X29 ← SP
add    x1, x2, #16      // X1 ← X2+16 (0x10)
mul    x1, x2, x3       // X1 ← X2*X3
blr    x8              // X8 already contains
                        //     the address of func (&func)
                        // LR ← PC+4; PC ← &func
sub    sp, sp, #48      // SP ← SP-48 (-0x30)
                        // make a room for local variables
```

This slide shows a few examples of CPU instructions that involve operations with registers, for example, moving a value and doing arithmetic. The direction of operands is the same as in the Intel x64 disassembly flavor if you are accustomed to WinDbg on Windows. It is equivalent to an assignment. **BLR** is a call of some function whose address is in the register. **BL** means Branch and Link.

45

Memory and Stack Addressing

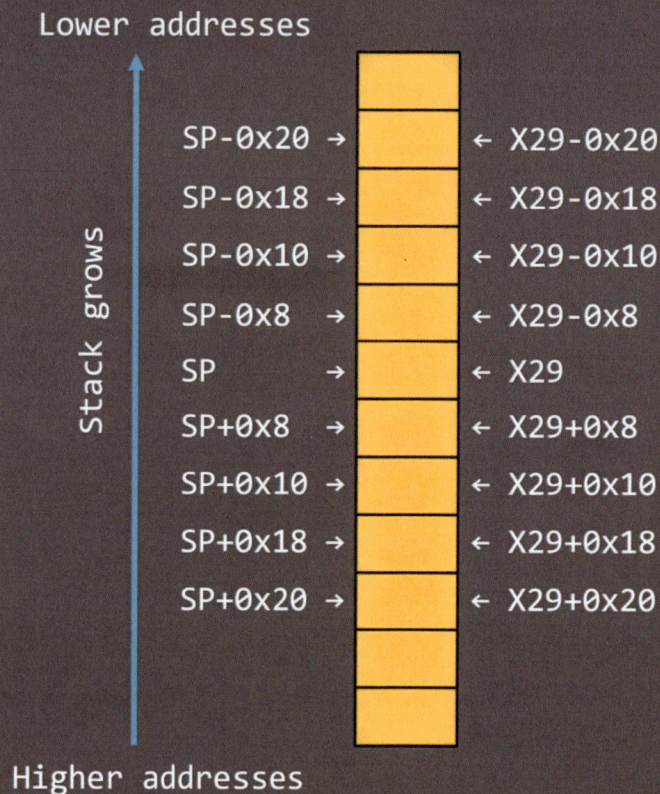

Lower addresses

SP-0x20 →	← X29-0x20
SP-0x18 →	← X29-0x18
SP-0x10 →	← X29-0x10
SP-0x8 →	← X29-0x8
SP →	← X29
SP+0x8 →	← X29+0x8
SP+0x10 →	← X29+0x10
SP+0x18 →	← X29+0x18
SP+0x20 →	← X29+0x20

Stack grows

Higher addresses

Before we look at operations with memory, let's look at a graphical representation of memory addressing. A thread stack is just any other memory region, so instead of **SP** and **X29** (**FP**), any other register can be used. Please note that the stack grows towards lower addresses, so to access the previously pushed values, you need to use positive offsets from **SP**.

Instructions: memory load (A64)

- Opcode DST, DST$_2$, [SRC, Offset]

- Opcode DST, DST$_2$, [SRC], Offset // Postincrement

- Examples:

```
ldr   x0, [sp]              // X0 ← value at address SP+0
ldr   x0, [x29, #-8]        // X0 ← value at address X29-0x8
ldp   x29, x30, [sp, #32]   // X29 ← value at address SP+32 (0x20)
                           // X30 ← value at address SP+40 (0x28)
ldp   x29, x30, [sp], #16   // X29 ← value at address SP+0
                           // X30 ← value at address SP+8
                           // SP ← SP+16 (0x10)
```

Constants are encoded in instructions, but if we need arbitrary values, we must get them from memory. Square brackets are used to show memory access relative to an address stored in some register. There's also an option to adjust the value of the register after load, the so-called **Postincrement**, which can be negative. As we see later, loading pairs of registers can be useful.

Instructions: memory store (A64)

- Opcode SRC, SRC$_2$, [DST, Offset]

- Opcode SRC, SRC$_2$, [DST, Offset]! // Preincrement

- Examples:

```
str    x0, [sp, #16]          // x0 → value at address SP+16 (0x10)
str    x0, [x29, #-8]         // x0 → value at address X29-8
stp    x29, x30, [sp, #32]    // x29 → value at address SP+32 (0x20)
                              // x30 → value at address SP+40 (0x28)
stp    x29, x30, [sp, #-16]!  // SP ← SP-16 (-0x10)
                              // x29 → set value at address SP
                              // x30 → set value at address SP+8
```

Storing operand order goes in the other direction compared to other instructions. There's a possibility to **Preincrement** the destination register before storing values.

Instructions: flow (A64)

- Opcode DST, SRC

- Examples:

```
adrp  x0, 0x420000      // x0 ← 0x420000

b     0x10493fc1c       // PC ← 0x10493fc1c
                        // (goto 0x10493fc1c)
br    x17               // PC ← the value of X17

0x10493fc14:            // PC == 0x10493fc14
bl    0x10493ff74       // LR ← PC+4 (0x10493fc18)
                        // PC ← 0x10493ff74
                        // (goto 0x10493ff74)
```

Because the size of every instruction is 4 bytes (32 bits), it is only possible to encode a part of a large 4GB address range, either as a relative offset to the current **PC** or via **ADRP** instruction. Goto (an unconditional branch) is implemented via the **B** instruction. Function calls are implemented via the **BL** (Branch and Link) instruction. For conditional branches, please look at the official documentation provided in the References slide. We don't use these instructions in our exercises.

Function Call and Prolog (A64)

GCC

```
// void proc(int p1, long p2);
mov   w0, #0x1
mov   x1, #0x2
bl    proc
addr:

// void proc2();
// void proc(int p1, long p2) {
//    long local = 0;
//    proc2();
// }
proc:
stp   x29, x30, [sp, #-32]!
mov   x29, sp
str   zxr, [x29, #16]
bl    proc2
adr2:
...
```

Lower addresses

X30   adr2

SP →	X29	← X29
SP-0x18 →	X30	← X29-0x18
SP+0x10 →	0	← X29+16
SP-0x8 →		← X29-0x8
SP →		← X29
SP+0x8 →		← X29+0x8
SP+0x10 →		← X29+0x10
SP+0x18 →		← X29+0x18
SP+0x20 →		← X29+0x20

Stack grows

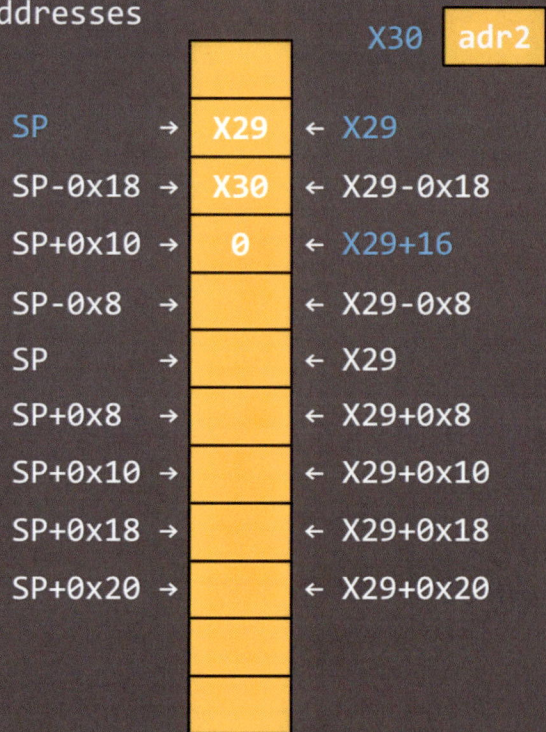

Higher addresses

When a function is called from the caller, a callee needs to do certain operations to make room for local variables on the thread stack and save **LR** if there are further calls in the function body. There are different ways to do that, and the assembly language code on the left is one of them GCC compiler uses by default. I use a different color in the diagram on the right to highlight the updated **SP** and **X29** (**FP**) values from the start of the *proc* function up to the moment when the *proc2* function is called. Please also note an example of zero register usage and the fact that both **SP** and **X29** point to the same memory location. Positive offsets from **X29** are used to address local variables. For simplicity of illustration, I only use 64-bit values.

Function Epilog and Return (A64)

GCC

```
// void proc(int p1, long p2);
mov  w0, #0x1
mov  x1, #0x2
bl   proc
addr:

// void proc2();
// void proc(int p1, long p2) {
//    long local = 0;
//    proc2();
// }
proc:
stp  x29, x30, [sp, #-32]!
mov  x29, sp
str  zxr, [x29, #16]
bl   proc2
adr2:

...
ldp     x29, x30, [sp], #32
ret
```

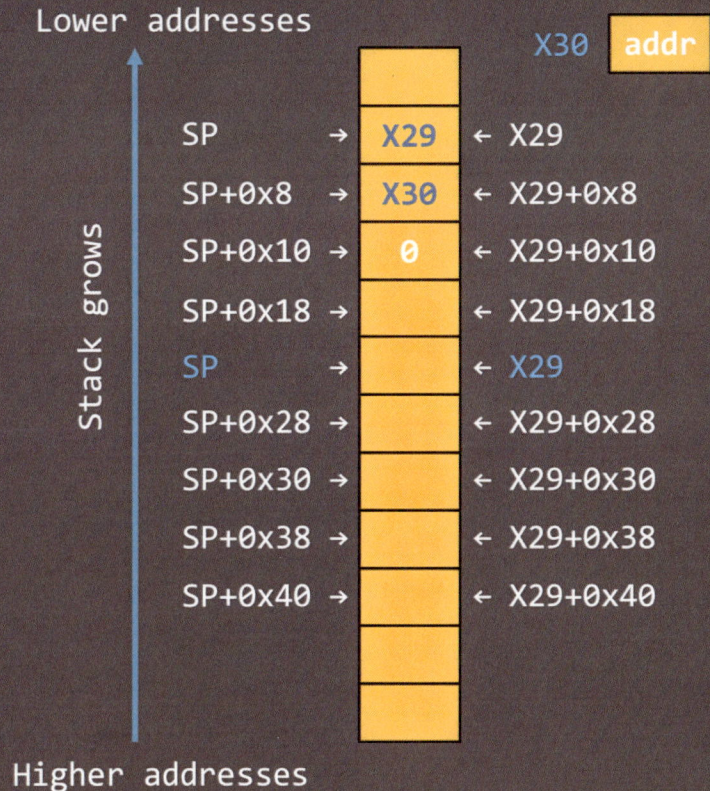

Before a function is returned back to the caller, a callee needs to do certain operations on the thread stack, for example, to adjust **SP** and restore saved **X29** and **X30**. There are different ways to do that, and the assembly language code on the left is one of them GCC compiler uses by default. I use a different color in the diagram on the right to highlight the updated **SP** and **X29** values after the return from the *proc2* function up to the moment when we return from the *proc* function. For simplicity of illustration, I only use 64-bit values.

Function Call and Prolog (A64)

Clang

```
// void proc(int p1, long p2);
mov   w0, #0x1
mov   x1, #0x2
bl    proc
addr:

// void proc2();
// void proc(int p1, long p2) {
//    long local = 0;
//    proc2();
// }
proc:
sub   sp, sp, #0x20
stp   x29, x30, [sp, #16]
add   x29, sp, #0x10
str   zxr, [x29, #-8]
bl    proc2
adr2:
...
```

Lower addresses

X30 adr2

SP →		← X29-0x20
SP-0x18 →	0	← X29-0x8
SP+0x10 →	X29	← X29
SP-0x8 →	X30	← X29-0x8
SP →		← X29
SP+0x8 →		← X29+0x8
SP+0x10 →		← X29+0x10
SP+0x18 →		← X29+0x18
SP+0x20 →		← X29+0x20

Stack grows

Higher addresses

Clang produces a slightly different code for the *proc* function prolog with **SP** and **X29** pointing to different memory locations. However, **X29** still points to the previous value of **X29**. Please note that negative offsets from **X29** are used to address local variables.

Function Epilog and Return (A64)

Clang

```
// void proc(int p1, long p2);
mov   w0, #0x1
mov   x1, #0x2
bl    proc
addr:

// void proc2();
// void proc(int p1, long p2) {
//    long local = 0;
//    proc2();
// }
proc:
sub   sp, sp, #0x20
stp   x29, x30, [sp, #16]
add   x29, sp, #0x10
str   zxr, [x29, #-8]
bl    proc2
adr2:

...
ldp       x29, x30, [sp, #16]
add       sp, sp, #0x20
ret
```

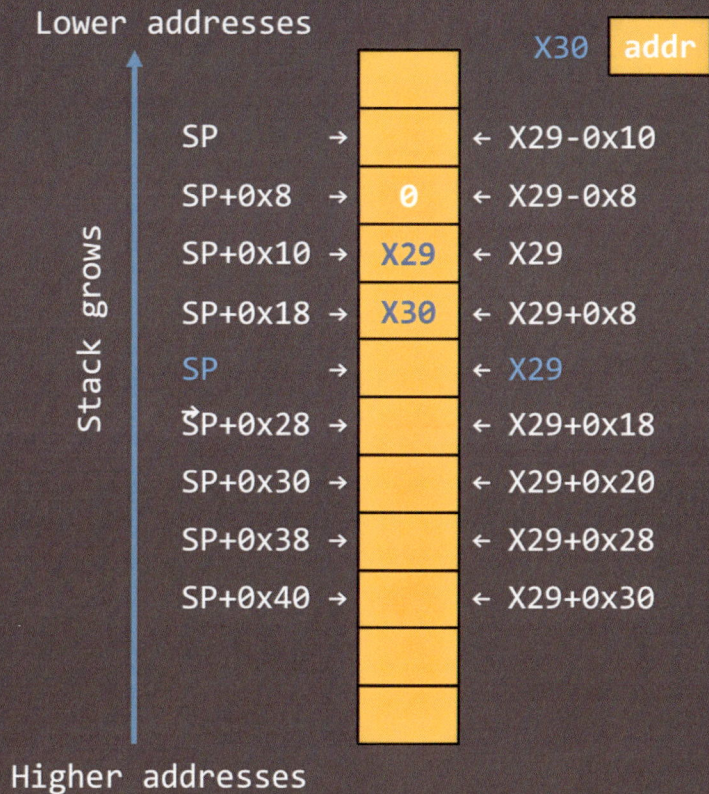

Lower addresses

X30 `addr`

```
SP        →           ← X29-0x10
SP+0x8    →    0       ← X29-0x8
SP+0x10   →    X29     ← X29
SP+0x18   →    X30     ← X29+0x8
SP        →            ← X29
SP+0x28   →            ← X29+0x18
SP+0x30   →            ← X29+0x20
SP+0x38   →            ← X29+0x28
SP+0x40   →            ← X29+0x30
```

Stack grows

Higher addresses

Clang produces a slightly different code for the *proc* function epilog to mirror its prolog code.

Stack Trace Reconstruction (A64)

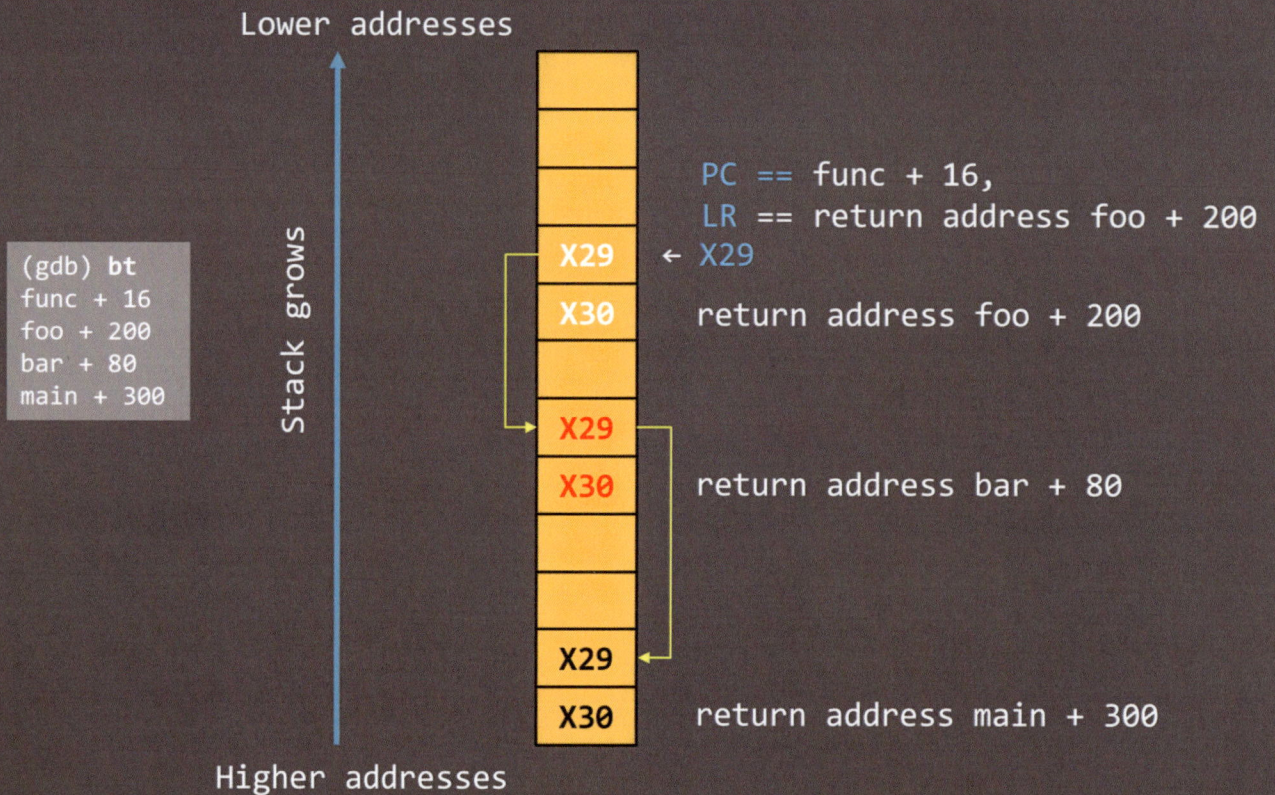

Lower addresses

Stack grows

```
(gdb) bt
func + 16
foo + 200
bar + 80
main + 300
```

PC == func + 16,
LR == return address foo + 200

X29 ← X29

X30   return address foo + 200

X29

X30   return address bar + 80

X29

X30   return address main + 300

Higher addresses

© 2023 Software Diagnostics Services

You may have noticed on the previous diagram that the new **X29** (**FP**) points to the **X29** of the caller, and below the previous **X29** is the return address of the caller. So, if you know either the return address in **LR** or **X29**, you can reconstruct the stack trace if the compiler follows the preceding function prolog convention.

54

Practice Exercises

Part 4: Practice Exercises

Now we start with practice exercises. The goal is to show essential GDB commands and techniques and how they help in disassembling, reversing, and reconstruction.

Links

⊙ **Memory dumps:**

Download links are in the exercise R0.

⊙ **Exercise Transcripts:**

Included in this book.

Note: Memory cell diagrams referenced in slides and exercises are included in this book.

Exercise R0

- **Goal:** Install GDB and check if GDB loads a core dump correctly

- \ADDR-Linux\Exercise-R0-x64-GDB.pdf

- \ADDR-Linux\Exercise-R0-ARM64-GDB.pdf

Exercise R0 (x64, GDB)

Goal: Install GDB and check if GDB loads a core dump correctly.

1.   Download core dump files if you haven't done that already and unpack the archives:

https://www.patterndiagnostics.com/Training/ADDR-Linux/ADDR-Linux-Dumps.tar.gz

2.   Download and install the latest version of GDB. For WSL2 Debian, we used the following commands:

```
$ sudo apt install build-essential
$ sudo apt install gdb
```

On RHEL-type systems, we may need to install the tools and GDB via:

```
$ sudo yum group install "Development Tools"
$ sudo yum install gdb
```

3.   Verify that GDB is accessible and then exit it (**q** command):

```
$ gdb
GNU gdb (Debian 8.2.1-2+b3) 8.2.1
Copyright (C) 2018 Free Software Foundation, Inc.
License GPLv3+: GNU GPL version 3 or later <http://gnu.org/licenses/gpl.html>
This is free software: you are free to change and redistribute it.
There is NO WARRANTY, to the extent permitted by law.
Type "show copying" and "show warranty" for details.
This GDB was configured as "x86_64-linux-gnu".
Type "show configuration" for configuration details.
For bug reporting instructions, please see:
<http://www.gnu.org/software/gdb/bugs/>.
Find the GDB manual and other documentation resources online at:
    <http://www.gnu.org/software/gdb/documentation/>.

For help, type "help".
Type "apropos word" to search for commands related to "word".

(gdb) q
$
```

4.   Load *notepad.61* dump file and *notepad* executable:

```
~/ADDR-Linux/x64/MemoryDumps$ gdb -c notepad.61 -se notepad
GNU gdb (Debian 8.2.1-2+b3) 8.2.1
Copyright (C) 2018 Free Software Foundation, Inc.
License GPLv3+: GNU GPL version 3 or later <http://gnu.org/licenses/gpl.html>
This is free software: you are free to change and redistribute it.
There is NO WARRANTY, to the extent permitted by law.
Type "show copying" and "show warranty" for details.
This GDB was configured as "x86_64-linux-gnu".
Type "show configuration" for configuration details.
For bug reporting instructions, please see:
```

```
<http://www.gnu.org/software/gdb/bugs/>.
Find the GDB manual and other documentation resources online at:
    <http://www.gnu.org/software/gdb/documentation/>.

For help, type "help".
Type "apropos word" to search for commands related to "word"...
Reading symbols from notepad...(no debugging symbols found)...done.
[New LWP 61]
Core was generated by `./notepad'.
#0  0x000000000043c4e1 in nanosleep ()
(gdb)
```

5.   Verify that the stack trace (back trace) is shown correctly with symbols:

```
(gdb) bt
#0  0x000000000043c4e1 in nanosleep ()
#1  0x000000000043c49a in sleep ()
#2  0x0000000000401c17 in internal_get_message ()
#3  0x0000000000401c57 in get_message ()
#4  0x0000000000401cea in main ()
```

6.   We exit GDB.

```
(gdb) q
~/ADDR-Linux/x64/MemoryDumps$
```

Exercise R0 (A64, GDB)

Goal: Install GDB and check if GDB loads a core dump correctly.

1.   Download core dump files if you haven't done that already and unpack the archives:

https://www.patterndiagnostics.com/Training/ADDR-Linux/ADDR-Linux-Dumps.tar.gz

2.   Download and install the latest version of GDB. For ARM64 Ubuntu, we used the following commands:

```
$ sudo apt install build-essential
$ sudo apt install gdb
```

On RHEL-type systems, we may need to install the tools and GDB via:

```
$ sudo yum group install "Development Tools"
$ sudo yum install gdb
```

3.   Verify that GDB is accessible and then exit it (**q** command):

```
$ gdb
GNU gdb (Ubuntu 12.0.90-0ubuntu1) 12.0.90
Copyright (C) 2022 Free Software Foundation, Inc.
License GPLv3+: GNU GPL version 3 or later <http://gnu.org/licenses/gpl.html>
This is free software: you are free to change and redistribute it.
There is NO WARRANTY, to the extent permitted by law.
Type "show copying" and "show warranty" for details.
This GDB was configured as "aarch64-linux-gnu".
Type "show configuration" for configuration details.
For bug reporting instructions, please see:
<https://www.gnu.org/software/gdb/bugs/>.
Find the GDB manual and other documentation resources online at:
    <http://www.gnu.org/software/gdb/documentation/>.

For help, type "help".
Type "apropos word" to search for commands related to "word".
(gdb)

(gdb) q
$
```

4.   Load *notepad.12315* dump file and *notepad* executable:

```
~/ADDR-Linux/A64/MemoryDumps$ gdb -c notepad.12315 -se notepad
GNU gdb (Ubuntu 12.0.90-0ubuntu1) 12.0.90
Copyright (C) 2022 Free Software Foundation, Inc.
License GPLv3+: GNU GPL version 3 or later <http://gnu.org/licenses/gpl.html>
This is free software: you are free to change and redistribute it.
There is NO WARRANTY, to the extent permitted by law.
Type "show copying" and "show warranty" for details.
This GDB was configured as "aarch64-linux-gnu".
Type "show configuration" for configuration details.
```

```
For bug reporting instructions, please see:
<https://www.gnu.org/software/gdb/bugs/>.
Find the GDB manual and other documentation resources online at:
    <http://www.gnu.org/software/gdb/documentation/>.

For help, type "help".
Type "apropos word" to search for commands related to "word"...
Reading symbols from notepad...
(No debugging symbols found in notepad)

warning: Can't open file /home/ubuntu/notepad during file-backed mapping note processing
[New LWP 12315]
Core was generated by `./notepad'.
#0  0x000000000043a3fc in clock_nanosleep ()
(gdb)
```

5.   Verify that the stack trace (back trace) is shown correctly with symbols:

```
(gdb) bt
#0  0x000000000043a3fc in clock_nanosleep ()
#1  0x0000000000418ffc in nanosleep ()
#2  0x0000000000418f98 in sleep ()
#3  0x00000000004007c4 in internal_get_message ()
#4  0x0000000000400808 in get_message ()
#5  0x00000000004008cc in main ()
```

6.   We exit GDB.

```
(gdb) q
~/ADDR-Linux/A64/MemoryDumps$
```

Exercise R1

- **Goal:** Review x64 and AArch64 assembly fundamentals; learn how to reconstruct stack trace manually

- **ADDR Patterns:** Universal Pointer, Symbolic Pointer S^2, Interpreted Pointer S^3, Context Pyramid

- **Memory Cell Diagrams:** Register, Pointer, Stack Frame

- \ADDR-Linux\Exercise-R1-x64-GDB.pdf
- \ADDR-Linux\MCD-R1-x64.xlsx

- \ADDR-Linux\Exercise-R1-ARM64-GDB.pdf
- \ADDR-Linux\MCD-R1-ARM64.xlsx

Here we review x64 (64-bit) and ARM64 CPU and assembly language fundamentals and introduce the simple Memory Cell Diagrams. We do such a review in the context of a manual memory dump from a running process that models UI messaging.

Exercise R1 (x64, GDB)

Goal: Review x64 assembly fundamentals; learn how to reconstruct stack trace manually.

ADDR Patterns: Universal Pointer, Symbolic Pointer S^2, Interpreted Pointer S^3, Context Pyramid.

Memory Cell Diagrams: Register, Pointer, Stack Frame.

1.　　Load a core dump *notepad.61* and *notepad* executable from x64/MemoryDumps directory:

```
~/ADDR-Linux/x64/MemoryDumps$ gdb -c notepad.61 -se notepad
GNU gdb (Debian 8.2.1-2+b3) 8.2.1
Copyright (C) 2018 Free Software Foundation, Inc.
License GPLv3+: GNU GPL version 3 or later <http://gnu.org/licenses/gpl.html>
This is free software: you are free to change and redistribute it.
There is NO WARRANTY, to the extent permitted by law.
Type "show copying" and "show warranty" for details.
This GDB was configured as "x86_64-linux-gnu".
Type "show configuration" for configuration details.
For bug reporting instructions, please see:
<http://www.gnu.org/software/gdb/bugs/>.
Find the GDB manual and other documentation resources online at:
    <http://www.gnu.org/software/gdb/documentation/>.

For help, type "help".
Type "apropos word" to search for commands related to "word"...
Reading symbols from notepad...(no debugging symbols found)...done.
[New LWP 61]
Core was generated by `./notepad'.
#0  0x000000000043c4e1 in nanosleep ()
```

2.　　We open a log file:

```
(gdb) set logging on R1.log
Copying output to R1.log.
```

3.　　We get this stack trace:

```
(gdb) bt
#0  0x000000000043c4e1 in nanosleep ()
#1  0x000000000043c49a in sleep ()
#2  0x0000000000401c17 in internal_get_message ()
#3  0x0000000000401c57 in get_message ()
#4  0x0000000000401cea in main ()
```

4.　　Let's check the main CPU registers:

```
(gdb) info registers
rax            0xfffffffffffffdfc     -516
rbx            0xffffffffffffffc0     -64
rcx            0x43c4e1               4441313
rdx            0x401b4d               4201293
rsi            0x7ffffe5129d0         140737460120016
rdi            0x7ffffe5129d0         140737460120016
rbp            0x0                    0x0
```

```
rsp            0x7ffffe5129c8       0x7ffffe5129c8
r8             0x2                  2
r9             0x2                  2
r10            0x7                  7
r11            0x246                582
r12            0x4029c0             4204992
r13            0x0                  0
r14            0x4a5018             4870168
r15            0x0                  0
rip            0x43c4e1             0x43c4e1 <nanosleep+17>
eflags         0x246                [ PF ZF IF ]
cs             0x33                 51
ss             0x2b                 43
ds             0x0                  0
es             0x0                  0
fs             0x0                  0
gs             0x0                  0
```

Note: The register parts and naming are illustrated in the MCD-R1-x64.xlsx A section.

5.   The current instruction registers (registers that are used and affected by the current instruction or semantically tied to it) can be checked by listing them individually:

```
(gdb) x/i $rip
=> 0x43c4e1 <nanosleep+17>:     cmp     $0xfffffffffffff000,%rax

(gdb) info registers rax
rax            0xfffffffffffffdfc   -516
```

Note: Most commands require $ to be prefixed to a register name; otherwise, they consider it a symbol name.

```
(gdb) x/i rip
No symbol table is loaded.  Use the "file" command.
```

6.   Any register value or its named parts can be checked with the **info registers** command (**i r**):

```
(gdb) i r r12
r12            0x4029c0             4204992

(gdb) i r r12d
r12d           0x4029c0             4204992

(gdb) i r r12w
r12w           0x29c0               10688

(gdb) i r r12l
r12l           0xc0                 -64
```

The original x86 registry set can be accessed using mnemonics:

```
(gdb) i r rbx
rbx            0xffffffffffffffc0   -64

(gdb) i r ebx
ebx            0xffffffc0           -64
```

66

```
(gdb) i r bx
bx              0xffc0              -64
(gdb) i r bh
bh              0xff                -1

(gdb) i r bl
bl              0xc0                -64

(gdb) i r rbp
rbp             0x0                 0x0

(gdb) i r ebp
ebp             0x0                 0

(gdb) i r rsi
rsi             0x7ffffe5129d0      140737460120016

(gdb) i r esi
esi             0xfe5129d0          -28235312

(gdb) i r si
si              0x29d0              10704

(gdb) i r sil
sil             0xd0                -48
```

7.   Individual parts can also be interpreted using the **print** command (**p**):

```
(gdb) p/z $r11
$1 = 0x0000000000000246

(gdb) p/z (int[2])$r11
$2 = {0x00000246, 0x00000000}

(gdb) p/z (short[4])$r11
$3 = {0x0246, 0x0000, 0x0000, 0x0000}

(gdb) p/z (char[8])$r11
$4 = {0x46, 0x02, 0x00, 0x00, 0x00, 0x00, 0x00, 0x00}

(gdb) p/d (char[8])$r11
$5 = {70, 2, 0, 0, 0, 0, 0, 0}
```

8.   Any registry value can be interpreted as a pointer to memory cells, a memory address (**Universal Pointer** pattern vs. a pointer originally designed to be such). However, memory contents at that address may be inaccessible or unknown, as in the case of RAX below.

```
(gdb) x $rax
0xfffffffffffffdfc:     Cannot access memory at address 0xfffffffffffffdfc
```

Note: The following output for RDI is illustrated in the MCD-R1-x64.xlsx B section.

```
(gdb) x/gx $rdi
0x7ffffe5129d0: 0x00000000fffffff0
```

67

9.   We can also specify value count or limit to just one value and use finer granularity for memory dumping:

```
(gdb) x/20gx $rdi
0x7ffffe5129d0: 0x00000000fffffff0      0x00000000130f2d88
0x7ffffe5129e0: 0x0000000000000140      0x3ebeea4a71786c00
0x7ffffe5129f0: 0x000000000000000a      0x0000000000400470
0x7ffffe512a00: 0x00007ffffe512a20      0x0000000000401c17
0x7ffffe512a10: 0x0000000000000000      0x00007ffffe512a80
0x7ffffe512a20: 0x00007ffffe512a60      0x0000000000401c57
0x7ffffe512a30: 0x0000000000000000      0x0000000000000000
0x7ffffe512a40: 0x0000000000000000      0x00007ffffe512a80
0x7ffffe512a50: 0x0000000000000001      0xfffffffffe512bd8
0x7ffffe512a60: 0x00007ffffe512ab0      0x0000000000401cea
```

```
(gdb) x/20wx $rdi
0x7ffffe5129d0: 0xfffffff0      0x00000000      0x130f2d88      0x00000000
0x7ffffe5129e0: 0x00000140      0x00000000      0x71786c00      0x3ebeea4a
0x7ffffe5129f0: 0x0000000a      0x00000000      0x00400470      0x00000000
0x7ffffe512a00: 0xfe512a20      0x00007fff      0x00401c17      0x00000000
0x7ffffe512a10: 0x00000000      0x00000000      0xfe512a80      0x00007fff
```

Note: The similar output for RDI as below is illustrated in the MCD-R1-x64.xlsx C section.

```
(gdb) x/20hx $rdi
0x7ffffe5129d0: 0xfff0  0xffff  0x0000  0x0000  0x2d88  0x130f  0x0000  0x0000
0x7ffffe5129e0: 0x0140  0x0000  0x0000  0x0000  0x6c00  0x7178  0xea4a  0x3ebe
0x7ffffe5129f0: 0x000a  0x0000  0x0000  0x0000
```

```
(gdb) x/20bx $rdi
0x7ffffe5129d0: 0xf0    0xff    0xff    0xff    0x00    0x00    0x00    0x00
0x7ffffe5129d8: 0x88    0x2d    0x0f    0x13    0x00    0x00    0x00    0x00
0x7ffffe5129e0: 0x40    0x01    0x00    0x00
```

Note: GDB remembers formatting:

```
(gdb) x/20 $rsp
0x7ffffe5129c8: 0x9a    0xc4    0x43    0x00    0x00    0x00    0x00    0x00
0x7ffffe5129d0: 0xf0    0xff    0xff    0xff    0x00    0x00    0x00    0x00
0x7ffffe5129d8: 0x88    0x2d    0x0f    0x13
```

10.   Notice a difference between a value and its organization in memory stemmed from the little-endian organization of the Intel x86-x64 platform (least significant parts are located at lower addresses):

```
(gdb) p/z $rsp
$6 = 0x00007ffffe5129c8
```

```
(gdb) p/z (int[2])$rsp
$7 = {0xfe5129c8, 0x00007fff}
```

```
(gdb) p/z $rsp
$8 = 0x00007ffffe5129c8
```

```
(gdb) p/z (short[4])$rsp
$9 = {0x29c8, 0xfe51, 0x7fff, 0x0000}
```

```
(gdb) p/z $rsp
$10 = 0x00007ffffe5129c8
```

68

```
(gdb) p/z (char[8])$rsp
$11 = {0xc8, 0x29, 0x51, 0xfe, 0xff, 0x7f, 0x00, 0x00}
```

11.   Every value can be associated with a symbolic value from symbol files or the binary (exported and included symbols) if available. We call this **Symbolic Pointer** or **S²**:

```
(gdb) x/40a $rsp
0x7ffffe5129c8: 0x43c49a <sleep+58>      0xfffffff0
0x7ffffe5129d8: 0x130f2d88       0x140
0x7ffffe5129e8: 0x3ebeea4a71786c00       0xa
0x7ffffe5129f8: 0x400470         0x7ffffe512a20
0x7ffffe512a08: 0x401c17 <internal_get_message+128>      0x0
0x7ffffe512a18: 0x7ffffe512a80   0x7ffffe512a60
0x7ffffe512a28: 0x401c57 <get_message+57>        0x0
0x7ffffe512a38: 0x0      0x0
0x7ffffe512a48: 0x7ffffe512a80   0x1
0x7ffffe512a58: 0xfffffffffe512bd8       0x7ffffe512ab0
0x7ffffe512a68: 0x401cea <main+56>       0x7ffffe512bd8
0x7ffffe512a78: 0x1004029a4      0x0
0x7ffffe512a88: 0x113    0x1
0x7ffffe512a98: 0x401b4d <time_proc>     0x9c04578350
0x7ffffe512aa8: 0x147    0x402930 <__libc_csu_init>
0x7ffffe512ab8: 0x402331 <__libc_start_main+977>         0x0
0x7ffffe512ac8: 0x100000000      0x7ffffe512bd8
0x7ffffe512ad8: 0x401cb2 <main> 0x0
0x7ffffe512ae8: 0x8e00000006     0xa00000080
0x7ffffe512af8: 0x0      0x0
```

```
(gdb) info symbol 0x401b4d
time_proc in section .text of /home/coredump/ADDR-Linux/x64/MemoryDumps/notepad
```

Note: The address 0x7ffffe512a98 that points to 0x401b4d doesn't have an associated symbol:

```
(gdb) info symbol 0x7ffffe512a98
No symbol matches 0x7ffffe512a98.
```

Note: The next instruction pointer address contained in RIP should have an associated symbol of the current function in our example because we have function symbols for *notepad*:

```
(gdb) p/z $rip
$12 = 0x000000000043c4e1
```

```
(gdb) info symbol 0x000000000043c4e1
nanosleep + 17 in section .text of /home/coredump/ADDR-Linux/x64/MemoryDumps/notepad
```

```
(gdb) info symbol $rip
nanosleep + 17 in section .text of /home/coredump/ADDR-Linux/x64/MemoryDumps/notepad
```

```
(gdb) i r $rip
rip            0x43c4e1              0x43c4e1 <nanosleep+17>
```

```
(gdb) x/i $rip
=> 0x43c4e1 <nanosleep+17>:      cmp     $0xfffffffffffff000,%rax
```

12.   Now we come to the next pointer level after its value and symbol: its interpretation. We call it an **Interpreted Pointer, S³**. Such interpretation is implemented either via typed structures (the **print** command) or via various debugger commands or scripts that format information for us. In our example, we would like to check the memory pointed to by the address 0x7ffffe512a80. We suspect it might be **msg_t** structure related to the "get message" loop:

```
typedef struct
{
  hwnd_t     hwnd;
  uint64_t  message;
  uint64_t  param1;
  uint64_t  param2;
  uint32_t  time;
  POINT      pt;
  uint32_t  private;
} msg_t, *p_msg_t;
```

```
(gdb) x/40a $rsp
0x7ffffe5129c8: 0x43c49a <sleep+58>      0xfffffff0
0x7ffffe5129d8: 0x130f2d88       0x140
0x7ffffe5129e8: 0x3ebeea4a71786c00      0xa
0x7ffffe5129f8: 0x400470        0x7ffffe512a20
0x7ffffe512a08: 0x401c17 <internal_get_message+128>      0x0
0x7ffffe512a18: 0x7ffffe512a80  0x7ffffe512a60
0x7ffffe512a28: 0x401c57 <get_message+57>        0x0
0x7ffffe512a38: 0x0      0x0
0x7ffffe512a48: 0x7ffffe512a80  0x1
0x7ffffe512a58: 0xfffffffffe512bd8        0x7ffffe512ab0
0x7ffffe512a68: 0x401cea <main+56>      0x7ffffe512bd8
0x7ffffe512a78: 0x1004029a4      0x0
0x7ffffe512a88: 0x113    0x1
0x7ffffe512a98: 0x401b4d <time_proc>      0x9c04578350
0x7ffffe512aa8: 0x147    0x402930 <__libc_csu_init>
0x7ffffe512ab8: 0x402331 <__libc_start_main+977>         0x0
0x7ffffe512ac8: 0x100000000      0x7ffffe512bd8
0x7ffffe512ad8: 0x401cb2 <main> 0x0
0x7ffffe512ae8: 0x8e00000006     0xa00000080
0x7ffffe512af8: 0x0      0x0
```

```
(gdb) x/20gx 0x7ffffe512a80
0x7ffffe512a80: 0x0000000000000000      0x0000000000000113
0x7ffffe512a90: 0x0000000000000001      0x0000000000401b4d
0x7ffffe512aa0: 0x0000009c04578350      0x0000000000000147
0x7ffffe512ab0: 0x0000000000402930      0x0000000000402331
0x7ffffe512ac0: 0x0000000000000000      0x0000000100000000
0x7ffffe512ad0: 0x00007ffffe512bd8      0x0000000000401cb2
0x7ffffe512ae0: 0x0000000000000000      0x0000008e00000006
0x7ffffe512af0: 0x0000000a00000080      0x0000000000000000
0x7ffffe512b00: 0x0000000000000000      0x0000000000000000
0x7ffffe512b10: 0x0000000000000000      0x0000000000000000
```

```
(gdb) x/20wx 0x7ffffe512a80
0x7ffffe512a80: 0x00000000    0x00000000    0x00000113    0x00000000
0x7ffffe512a90: 0x00000001    0x00000000    0x00401b4d    0x00000000
0x7ffffe512aa0: 0x04578350    0x0000009c    0x00000147    0x00000000
0x7ffffe512ab0: 0x00402930    0x00000000    0x00402331    0x00000000
0x7ffffe512ac0: 0x00000000    0x00000000    0x00000000    0x00000001
```

```
(gdb) x/20wd 0x7ffffe512a80
0x7ffffe512a80: 0          0          275       0
0x7ffffe512a90: 1          0          4201293   0
0x7ffffe512aa0: 72844112              156       327       0
0x7ffffe512ab0: 4204848    0          4203313   0
0x7ffffe512ac0: 0          0          0         1

(gdb) p *(msg_t *)0x7ffffe512a80
No symbol table is loaded.  Use the "file" command.

(gdb) info types msg_t
All types matching regular expression "msg_t":
```

Note: Suppose that the raw structure makes sense for a timer message (**0x113**) where param1 is a timer ID (**1**), and usually a callback function (param2) is NULL (0x0), but in our case, it is not (**0x0000000000401b4d**, as we saw previously, *time_proc*). Also, mouse pointer data makes sense (**0x9c, 0x147**). Unfortunately, the **msg_t** structure type is not available in the *notepad* memory dump and executable, and suppose we don't have a debug symbol file for it either. However, we can add a different unrelated symbol file, for example, *extra-symbols* from x64/MemoryDumps/ExtraSymbols, which was compiled with full debug symbols and should have structures necessary for this message loop processing (**Injected Symbols** memory analysis pattern).

13.   We specify an additional symbol file path:

```
(gdb) add-symbol-file ./ExtraSymbols/extra-symbols
add symbol table from file "./ExtraSymbols/extra-symbols"
(y or n) y
Reading symbols from ./ExtraSymbols/extra-symbols...done.
```

14.   Now we can use the **msg_t** structure:

```
(gdb) info types msg_t
All types matching regular expression "msg_t":

File extra-symbols.c:
26:     typedef struct {
    hwnd_t hwnd;
    uint64_t message;
    uint64_t param1;
    uint64_t param2;
    uint32_t time;
    POINT pt;
    uint32_t private;
} msg_t;

(gdb) p *(msg_t *)0x7ffffe512a80
$13 = {hwnd = 0, message = 275, param1 = 1, param2 = 4201293, time = 72844112, pt = {x = 156, y
= 327}, private = 0}

(gdb) set print pretty on
```

```
(gdb) p *(msg_t *)0x7ffffe512a80
$14 = {
  hwnd = 0,
  message = 275,
  param1 = 1,
  param2 = 4201293,
  time = 72844112,
  pt = {
    x = 156,
    y = 327
  },
  private = 0
}
```

```
(gdb) p/x *(msg_t *)0x7ffffe512a80
$15 = {
  hwnd = 0x0,
  message = 0x113,
  param1 = 0x1,
  param2 = 0x401b4d,
  time = 0x4578350,
  pt = {
    x = 0x9c,
    y = 0x147
  },
  private = 0x0
}
```

```
(gdb) p/z *(msg_t *)0x7ffffe512a80
$16 = {
  hwnd = 0x0000000000000000,
  message = 0x0000000000000113,
  param1 = 0x0000000000000001,
  param2 = 0x0000000000401b4d,
  time = 0x04578350,
  pt = {
    x = 0x0000009c,
    y = 0x00000147
  },
  private = 0x00000000
}
```

Note: Don't forget to unload the loaded symbol file if it interferes with the original section symbols:

```
(gdb) disassemble main
Dump of assembler code for function main:
   0x0000000000401b4d <+0>:     push   %rbp
   0x0000000000401b4e <+1>:     mov    %rsp,%rbp
   0x0000000000401b51 <+4>:     mov    $0x1,%eax
   0x0000000000401b56 <+9>:     pop    %rbp
   0x0000000000401b57 <+10>:    retq
   0x0000000000401b58 <+0>:     push   %rbp
   0x0000000000401b59 <+1>:     mov    %rsp,%rbp
   0x0000000000401b5c <+4>:     mov    %edi,-0x4(%rbp)
End of assembler dump.
```

```
(gdb) info symbol main
time_proc in section .text of /home/coredump/ADDR-Linux/x64/MemoryDumps/notepad
main in section .text of /home/coredump/ADDR-Linux/x64/MemoryDumps/ExtraSymbols/extra-symbols

(gdb) remove-symbol-file /home/coredump/ADDR-Linux/x64/MemoryDumps/ExtraSymbols/extra-symbols
Remove symbol table from file "/home/coredump/ADDR-Linux/x64/MemoryDumps/ExtraSymbols/extra-
symbols"? (y or n) y

(gdb) info symbol main
main in section .text of /home/coredump/ADDR-Linux/x64/MemoryDumps/notepad

(gdb) disassemble main
Dump of assembler code for function main:
   0x0000000000401cb2 <+0>:     push   %rbp
   0x0000000000401cb3 <+1>:     mov    %rsp,%rbp
   0x0000000000401cb6 <+4>:     sub    $0x40,%rsp
   0x0000000000401cba <+8>:     mov    %edi,-0x34(%rbp)
   0x0000000000401cbd <+11>:    mov    %rsi,-0x40(%rbp)
   0x0000000000401cc1 <+15>:    jmp    0x401ccf <main+29>
   0x0000000000401cc3 <+17>:    lea    -0x30(%rbp),%rax
   0x0000000000401cc7 <+21>:    mov    %rax,%rdi
   0x0000000000401cca <+24>:    callq  0x401c87 <dispatch_message>
   0x0000000000401ccf <+29>:    lea    -0x30(%rbp),%rax
   0x0000000000401cd3 <+33>:    mov    $0x0,%ecx
   0x0000000000401cd8 <+38>:    mov    $0x0,%edx
   0x0000000000401cdd <+43>:    mov    $0x0,%esi
   0x0000000000401ce2 <+48>:    mov    %rax,%rdi
   0x0000000000401ce5 <+51>:    callq  0x401c1e <get_message>
   0x0000000000401cea <+56>:    test   %eax,%eax
   0x0000000000401cec <+58>:    jne    0x401cc3 <main+17>
   0x0000000000401cee <+60>:    mov    $0x0,%eax
   0x0000000000401cf3 <+65>:    leaveq
   0x0000000000401cf4 <+66>:    retq
End of assembler dump.
```

15.   When we have an exception such as a breakpoint or access violation, the values of the thread CPU registers are saved, and valid for the currently executing function and the instruction pointed to by the RIP register (the topmost frame). In other situations, such as a manual memory dump, we can only be sure about some registers such as RIP and RSP:

```
(gdb) bt
#0  0x000000000043c4e1 in nanosleep ()
#1  0x000000000043c49a in sleep ()
#2  0x0000000000401c17 in internal_get_message ()
#3  0x0000000000401c57 in get_message ()
#4  0x0000000000401cea in main ()

(gdb) i r
rax            0xfffffffffffffdfc   -516
rbx            0xffffffffffffffc0   -64
rcx            0x43c4e1             4441313
rdx            0x401b4d             4201293
rsi            0x7ffffe5129d0       140737460120016
rdi            0x7ffffe5129d0       140737460120016
rbp            0x0                  0x0
rsp            0x7ffffe5129c8       0x7ffffe5129c8
r8             0x2                  2
```

```
r9              0x2                     2
r10             0x7                     7
r11             0x246                   582
r12·            0x4029c0                4204992
r13             0x0                     0
r14             0x4a5018                4870168
r15             0x0                     0
rip             0x43c4e1                0x43c4e1 <nanosleep+17>
eflags          0x246                   [ PF ZF IF ]
cs              0x33                    51
ss              0x2b                    43
ds              0x0                     0
es              0x0                     0
fs              0x0                     0
gs              0x0                     0
```

16.   In any situation when we move down to the next frame, for example, to *sleep* (0x000000000043c49a points to the next instruction after *nanosleep* was called) and to *main*, we don't have most CPU registers' values saved previously (**i r** command gives accurate values only for the topmost frame 0 except RIP and RSP and perhaps a few other registers such as RBP):

```
(gdb) bt
#0  0x000000000043c4e1 in nanosleep ()
#1  0x000000000043c49a in sleep ()
#2  0x0000000000401c17 in internal_get_message ()
#3  0x0000000000401c57 in get_message ()
#4  0x0000000000401cea in main ()

(gdb) disassemble 0x000000000043c49a
Dump of assembler code for function sleep:
   0x000000000043c460 <+0>:     push   %rbp
   0x000000000043c461 <+1>:     push   %rbx
   0x000000000043c462 <+2>:     sub    $0x28,%rsp
   0x000000000043c466 <+6>:     mov    $0xffffffffffffffc0,%rbx
   0x000000000043c46d <+13>:    mov    %fs:0x28,%rax
   0x000000000043c476 <+22>:    mov    %rax,0x18(%rsp)
   0x000000000043c47b <+27>:    xor    %eax,%eax
   0x000000000043c47d <+29>:    mov    %edi,%eax
   0x000000000043c47f <+31>:    mov    %rsp,%rdi
   0x000000000043c482 <+34>:    mov    %rdi,%rsi
   0x000000000043c485 <+37>:    mov    %fs:(%rbx),%ebp
   0x000000000043c488 <+40>:    mov    %rax,(%rsp)
   0x000000000043c48c <+44>:    movq   $0x0,0x8(%rsp)
   0x000000000043c495 <+53>:    callq  0x43c4d0 <nanosleep>
   0x000000000043c49a <+58>:    test   %eax,%eax
   0x000000000043c49c <+60>:    js     0x43c4c0 <sleep+96>
   0x000000000043c49e <+62>:    mov    %ebp,%fs:(%rbx)
   0x000000000043c4a1 <+65>:    xor    %eax,%eax
   0x000000000043c4a3 <+67>:    mov    0x18(%rsp),%rdx
   0x000000000043c4a8 <+72>:    xor    %fs:0x28,%rdx
   0x000000000043c4b1 <+81>:    jne    0x43c4c5 <sleep+101>
   0x000000000043c4b3 <+83>:    add    $0x28,%rsp
   0x000000000043c4b7 <+87>:    pop    %rbx
   0x000000000043c4b8 <+88>:    pop    %rbp
   0x000000000043c4b9 <+89>:    retq
   0x000000000043c4ba <+90>:    nopw   0x0(%rax,%rax,1)
   0x000000000043c4c0 <+96>:    mov    (%rsp),%eax
```

```
   0x000000000043c4c3 <+99>:    jmp    0x43c4a3 <sleep+67>
   0x000000000043c4c5 <+101>:   callq  0x43edd0 <__stack_chk_fail_local>
End of assembler dump.
```

```
(gdb) i r
rax            0xfffffffffffffdfc    -516
rbx            0xffffffffffffffc0    -64
rcx            0x43c4e1              4441313
rdx            0x401b4d              4201293
rsi            0x7ffffe5129d0        140737460120016
rdi            0x7ffffe5129d0        140737460120016
rbp            0x0                   0x0
rsp            0x7ffffe5129c8        0x7ffffe5129c8
r8             0x2                   2
r9             0x2                   2
r10            0x7                   7
r11            0x246                 582
r12            0x4029c0              4204992
r13            0x0                   0
r14            0x4a5018              4870168
r15            0x0                   0
rip            0x43c4e1              0x43c4e1 <nanosleep+17>
eflags         0x246                 [ PF ZF IF ]
cs             0x33                  51
ss             0x2b                  43
ds             0x0                   0
es             0x0                   0
fs             0x0                   0
gs             0x0                   0
```

```
(gdb) frame 1
#1  0x000000000043c49a in sleep ()
```

```
(gdb) i r
rax            0xfffffffffffffdfc    -516
rbx            0xffffffffffffffc0    -64
rcx            0x43c4e1              4441313
rdx            0x401b4d              4201293
rsi            0x7ffffe5129d0        140737460120016
rdi            0x7ffffe5129d0        140737460120016
rbp            0x0                   0x0
rsp            0x7ffffe5129d0        0x7ffffe5129d0
r8             0x2                   2
r9             0x2                   2
r10            0x7                   7
r11            0x246                 582
r12            0x4029c0              4204992
r13            0x0                   0
r14            0x4a5018              4870168
r15            0x0                   0
rip            0x43c49a              0x43c49a <sleep+58>
eflags         0x246                 [ PF ZF IF ]
cs             0x33                  51
ss             0x2b                  43
ds             0x0                   0
es             0x0                   0
fs             0x0                   0
gs             0x0                   0
```

```
(gdb) frame 2
#2  0x0000000000401c17 in internal_get_message ()

(gdb) i r
rax            0xfffffffffffffdfc   -516
rbx            0x400470             4195440
rcx            0x43c4e1             4441313
rdx            0x401b4d             4201293
rsi            0x7ffffe5129d0       140737460120016
rdi            0x7ffffe5129d0       140737460120016
rbp            0x7ffffe512a20       0x7ffffe512a20
rsp            0x7ffffe512a10       0x7ffffe512a10
r8             0x2                  2
r9             0x2                  2
r10            0x7                  7
r11            0x246                582
r12            0x4029c0             4204992
r13            0x0                  0
r14            0x4a5018             4870168
r15            0x0                  0
rip            0x401c17             0x401c17 <internal_get_message+128>
eflags         0x246                [ PF ZF IF ]
cs             0x33                 51
ss             0x2b                 43
ds             0x0                  0
es             0x0                  0
fs             0x0                  0
gs             0x0                  0

(gdb) frame 3
#3  0x0000000000401c57 in get_message ()

(gdb) i r
rax            0xfffffffffffffdfc   -516
rbx            0x400470             4195440
rcx            0x43c4e1             4441313
rdx            0x401b4d             4201293
rsi            0x7ffffe5129d0       140737460120016
rdi            0x7ffffe5129d0       140737460120016
rbp            0x7ffffe512a60       0x7ffffe512a60
rsp            0x7ffffe512a30       0x7ffffe512a30
r8             0x2                  2
r9             0x2                  2
r10            0x7                  7
r11            0x246                582
r12            0x4029c0             4204992
r13            0x0                  0
r14            0x4a5018             4870168
r15            0x0                  0
rip            0x401c57             0x401c57 <get_message+57>
eflags         0x246                [ PF ZF IF ]
cs             0x33                 51
ss             0x2b                 43
ds             0x0                  0
es             0x0                  0
fs             0x0                  0
gs             0x0                  0

(gdb) frame 4
```

```
#4  0x0000000000401cea in main ()
```

```
(gdb) i r
rax            0xfffffffffffffdfc    -516
rbx            0x400470             4195440
rcx            0x43c4e1             4441313
rdx            0x401b4d             4201293
rsi            0x7ffffe5129d0       140737460120016
rdi            0x7ffffe5129d0       140737460120016
rbp            0x7ffffe512ab0       0x7ffffe512ab0
rsp            0x7ffffe512a70       0x7ffffe512a70
r8             0x2                  2
r9             0x2                  2
r10            0x7                  7
r11            0x246                582
r12            0x4029c0             4204992
r13            0x0                  0
r14            0x4a5018             4870168
r15            0x0                  0
rip            0x401cea             0x401cea <main+56>
eflags         0x246                [ PF ZF IF ]
cs             0x33                 51
ss             0x2b                 43
ds             0x0                  0
es             0x0                  0
fs             0x0                  0
gs             0x0                  0
```

Note: It also appears that RBX changed between frame 1 and frame 2. This is because it was previously saved on the stack, so its value is taken from that location:

```
(gdb) disassemble sleep
Dump of assembler code for function sleep:
   0x000000000043c460 <+0>:    push   %rbp
   0x000000000043c461 <+1>:    push   %rbx
   0x000000000043c462 <+2>:    sub    $0x28,%rsp
   0x000000000043c466 <+6>:    mov    $0xffffffffffffffc0,%rbx
   0x000000000043c46d <+13>:   mov    %fs:0x28,%rax
   0x000000000043c476 <+22>:   mov    %rax,0x18(%rsp)
   0x000000000043c47b <+27>:   xor    %eax,%eax
   0x000000000043c47d <+29>:   mov    %edi,%eax
   0x000000000043c47f <+31>:   mov    %rsp,%rdi
   0x000000000043c482 <+34>:   mov    %rdi,%rsi
   0x000000000043c485 <+37>:   mov    %fs:(%rbx),%ebp
   0x000000000043c488 <+40>:   mov    %rax,(%rsp)
   0x000000000043c48c <+44>:   movq   $0x0,0x8(%rsp)
   0x000000000043c495 <+53>:   callq  0x43c4d0 <nanosleep>
   0x000000000043c49a <+58>:   test   %eax,%eax
   0x000000000043c49c <+60>:   js     0x43c4c0 <sleep+96>
   0x000000000043c49e <+62>:   mov    %ebp,%fs:(%rbx)
   0x000000000043c4a1 <+65>:   xor    %eax,%eax
   0x000000000043c4a3 <+67>:   mov    0x18(%rsp),%rdx
   0x000000000043c4a8 <+72>:   xor    %fs:0x28,%rdx
   0x000000000043c4b1 <+81>:   jne    0x43c4c5 <sleep+101>
   0x000000000043c4b3 <+83>:   add    $0x28,%rsp
   0x000000000043c4b7 <+87>:   pop    %rbx
   0x000000000043c4b8 <+88>:   pop    %rbp
   0x000000000043c4b9 <+89>:   retq
```

```
   0x000000000043c4ba <+90>:    nopw   0x0(%rax,%rax,1)
   0x000000000043c4c0 <+96>:    mov    (%rsp),%eax
   0x000000000043c4c3 <+99>:    jmp    0x43c4a3 <sleep+67>
   0x000000000043c4c5 <+101>:   callq  0x43edd0 <__stack_chk_fail_local>
End of assembler dump.
```

17.   Some CPU registers can be recovered manually, such as RIP (saved address when using *call* instruction) and RSP (the stack pointer value before saving that RIP address). Other register values can be recovered manually, too, if they were not used in called frames or were saved in temporary memory cells (such as on stack, as we saw in the case of RBX). Let's recover some registers for the first few frames.

```
(gdb) frame 0
#0  0x000000000043c4e1 in nanosleep ()
```

Let's disassemble the current function:

```
(gdb) disassemble nanosleep
Dump of assembler code for function nanosleep:
   0x000000000043c4d0 <+0>:     mov    0x6c356(%rip),%eax        # 0x4a882c
<__libc_multiple_threads>
   0x000000000043c4d6 <+6>:     test   %eax,%eax
   0x000000000043c4d8 <+8>:     jne    0x43c4f0 <nanosleep+32>
   0x000000000043c4da <+10>:    mov    $0x23,%eax
   0x000000000043c4df <+15>:    syscall
=> 0x000000000043c4e1 <+17>:    cmp    $0xfffffffffffff000,%rax
   0x000000000043c4e7 <+23>:    ja     0x43c530 <nanosleep+96>
   0x000000000043c4e9 <+25>:    retq
   0x000000000043c4ea <+26>:    nopw   0x0(%rax,%rax,1)
   0x000000000043c4f0 <+32>:    push   %rbp
   0x000000000043c4f1 <+33>:    mov    %rsi,%rbp
   0x000000000043c4f4 <+36>:    push   %rbx
   0x000000000043c4f5 <+37>:    mov    %rdi,%rbx
   0x000000000043c4f8 <+40>:    sub    $0x18,%rsp
   0x000000000043c4fc <+44>:    callq  0x43ed00 <__libc_enable_asynccancel>
   0x000000000043c501 <+49>:    mov    %rbp,%rsi
   0x000000000043c504 <+52>:    mov    %rbx,%rdi
   0x000000000043c507 <+55>:    mov    %eax,%edx
   0x000000000043c509 <+57>:    mov    $0x23,%eax
   0x000000000043c50e <+62>:    syscall
   0x000000000043c510 <+64>:    cmp    $0xfffffffffffff000,%rax
   0x000000000043c516 <+70>:    ja     0x43c542 <nanosleep+114>
   0x000000000043c518 <+72>:    mov    %edx,%edi
   0x000000000043c51a <+74>:    mov    %eax,0xc(%rsp)
   0x000000000043c51e <+78>:    callq  0x43ed60 <__libc_disable_asynccancel>
   0x000000000043c523 <+83>:    mov    0xc(%rsp),%eax
   0x000000000043c527 <+87>:    add    $0x18,%rsp
   0x000000000043c52b <+91>:    pop    %rbx
   0x000000000043c52c <+92>:    pop    %rbp
   0x000000000043c52d <+93>:    retq
   0x000000000043c52e <+94>:    xchg   %ax,%ax
   0x000000000043c530 <+96>:    mov    $0xffffffffffffffc0,%rdx
   0x000000000043c537 <+103>:   neg    %eax
   0x000000000043c539 <+105>:   mov    %eax,%fs:(%rdx)
   0x000000000043c53c <+108>:   mov    $0xffffffff,%eax
   0x000000000043c541 <+113>:   retq
   0x000000000043c542 <+114>:   mov    $0xffffffffffffffc0,%rcx
   0x000000000043c549 <+121>:   neg    %eax
```

```
   0x000000000043c54b <+123>:    mov     %eax,%fs:(%rcx)
   0x000000000043c54e <+126>:    mov     $0xffffffff,%eax
   0x000000000043c553 <+131>:    jmp     0x43c518 <nanosleep+72>
End of assembler dump.
```

It is a short function. We see it overwrites EAX. Note that the EAX value is different:

```
(gdb) i r $rax
rax              0xfffffffffffffdfc   -516
```

We see that RSP is not used inside the *nanosleep* function, and its value should point to the return address of the caller, *sleep* function during the execution of the **call** instruction:

```
(gdb) x/a $rsp
0x7ffffe5129c8: 0x43c49a <sleep+58>
```

Note: The RIP value of the caller, `0x43c49a`, is saved before the call, and RSP for the caller should be the value before the **call** instruction was executed. When a return address is saved, RSP is decremented by 8, so the value of RSP before the *nanosleep* call should be the current value of RSP pointing to the saved return address + 8:

```
(gdb) p/x $rsp+8
$17 = 0x7ffffe5129d0
```

Note: We see that for the next frame RIP is `0x43c49a <sleep+58>` and RSP is `0x7ffffe5129d0`. Let's now find out RIP and RSP for the next frame (the caller of the *sleep* function). To find out RSP pointing to the caller's saved RIP, we need to see how it was used in the callee, the *sleep* function, before the callee called *nanosleep*. We disassemble the *sleep* function:

```
(gdb) disassemble sleep
Dump of assembler code for function sleep:
   0x000000000043c460 <+0>:     push    %rbp
   0x000000000043c461 <+1>:     push    %rbx
   0x000000000043c462 <+2>:     sub     $0x28,%rsp
   0x000000000043c466 <+6>:     mov     $0xffffffffffffffc0,%rbx
   0x000000000043c46d <+13>:    mov     %fs:0x28,%rax
   0x000000000043c476 <+22>:    mov     %rax,0x18(%rsp)
   0x000000000043c47b <+27>:    xor     %eax,%eax
   0x000000000043c47d <+29>:    mov     %edi,%eax
   0x000000000043c47f <+31>:    mov     %rsp,%rdi
   0x000000000043c482 <+34>:    mov     %rdi,%rsi
   0x000000000043c485 <+37>:    mov     %fs:(%rbx),%ebp
   0x000000000043c488 <+40>:    mov     %rax,(%rsp)
   0x000000000043c48c <+44>:    movq    $0x0,0x8(%rsp)
   0x000000000043c495 <+53>:    callq   0x43c4d0 <nanosleep>
   0x000000000043c49a <+58>:    test    %eax,%eax
   0x000000000043c49c <+60>:    js      0x43c4c0 <sleep+96>
   0x000000000043c49e <+62>:    mov     %ebp,%fs:(%rbx)
   0x000000000043c4a1 <+65>:    xor     %eax,%eax
   0x000000000043c4a3 <+67>:    mov     0x18(%rsp),%rdx
   0x000000000043c4a8 <+72>:    xor     %fs:0x28,%rdx
   0x000000000043c4b1 <+81>:    jne     0x43c4c5 <sleep+101>
   0x000000000043c4b3 <+83>:    add     $0x28,%rsp
   0x000000000043c4b7 <+87>:    pop     %rbx
   0x000000000043c4b8 <+88>:    pop     %rbp
   0x000000000043c4b9 <+89>:    retq
```

```
      0x000000000043c4ba <+90>:     nopw    0x0(%rax,%rax,1)
      0x000000000043c4c0 <+96>:     mov     (%rsp),%eax
      0x000000000043c4c3 <+99>:     jmp     0x43c4a3 <sleep+67>
      0x000000000043c4c5 <+101>:    callq   0x43edd0 <__stack_chk_fail_local>
End of assembler dump.
```

We see that the stack pointer was decremented by 0x28 (*sub* instruction) and also by 16 (two *push* instructions), and so we add these values to RSP we found out previously for the *nanosleep* call, **0x7ffffe5129d0**:

```
(gdb) x/a 0x7ffffe5129d0 + 0x28 + 16
0x7ffffe512a08: 0x401c17 <internal_get_message+128>
```

We see that *sleep* was called from the *internal_get_message* function. The value of RSP before the call should be adjusted by 8 because of the saved return address:

```
(gdb) p/x 0x7ffffe512a08+8
$18 = 0x7ffffe512a10
```

18.   We continue with a few more frames. We disassemble the caller of *sleep*, *internal_get_message*:

```
(gdb) disassemble internal_get_message
Dump of assembler code for function internal_get_message:
   0x0000000000401b97 <+0>:      push    %rbp
   0x0000000000401b98 <+1>:      mov     %rsp,%rbp
   0x0000000000401b9b <+4>:      sub     $0x10,%rsp
   0x0000000000401b9f <+8>:      mov     %rdi,-0x8(%rbp)
   0x0000000000401ba3 <+12>:     mov     %rsi,-0x10(%rbp)
   0x0000000000401ba7 <+16>:     cmpq    $0x0,-0x8(%rbp)
   0x0000000000401bac <+21>:     je      0x401c0d <internal_get_message+118>
   0x0000000000401bae <+23>:     mov     -0x8(%rbp),%rax
   0x0000000000401bb2 <+27>:     movq    $0x0,(%rax)
   0x0000000000401bb9 <+34>:     mov     -0x8(%rbp),%rax
   0x0000000000401bbd <+38>:     movq    $0x113,0x8(%rax)
   0x0000000000401bc5 <+46>:     mov     $0x1,%edx
   0x0000000000401bca <+51>:     mov     -0x8(%rbp),%rax
   0x0000000000401bce <+55>:     mov     %rdx,0x10(%rax)
   0x0000000000401bd2 <+59>:     lea     -0x8c(%rip),%rdx         # 0x401b4d <time_proc>
   0x0000000000401bd9 <+66>:     mov     -0x8(%rbp),%rax
   0x0000000000401bdd <+70>:     mov     %rdx,0x18(%rax)
   0x0000000000401be1 <+74>:     mov     -0x8(%rbp),%rax
   0x0000000000401be5 <+78>:     movl    $0x4578350,0x20(%rax)
   0x0000000000401bec <+85>:     mov     -0x8(%rbp),%rax
   0x0000000000401bf0 <+89>:     movl    $0x9c,0x24(%rax)
   0x0000000000401bf7 <+96>:     mov     -0x8(%rbp),%rax
   0x0000000000401bfb <+100>:    movl    $0x147,0x28(%rax)
   0x0000000000401c02 <+107>:    mov     -0x8(%rbp),%rax
   0x0000000000401c06 <+111>:    movl    $0x0,0x2c(%rax)
   0x0000000000401c0d <+118>:    mov     $0xffffffff,%edi
   0x0000000000401c12 <+123>:    callq   0x43c460 <sleep>
   0x0000000000401c17 <+128>:    mov     $0x0,%eax
   0x0000000000401c1c <+133>:    leaveq
   0x0000000000401c1d <+134>:    retq
End of assembler dump.
```

We see that the stack pointer was decremented by 0x10 (*sub* instruction) and also by 8 (*push* instruction), and so we add these values to RSP we found out previously for the *sleep* call, **0x7ffffe512a10**:

```
(gdb) x/a 0x7ffffe512a10 + 0x10 + 8
0x7ffffe512a28: 0x401c57 <get_message+57>
```

We see that *internal_get_message* was called from the *get_message* function. The value of RSP before the call should be adjusted by 8 because of the saved return address:

```
(gdb) p/x 0x7ffffe512a28+8
$19 = 0x7ffffe512a30
```

Now we disassemble the caller of *internal_get_message*, *get_message*:

```
(gdb) disassemble get_message
Dump of assembler code for function get_message:
   0x0000000000401c1e <+0>:     push   %rbp
   0x0000000000401c1f <+1>:     mov    %rsp,%rbp
   0x0000000000401c22 <+4>:     sub    $0x30,%rsp
   0x0000000000401c26 <+8>:     mov    %rdi,-0x18(%rbp)
   0x0000000000401c2a <+12>:    mov    %rsi,-0x20(%rbp)
   0x0000000000401c2e <+16>:    mov    %rdx,-0x28(%rbp)
   0x0000000000401c32 <+20>:    mov    %rcx,-0x30(%rbp)
   0x0000000000401c36 <+24>:    movl   $0xffffffff,-0x4(%rbp)
   0x0000000000401c3d <+31>:    cmpq   $0x0,-0x18(%rbp)
   0x0000000000401c42 <+36>:    je     0x401c5a <get_message+60>
   0x0000000000401c44 <+38>:    mov    -0x20(%rbp),%rdx
   0x0000000000401c48 <+42>:    mov    -0x18(%rbp),%rax
   0x0000000000401c4c <+46>:    mov    %rdx,%rsi
   0x0000000000401c4f <+49>:    mov    %rax,%rdi
   0x0000000000401c52 <+52>:    callq  0x401b97 <internal_get_message>
   0x0000000000401c57 <+57>:    mov    %eax,-0x4(%rbp)
   0x0000000000401c5a <+60>:    cmpl   $0x0,-0x4(%rbp)
   0x0000000000401c5e <+64>:    je     0x401c6c <get_message+78>
   0x0000000000401c60 <+66>:    mov    -0x4(%rbp),%eax
   0x0000000000401c63 <+69>:    mov    %eax,%edi
   0x0000000000401c65 <+71>:    callq  0x401b58 <set_last_ui_error>
   0x0000000000401c6a <+76>:    jmp    0x401c7b <get_message+93>
   0x0000000000401c6c <+78>:    mov    -0x20(%rbp),%rax
   0x0000000000401c70 <+82>:    mov    %rax,%rdi
   0x0000000000401c73 <+85>:    callq  0x401b6b <call_ui_hooks>
   0x0000000000401c78 <+90>:    mov    %eax,-0x4(%rbp)
   0x0000000000401c7b <+93>:    cmpl   $0x0,-0x4(%rbp)
   0x0000000000401c7f <+97>:    sete   %al
   0x0000000000401c82 <+100>:   movzbl %al,%eax
   0x0000000000401c85 <+103>:   leaveq
   0x0000000000401c86 <+104>:   retq
End of assembler dump.
```

We see that the stack pointer was decremented by 0x30 (*sub* instruction) and also by 8 (*push* instruction), and so we add these values to RSP we found out previously for the *sleep* call, 0x7ffffe512a30:

```
(gdb) x/a 0x7ffffe512a30 + 0x30 + 8
0x7ffffe512a68: 0x401cea <main+56>
```

We see that *get_message* was called from the *main* function.

Note: We can reconstruct the stack trace like a debugger. It works whether or not the RBP pointer is used to track the previous RSP. Note that we can correctly disassemble functions using the **disassemble** command because function boundaries are saved in symbol files, or the start of the function is available from the image file section. If such information is not available, we would most likely have a truncated or incorrect stack trace:

```
(gdb) symbol-file
No symbol file now.
```

```
(gdb) bt
#0  0x000000000043c4e1 in ?? ()
#1  0x000000000043c49a in ?? ()
#2  0x00000000fffffff0 in ?? ()
#3  0x00000000130f2d88 in ?? ()
#4  0x0000000000000140 in ?? ()
#5  0x3ebeea4a71786c00 in ?? ()
#6  0x000000000000000a in ?? ()
#7  0x0000000000400470 in ?? ()
#8  0x00007ffffe512a20 in ?? ()
#9  0x0000000000401c17 in ?? ()
#10 0x0000000000000000 in ?? ()
```

Note: In such a case, we may still find the beginning of the function heuristically by disassembling the return address backward and looking for the possible function prologue, for example:

```
(gdb) x/20i 0x43c49a-72
   0x43c452:    lea     0x43cbb(%rip),%edi        # 0x480113
   0x43c458:    callq   0x402b70
   0x43c45d:    nopl    (%rax)
   0x43c460:    push    %rbp
   0x43c461:    push    %rbx
   0x43c462:    sub     $0x28,%rsp
   0x43c466:    mov     $0xffffffffffffffc0,%rbx
   0x43c46d:    mov     %fs:0x28,%rax
   0x43c476:    mov     %rax,0x18(%rsp)
   0x43c47b:    xor     %eax,%eax
   0x43c47d:    mov     %edi,%eax
   0x43c47f:    mov     %rsp,%rdi
   0x43c482:    mov     %rdi,%rsi
   0x43c485:    mov     %fs:(%rbx),%ebp
   0x43c488:    mov     %rax,(%rsp)
   0x43c48c:    movq    $0x0,0x8(%rsp)
   0x43c495:    callq   0x43c4d0
   0x43c49a:    test    %eax,%eax
   0x43c49c:    js      0x43c4c0
   0x43c49e:    mov     %ebp,%fs:(%rbx)
```

19.   Other registers and memory values are reused and overwritten when we move down the frames, so less and less information can be recovered. We call this ADDR pattern (Inverse) **Context Pyramid**.

20.   We also introduce special **Stack Frame** memory cell diagrams. For example, the case of the stack frame for the *get_message* function before calling *internal_get_message* is illustrated in the MCD-R1.xlsx section D (offsets are hexadecimal), where [RSP+38] corresponds to the stored return address of the *get_message* caller, *main*.

Stack Reconstruction (x64)

1. Top frame from the current RIP_1, RSP_1 (**info reg**)
2. Disassemble around the current RIP_n (**disass** RIP_n)*
3. Find out the beginning of the function prologue*
4. Check RSP_n usage (**sub**, **push**) and count offsets
5. Get RIP_{n+1} for the next frame (**x/a** RSP_n + offset)
6. Get RSP_{n+1} for the next frame (RSP_n + offset + 8)
7. ++n
8. goto #2

* If symbols are available, disassemble the function corresponding to RIP_n (**disass name**)
If symbols are not available, disassemble backwards until the function prologue is found

The slide shows an algorithm for reconstructing stack traces on the Linux x64 platform. It should also work on 32-bit x86 Linux platforms (with a +4 pointer size change, of course). Stack reconstruction is more straightforward when the RBP register is used as a stack frame pointer since it is also saved in every function prologue.

Exercise R1 (A64, GDB)

Goal: Review A64 assembly fundamentals; learn how to reconstruct stack trace manually.

ADDR Patterns: Universal Pointer, Symbolic Pointer S^2, Interpreted Pointer S^3, Context Pyramid.

Memory Cell Diagrams: Register, Pointer, Stack Frame.

1. Load a core dump *notepad.12315* and *notepad* executable from A64/MemoryDumps directory:

```
~/ADDR-Linux/A64/MemoryDumps$ gdb -c notepad.12315 -se notepad
GNU gdb (Ubuntu 12.0.90-0ubuntu1) 12.0.90
Copyright (C) 2022 Free Software Foundation, Inc.
License GPLv3+: GNU GPL version 3 or later <http://gnu.org/licenses/gpl.html>
This is free software: you are free to change and redistribute it.
There is NO WARRANTY, to the extent permitted by law.
Type "show copying" and "show warranty" for details.
This GDB was configured as "aarch64-linux-gnu".
Type "show configuration" for configuration details.
For bug reporting instructions, please see:
<https://www.gnu.org/software/gdb/bugs/>.
Find the GDB manual and other documentation resources online at:
    <http://www.gnu.org/software/gdb/documentation/>.

For help, type "help".
Type "apropos word" to search for commands related to "word"...
Reading symbols from notepad...
(No debugging symbols found in notepad)

warning: Can't open file /home/ubuntu/notepad during file-backed mapping note processing
[New LWP 12315]
Core was generated by `./notepad'.
#0  0x000000000043a3fc in clock_nanosleep ()
```

2. We open a log file and set color highlighting off:

```
(gdb) set logging file R1.log
```

```
(gdb) set logging enabled on
Copying output to R1.log.
Copying debug output to R1.log.
```

```
(gdb) set style enabled off
```

3. We get this stack trace:

```
(gdb) bt
#0  0x000000000043a3fc in clock_nanosleep ()
#1  0x0000000000418ffc in nanosleep ()
#2  0x0000000000418f98 in sleep ()
#3  0x00000000004007c4 in internal_get_message ()
#4  0x0000000000400808 in get_message ()
#5  0x00000000004008cc in main ()
```

84

4.   Let's check the main CPU registers:

```
(gdb) info registers
x0              0x0                 0
x1              0x0                 0
x2              0xffffd9cbc488      281474335753352
x3              0xffffd9cbc488      281474335753352
x4              0x4919e8            4790760
x5              0xc4c3d06c44caa706  -4268338858387921146
x6              0x495a58            4807256
x7              0x2                 2
x8              0x73                115
x9              0x2                 2
x10             0x0                 0
x11             0x49a000            4825088
x12             0x46d244            4641348
x13             0x0                 0
x14             0x70                112
x15             0x0                 0
x16             0x0                 0
x17             0x0                 0
x18             0x0                 0
x19             0x0                 0
x20             0x492000            4792320
x21             0x33e4a000          870621184
x22             0xffffd9cbc488      281474335753352
x23             0xffffd9cbc488      281474335753352
x24             0x0                 0
x25             0x0                 0
x26             0x1                 1
x27             0x400280            4194944
x28             0x493030            4796464
x29             0xffffd9cbc3c0      281474335753152
x30             0x418ffc            4296700
sp              0xffffd9cbc3c0      0xffffd9cbc3c0
pc              0x43a3fc            0x43a3fc <clock_nanosleep+124>
cpsr            0x60001000          [ EL=0 BTYPE=0 SSBS C Z ]
fpsr            0x0                 [ ]
fpcr            0x0                 [ RMode=0 ]
```

Note: The register parts and naming are illustrated in the MCD-R1-A64.xlsx A section.

5.   The current instruction registers (registers that are used and affected by the current instruction or semantically tied to it) can be checked by listing them individually:

```
(gdb) x/i $pc
=> 0x43a3fc <clock_nanosleep+124>:      svc     #0x0

(gdb) info registers x8
x8              0x73                115
```

Note: Most commands require $ to be prefixed to a register name; otherwise, they consider it a symbol name.

```
(gdb) x/i pc
No symbol table is loaded.  Use the "file" command.
```

85

6.   Any register value can be checked with the **info registers** command (**i r**):

```
(gdb) i r x22
x22             0xffffd9cbc488        281474335753352
```

```
(gdb) i r w22
w22             0xffffd9cbc488        281474335753352
```

7.   Individual parts can also be interpreted using the **print** command (**p**):

```
(gdb) p/z $x22
$5 = 0x0000ffffd9cbc488
```

```
(gdb) p/z (int[2])$x22
$6 = {0xd9cbc488, 0x0000ffff}
```

```
(gdb) p/z (short[4])$x22
$7 = {0xc488, 0xd9cb, 0xffff, 0x0000}
```

```
(gdb) p/z (char[8])$x22
$8 = {0x88, 0xc4, 0xcb, 0xd9, 0xff, 0xff, 0x00, 0x00}
```

8.   Any registry value can be interpreted as a pointer to memory cells, a memory address (**Universal Pointer** pattern vs. a pointer originally designed to be such). However, memory contents at that address may be inaccessible or unknown, as in the case of X5 below.

```
(gdb) x $x5
0xc4c3d06c44caa706:     Cannot access memory at address 0xc4c3d06c44caa706
```

Note: The following output for X22 is illustrated in the MCD-R1-A64.xlsx B section.

```
(gdb) x/gx $x22
0xffffd9cbc488: 0x00000000ffffffd7
```

9.   We can also specify value count or limit to just one value and use finer granularity for memory dumping:

```
(gdb) x/20gx $x22
0xffffd9cbc488: 0x00000000ffffffd7      0x000000003110ad3d
0xffffd9cbc498: 0xca3b4bf9224d6b00      0x0000ffffd9cbc4c0
0xffffd9cbc4a8: 0x0000000000400808      0x0000000000000000
0xffffd9cbc4b8: 0x0000ffffd9cbc528      0x0000ffffd9cbc500
0xffffd9cbc4c8: 0x00000000004008cc      0x0000000000000000
0xffffd9cbc4d8: 0x0000000000000000      0x0000000000000000
0xffffd9cbc4e8: 0x0000ffffd9cbc528      0x0000000000493678
0xffffd9cbc4f8: 0xffffffff00000001      0x0000ffffd9cbc560
0xffffd9cbc508: 0x00000000004009b4      0x0000ffffd9cbc718
0xffffd9cbc518: 0x0000000100000000      0x000000770000007c
```

Note: The similar output for X22 as below is illustrated in the MCD-R1-A64.xlsx C section.

```
(gdb) x/20wx $x22
0xffffd9cbc488: 0xffffffd7      0x00000000      0x3110ad3d      0x00000000
0xffffd9cbc498: 0x224d6b00      0xca3b4bf9      0xd9cbc4c0      0x0000ffff
0xffffd9cbc4a8: 0x00400808      0x00000000      0x00000000      0x00000000
0xffffd9cbc4b8: 0xd9cbc528      0x0000ffff      0xd9cbc500      0x0000ffff
0xffffd9cbc4c8: 0x004008cc      0x00000000      0x00000000      0x00000000
```

```
(gdb) x/20hx $x22
0xffffd9cbc488:  0xffd7   0xffff   0x0000   0x0000   0xad3d   0x3110   0x0000   0x0000
0xffffd9cbc498:  0x6b00   0x224d   0x4bf9   0xca3b   0xc4c0   0xd9cb   0xffff   0x0000
0xffffd9cbc4a8:  0x0808   0x0040   0x0000   0x0000

(gdb) x/20bx $x22
0xffffd9cbc488:  0xd7   0xff   0xff   0xff   0x00   0x00   0x00   0x00
0xffffd9cbc490:  0x3d   0xad   0x10   0x31   0x00   0x00   0x00   0x00
0xffffd9cbc498:  0x00   0x6b   0x4d   0x22
```

Note: GDB remembers formatting:

```
(gdb) x/20 $sp
0xffffd9cbc3c0:  0x40   0xc4   0xcb   0xd9   0xff   0xff   0x00   0x00
0xffffd9cbc3c8:  0xfc   0x8f   0x41   0x00   0x00   0x00   0x00   0x00
0xffffd9cbc3d0:  0x00   0x20   0x49   0x00
```

10.   Notice a difference between a value and its organization in memory stemmed from the little-endian organization of the ARM64 platform (least significant parts are located at lower addresses):

```
(gdb) p/z $sp
$37 = 0x0000ffffd9cbc3c0

(gdb) p/z (int[2])$sp
$38 = {0xd9cbc3c0, 0x0000ffff}

(gdb) p/z $sp
$43 = 0x0000ffffd9cbc3c0

(gdb) p/z (short[4])$sp
$44 = {0xc3c0, 0xd9cb, 0xffff, 0x0000}

(gdb) p/z $rsp
$45 = 0x0000ffffd9cbc3c0

(gdb) p/z (char[8])$rsp
$46 = {0xc0, 0xc3, 0xcb, 0xd9, 0xff, 0xff, 0x00, 0x00}
```

11.   Every value can be associated with a symbolic value from symbol files or the binary (exported and included symbols) if available. We call this **Symbolic Pointer** or S^2:

```
(gdb) x/60a $sp
0xffffd9cbc3c0:  0xffffd9cbc440   0x418ffc <nanosleep+28>
0xffffd9cbc3d0:  0x492000 <tunable_list+1320>   0x30
0xffffd9cbc3e0:  0x33e4a7c0   0x0
0xffffd9cbc3f0:  0x2   0x48f850
0xffffd9cbc400:  0x18   0x0
0xffffd9cbc410:  0x0   0x499fb0 <_dl_debug_mask>
0xffffd9cbc420:  0x360ed96   0xffffd9cbc494
0xffffd9cbc430:  0x492000 <tunable_list+1320>   0xca3b4bf9224d6b00
0xffffd9cbc440:  0xffffd9cbc450   0x418f98 <sleep+72>
0xffffd9cbc450:  0xffffd9cbc4a0   0x4007c4 <internal_get_message+132>
0xffffd9cbc460:  0x1   0xffffd9cbc718
0xffffd9cbc470:  0x2   0xffffd9cbc728
0xffffd9cbc480:  0xffffd9cbc540   0xffffffd7
0xffffd9cbc490:  0x3110ad3d   0xca3b4bf9224d6b00
0xffffd9cbc4a0:  0xffffd9cbc4c0   0x400808 <get_message+56>
```

```
0xffffd9cbc4b0: 0x0      0xffffd9cbc528
0xffffd9cbc4c0: 0xffffd9cbc500  0x4008cc <main+68>
0xffffd9cbc4d0: 0x0      0x0
0xffffd9cbc4e0: 0x0      0xffffd9cbc528
0xffffd9cbc4f0: 0x493678 <main_arena>   0xffffffff00000001
0xffffd9cbc500: 0xffffd9cbc560  0x4009b4 <__libc_start_call_main+84>
0xffffd9cbc510: 0xffffd9cbc718  0x100000000
0xffffd9cbc520: 0x770000007c     0x0
0xffffd9cbc530: 0x113    0x1
0xffffd9cbc540: 0x4006d4 <time_proc>    0x9c04578350
0xffffd9cbc550: 0x147    0xca3b4bf9224d6b00
0xffffd9cbc560: 0xffffd9cbc670  0x400d34 <__libc_start_main_impl+836>
0xffffd9cbc570: 0xffffd9cbc5a0  0x4005b4 <_start+52>
0xffffd9cbc580: 0x100499f68      0xffffd9cbc718
0xffffd9cbc590: 0x494000 <_dl_main_map> 0x1
```

```
(gdb) info symbol 0x4006d4
time_proc in section .text of /home/ubuntu/ADDR-Linux/A64/MemoryDumps/notepad
```

Note: The address 0xffffd9cbc540 that points to 0x4006d4 doesn't have an associated symbol:

```
(gdb) info symbol 0xffffd9cbc540
No symbol matches 0xffffd9cbc540.
```

Note: The current instruction pointer address contained in PC should have an associated symbol of the current function in our example because we have function symbols for *notepad*:

```
(gdb) p/z $pc
$4 = 0x000000000043a3fc
```

```
(gdb) info symbol 0x000000000043a3fc
clock_nanosleep + 124 in section .text of /home/ubuntu/ADDR-Linux/A64/MemoryDumps/notepad
```

```
(gdb) info symbol $pc
clock_nanosleep + 124 in section .text of /home/ubuntu/ADDR-Linux/A64/MemoryDumps/notepad
```

```
(gdb) i r $pc
pc              0x43a3fc                0x43a3fc <clock_nanosleep+124>
```

```
(gdb) x/i $pc
=> 0x43a3fc <clock_nanosleep+124>:      svc     #0x0
```

12.   Now we come to the next pointer level after its value and symbol: its interpretation. We call it an **Interpreted Pointer**, S^3. Such interpretation is implemented either via typed structures (the **print** command) or via various debugger commands or scripts that format information for us. In our example, we would like to check the memory pointed to by the address 0xffffd9cbc528. We suspect it might be **msg_t** structure related to the "get message" loop:

```
typedef struct
{
  hwnd_t    hwnd;
  uint64_t  message;
  uint64_t  param1;
  uint64_t  param2;
  uint32_t  time;
  POINT     pt;
```

```
    uint32_t  private;
} msg_t, *p_msg_t;

(gdb) x/60a $sp
0xffffd9cbc3c0: 0xffffd9cbc440  0x418ffc <nanosleep+28>
0xffffd9cbc3d0: 0x492000 <tunable_list+1320>      0x30
0xffffd9cbc3e0: 0x33e4a7c0       0x0
0xffffd9cbc3f0: 0x2      0x48f850
0xffffd9cbc400: 0x18      0x0
0xffffd9cbc410: 0x0        0x499fb0 <_dl_debug_mask>
0xffffd9cbc420: 0x360ed96        0xffffd9cbc494
0xffffd9cbc430: 0x492000 <tunable_list+1320>      0xca3b4bf9224d6b00
0xffffd9cbc440: 0xffffd9cbc450  0x418f98 <sleep+72>
0xffffd9cbc450: 0xffffd9cbc4a0  0x4007c4 <internal_get_message+132>
0xffffd9cbc460: 0x1      0xffffd9cbc718
0xffffd9cbc470: 0x2      0xffffd9cbc728
0xffffd9cbc480: 0xffffd9cbc540  0xfffffffd7
0xffffd9cbc490: 0x3110ad3d        0xca3b4bf9224d6b00
0xffffd9cbc4a0: 0xffffd9cbc4c0  0x400808 <get_message+56>
0xffffd9cbc4b0: 0x0        0xffffd9cbc528
0xffffd9cbc4c0: 0xffffd9cbc500  0x4008cc <main+68>
0xffffd9cbc4d0: 0x0        0x0
0xffffd9cbc4e0: 0x0        0xffffd9cbc528
0xffffd9cbc4f0: 0x493678 <main_arena>     0xffffffff00000001
0xffffd9cbc500: 0xffffd9cbc560  0x4009b4 <__libc_start_call_main+84>
0xffffd9cbc510: 0xffffd9cbc718  0x100000000
0xffffd9cbc520: 0x770000007c      0x0
0xffffd9cbc530: 0x113    0x1
0xffffd9cbc540: 0x4006d4 <time_proc>      0x9c04578350
0xffffd9cbc550: 0x147    0xca3b4bf9224d6b00
0xffffd9cbc560: 0xffffd9cbc670  0x400d34 <__libc_start_main_impl+836>
0xffffd9cbc570: 0xffffd9cbc5a0  0x4005b4 <_start+52>
0xffffd9cbc580: 0x100499f68      0xffffd9cbc718
0xffffd9cbc590: 0x494000 <_dl_main_map> 0x1

(gdb) x/20gx 0xffffd9cbc528
0xffffd9cbc528: 0x0000000000000000      0x0000000000000113
0xffffd9cbc538: 0x0000000000000001      0x00000000004006d4
0xffffd9cbc548: 0x0000009c04578350      0x0000000000000147
0xffffd9cbc558: 0xca3b4bf9224d6b00      0x0000ffffd9cbc670
0xffffd9cbc568: 0x0000000000400d34      0x0000ffffd9cbc5a0
0xffffd9cbc578: 0x00000000004005b4      0x0000000100499f68
0xffffd9cbc588: 0x0000ffffd9cbc718      0x0000000000494000
0xffffd9cbc598: 0x0000000000000001      0x0000ffffd9cbc718
0xffffd9cbc5a8: 0x0000000000000002      0x0000ffffd9cbc728
0xffffd9cbc5b8: 0x0000000000000002      0x000000000048f850

(gdb) x/20wx 0xffffd9cbc528
0xffffd9cbc528: 0x00000000      0x00000000      0x00000113      0x00000000
0xffffd9cbc538: 0x00000001      0x00000000      0x004006d4      0x00000000
0xffffd9cbc548: 0x04578350      0x0000009c      0x00000147      0x00000000
0xffffd9cbc558: 0x224d6b00      0xca3b4bf9      0xd9cbc670      0x0000ffff
0xffffd9cbc568: 0x00400d34      0x00000000      0xd9cbc5a0      0x0000ffff

(gdb) x/20wd 0xffffd9cbc528
0xffffd9cbc528: 0        0        275      0
0xffffd9cbc538: 1        0        4196052  0
0xffffd9cbc548: 72844112         156      327      0
0xffffd9cbc558: 575499008        -902083591       -640956816       65535
```

```
0xffffd9cbc568: 4197684 0         -640957024      65535
```

```
(gdb) p *(msg_t *)0xffffd9cbc528
No symbol table is loaded.  Use the "file" command.
```

```
(gdb) info types msg_t
All types matching regular expression "msg_t":
```

Note: Suppose that the raw structure makes sense for a timer message (**0x113**) where param1 is a timer ID (**1**), and usually a callback function (param2) is NULL (0x0), but in our case, it is not (0x000000000004006d4, as we saw previously, *time_proc*). Also, mouse pointer data makes sense (**0x9c, 0x147**). Unfortunately, the **msg_t** structure type is not available in the *notepad* memory dump, and suppose we don't have a debug symbol file for it either. However, we can add a different unrelated symbol file, for example, *extra-symbols* from x64/MemoryDumps/ExtraSymbols, which was compiled with full debug symbols and should have structures necessary for this message loop processing (**Injected Symbols** memory analysis pattern).

13.   We specify an additional symbol file path:

```
(gdb) add-symbol-file ./ExtraSymbols/extra-symbols
add symbol table from file "./ExtraSymbols/extra-symbols"
(y or n) y
Reading symbols from ./ExtraSymbols/extra-symbols...done.
```

14.   Now we can use the **msg_t** structure:

```
(gdb) info types msg_t
All types matching regular expression "msg_t":

File extra-symbols.c:
26:     typedef struct {...} msg_t;
```

```
(gdb) ptype msg_t
type = struct {
    hwnd_t hwnd;
    uint64_t message;
    uint64_t param1;
    uint64_t param2;
    uint32_t time;
    POINT pt;
    uint32_t private;
}
```

```
(gdb) p *(msg_t *)0xffffd9cbc528
$1 = {hwnd = 0, message = 275, param1 = 1, param2 = 4196052, time = 72844112, pt = {x = 156, y
= 327}, private = 0}
```

```
(gdb) set print pretty on
```

```
(gdb) p *(msg_t *)0xffffd9cbc528
$3 = {
  hwnd = 0,
  message = 275,
  param1 = 1,
  param2 = 4201293,
  time = 72844112,
```

```
  pt = {
    x = 156,
    y = 327
  },
  private = 0
}

(gdb) p/x *(msg_t *)0xffffd9cbc528
$3 = {
  hwnd = 0x0,
  message = 0x113,
  param1 = 0x1,
  param2 = 0x401b4d,
  time = 0x4578350,
  pt = {
    x = 0x9c,
    y = 0x147
  },
  private = 0x0
}

(gdb) p/z *(msg_t *)0xffffd9cbc528
$4 = {
  hwnd = 0x0000000000000000,
  message = 0x0000000000000113,
  param1 = 0x0000000000000001,
  param2 = 0x0000000000401b4d,
  time = 0x04578350,
  pt = {
    x = 0x0000009c,
    y = 0x00000147
  },
  private = 0x00000000
}
```

Note: Don't forget to unload the loaded symbol file if it interferes with the original section symbols:

```
(gdb) disassemble main
Dump of assembler code for function main:
   0x00000000004006d4 <+0>:     mov     x0, #0x1                          // #1
   0x00000000004006d8 <+4>:     ret
   0x00000000004006dc <+8>:     sub     sp, sp, #0x10
   0x00000000004006e0 <+12>:    str     w0, [sp, #12]
   0x00000000004006e4 <+16>:    adrp    x0, 0x495000 <__pthread_keys-3784>
   0x00000000004006e8 <+20>:    add     x0, x0, #0x60
End of assembler dump.

(gdb) info symbol main
time_proc in section .text of /home/ubuntu/ADDR-Linux/A64/MemoryDumps/notepad
main in section .text of /home/ubuntu/ADDR-Linux/A64/MemoryDumps/ExtraSymbols/extra-symbols

(gdb) remove-symbol-file /home/ubuntu/ADDR-Linux/A64/MemoryDumps/ExtraSymbols/extra-symbols
Remove symbol table from file "/home/ubuntu/ADDR-Linux/A64/MemoryDumps/ExtraSymbols/extra-
symbols"? (y or n) y

(gdb) info symbol main
main in section .text of /home/ubuntu/ADDR-Linux/A64/MemoryDumps/notepad
```

```
(gdb) disassemble main
Dump of assembler code for function main:
    0x0000000000400888 <+0>:     stp     x29, x30, [sp, #-96]!
    0x000000000040088c <+4>:     mov     x29, sp
    0x0000000000400890 <+8>:     str     w0, [sp, #28]
    0x0000000000400894 <+12>:    str     x1, [sp, #16]
    0x0000000000400898 <+16>:    adrp    x0, 0x492000 <tunable_list+1320>
    0x000000000040089c <+20>:    ldr     x0, [x0, #3056]
    0x00000000004008a0 <+24>:    ldr     x1, [x0]
    0x00000000004008a4 <+28>:    str     x1, [sp, #88]
    0x00000000004008a8 <+32>:    mov     x1, #0x0                     // #0
    0x00000000004008ac <+36>:    b       0x4008b8 <main+48>
    0x00000000004008b0 <+40>:    add     x0, sp, #0x28
    0x00000000004008b4 <+44>:    bl      0x400848 <dispatch_message>
    0x00000000004008b8 <+48>:    add     x0, sp, #0x28
    0x00000000004008bc <+52>:    mov     x3, #0x0                     // #0
    0x00000000004008c0 <+56>:    mov     x2, #0x0                     // #0
    0x00000000004008c4 <+60>:    mov     x1, #0x0                     // #0
    0x00000000004008c8 <+64>:    bl      0x4007d0 <get_message>
    0x00000000004008cc <+68>:    cmp     w0, #0x0
    0x00000000004008d0 <+72>:    b.ne    0x4008b0 <main+40>   // b.any
    0x00000000004008d4 <+76>:    mov     w0, #0x0                     // #0
    0x00000000004008d8 <+80>:    mov     w1, w0
    0x00000000004008dc <+84>:    adrp    x0, 0x492000 <tunable_list+1320>
    0x00000000004008e0 <+88>:    ldr     x0, [x0, #3056]
    0x00000000004008e4 <+92>:    ldr     x3, [sp, #88]
    0x00000000004008e8 <+96>:    ldr     x2, [x0]
    0x00000000004008ec <+100>:   subs    x3, x3, x2
    0x00000000004008f0 <+104>:   mov     x2, #0x0                     // #0
    0x00000000004008f4 <+108>:   b.eq    0x4008fc <main+116>   // b.none
    0x00000000004008f8 <+112>:   bl      0x41c270 <__stack_chk_fail_local>
    0x00000000004008fc <+116>:   mov     w0, w1
    0x0000000000400900 <+120>:   ldp     x29, x30, [sp], #96
    0x0000000000400904 <+124>:   ret
End of assembler dump.
```

15.   When we have an exception such as a breakpoint or access violation, the values of the thread CPU registers are saved and valid for the currently executing function and the instruction pointed to by the PC register (the topmost frame). However, in other situations, such as a manual memory dump, we can only be sure about some registers such as PC, SP, FP (X29), and LR (X30):

```
(gdb) bt
#0  0x000000000043a3fc in clock_nanosleep ()
#1  0x0000000000418ffc in nanosleep ()
#2  0x0000000000418f98 in sleep ()
#3  0x00000000004007c4 in internal_get_message ()
#4  0x0000000000400808 in get_message ()
#5  0x00000000004008cc in main ()

(gdb) i r
x0             0x0                    0
x1             0x0                    0
x2             0xffffd9cbc488         281474335753352
x3             0xffffd9cbc488         281474335753352
x4             0x4919e8               4790760
x5             0xc4c3d06c44caa706     -4268338858387921146
x6             0x495a58               4807256
```

```
x7              0x2                 2
x8              0x73                115
x9              0x2                 2
x10             0x0                 0
x11             0x49a000            4825088
x12             0x46d244            4641348
x13             0x0                 0
x14             0x70                112
x15             0x0                 0
x16             0x0                 0
x17             0x0                 0
x18             0x0                 0
x19             0x0                 0
x20             0x492000            4792320
x21             0x33e4a000          870621184
x22             0xffffd9cbc488      281474335753352
x23             0xffffd9cbc488      281474335753352
x24             0x0                 0
x25             0x0                 0
x26             0x1                 1
x27             0x400280            4194944
x28             0x493030            4796464
x29             0xffffd9cbc3c0      281474335753152
x30             0x418ffc            4296700
sp              0xffffd9cbc3c0      0xffffd9cbc3c0
pc              0x43a3fc            0x43a3fc <clock_nanosleep+124>
cpsr            0x60001000          [ EL=0 BTYPE=0 SSBS C Z ]
fpsr            0x0                 [ ]
fpcr            0x0                 [ RMode=0 ]
```

16.   In any situation when we move down to the next frame, for example, to *nanosleep* (0x0000000000418ffc points to the next instruction after *clock_nanosleep* was called) and to *main*, we don't have most CPU registers' values saved previously (**i r** command gives accurate values only for the topmost frame 0) except PC and SP and perhaps a few other registers such as FP and LR:

```
(gdb) bt
#0  0x000000000043a3fc in clock_nanosleep ()
#1  0x0000000000418ffc in nanosleep ()
#2  0x0000000000418f98 in sleep ()
#3  0x00000000004007c4 in internal_get_message ()
#4  0x0000000000400808 in get_message ()
#5  0x00000000004008cc in main ()

(gdb) disassemble 0x0000000000418ffc
Dump of assembler code for function nanosleep:
   0x0000000000418fe0 <+0>:     stp     x29, x30, [sp, #-16]!
   0x0000000000418fe4 <+4>:     mov     x2, x0
   0x0000000000418fe8 <+8>:     mov     x3, x1
   0x0000000000418fec <+12>:    mov     x29, sp
   0x0000000000418ff0 <+16>:    mov     w1, #0x0                        // #0
   0x0000000000418ff4 <+20>:    mov     w0, #0x0                        // #0
   0x0000000000418ff8 <+24>:    bl      0x43a380 <clock_nanosleep>
   0x0000000000418ffc <+28>:    cbnz    w0, 0x419008 <nanosleep+40>
   0x0000000000419000 <+32>:    ldp     x29, x30, [sp], #16
   0x0000000000419004 <+36>:    ret
   0x0000000000419008 <+40>:    adrp    x1, 0x492000 <tunable_list+1320>
   0x000000000041900c <+44>:    ldr     x1, [x1, #3552]
   0x0000000000419010 <+48>:    mrs     x2, tpidr_el0
```

```
   0x0000000000419014 <+52>:     str     w0, [x2, x1]
   0x0000000000419018 <+56>:     mov     w0, #0xffffffff              // #-1
   0x000000000041901c <+60>:     b       0x419000 <nanosleep+32>
End of assembler dump.
```

```
(gdb) i r
x0              0x0                 0
x1              0x0                 0
x2              0xffffd9cbc488      281474335753352
x3              0xffffd9cbc488      281474335753352
x4              0x4919e8            4790760
x5              0xc4c3d06c44caa706  -4268338858387921146
x6              0x495a58            4807256
x7              0x2                 2
x8              0x73                115
x9              0x2                 2
x10             0x0                 0
x11             0x49a000            4825088
x12             0x46d244            4641348
x13             0x0                 0
x14             0x70                112
x15             0x0                 0
x16             0x0                 0
x17             0x0                 0
x18             0x0                 0
x19             0x0                 0
x20             0x492000            4792320
x21             0x33e4a000          870621184
x22             0xffffd9cbc488      281474335753352
x23             0xffffd9cbc488      281474335753352
x24             0x0                 0
x25             0x0                 0
x26             0x1                 1
x27             0x400280            4194944
x28             0x493030            4796464
x29             0xffffd9cbc3c0      281474335753152
x30             0x418ffc            4296700
sp              0xffffd9cbc3c0      0xffffd9cbc3c0
pc              0x43a3fc            0x43a3fc <clock_nanosleep+124>
cpsr            0x60001000          [ EL=0 BTYPE=0 SSBS C Z ]
fpsr            0x0                 [ ]
fpcr            0x0                 [ RMode=0 ]
```

```
(gdb) frame 1
#1  0x0000000000418ffc in nanosleep ()
```

```
(gdb) i r
x0              0x0                 0
x1              0x0                 0
x2              0xffffd9cbc488      281474335753352
x3              0xffffd9cbc488      281474335753352
x4              0x4919e8            4790760
x5              0xc4c3d06c44caa706  -4268338858387921146
x6              0x495a58            4807256
x7              0x2                 2
x8              0x73                115
x9              0x2                 2
x10             0x0                 0
x11             0x49a000            4825088
```

```
x12          0x46d244                 4641348
x13          0x0                      0
x14          0x70                     112
x15          0x0                      0
x16          0x0                      0
x17          0x0                      0
x18          0x0                      0
x19          0x492000                 4792320
x20          0x30                     48
x21          0x33e4a7c0               870623168
x22          0x0                      0
x23          0x2                      2
x24          0x48f850                 4782160
x25          0x18                     24
x26          0x0                      0
x27          0x400280                 4194944
x28          0x493030                 4796464
x29          0xffffd9cbc440           281474335753280
x30          0x418ffc                 4296700
sp           0xffffd9cbc440           0xffffd9cbc440
pc           0x418ffc                 0x418ffc <nanosleep+28>
cpsr         0x60001000               [ EL=0 BTYPE=0 SSBS C Z ]
fpsr         0x0                      [ ]
fpcr         0x0                      [ RMode=0 ]
```

(gdb) **frame** 2
#2 0x0000000000418f98 in sleep ()

(gdb) **i r**
```
x0           0x0                      0
x1           0x0                      0
x2           0xffffd9cbc488           281474335753352
x3           0xffffd9cbc488           281474335753352
x4           0x4919e8                 4790760
x5           0xc4c3d06c44caa706       -4268338858387921146
x6           0x495a58                 4807256
x7           0x2                      2
x8           0x73                     115
x9           0x2                      2
x10          0x0                      0
x11          0x49a000                 4825088
x12          0x46d244                 4641348
x13          0x0                      0
x14          0x70                     112
x15          0x0                      0
x16          0x0                      0
x17          0x0                      0
x18          0x0                      0
x19          0x492000                 4792320
x20          0x30                     48
x21          0x33e4a7c0               870623168
x22          0x0                      0
x23          0x2                      2
x24          0x48f850                 4782160
x25          0x18                     24
x26          0x0                      0
x27          0x400280                 4194944
x28          0x493030                 4796464
x29          0xffffd9cbc450           281474335753296
```

95

```
x30           0x418f98              4296600
sp            0xffffd9cbc450        0xffffd9cbc450
pc            0x418f98              0x418f98 <sleep+72>
cpsr          0x60001000            [ EL=0 BTYPE=0 SSBS C Z ]
fpsr          0x0                   [ ]
fpcr          0x0                   [ RMode=0 ]
```

(gdb) frame 3
#3 0x00000000004007c4 in internal_get_message ()

(gdb) i r
```
x0            0x0                   0
x1            0x0                   0
x2            0xffffd9cbc488        281474335753352
x3            0xffffd9cbc488        281474335753352
x4            0x4919e8              4790760
x5            0xc4c3d06c44caa706    -4268338858387921146
x6            0x495a58              4807256
x7            0x2                   2
x8            0x73                  115
x9            0x2                   2
x10           0x0                   0
x11           0x49a000              4825088
x12           0x46d244              4641348
x13           0x0                   0
x14           0x70                  112
x15           0x0                   0
x16           0x0                   0
x17           0x0                   0
x18           0x0                   0
x19           0x1                   1
x20           0xffffd9cbc718        281474335754008
x21           0x2                   2
x22           0xffffd9cbc728        281474335754024
x23           0x2                   2
x24           0x48f850              4782160
x25           0x18                  24
x26           0x0                   0
x27           0x400280              4194944
x28           0x493030              4796464
x29           0xffffd9cbc4a0        281474335753376
x30           0x4007c4              4196292
sp            0xffffd9cbc4a0        0xffffd9cbc4a0
pc            0x4007c4              0x4007c4 <internal_get_message+132>
cpsr          0x60001000            [ EL=0 BTYPE=0 SSBS C Z ]
fpsr          0x0                   [ ]
fpcr          0x0                   [ RMode=0 ]
```

(gdb) frame 4
#4 0x0000000000400808 in get_message ()

(gdb) i r
```
x0            0x0                   0
x1            0x0                   0
x2            0xffffd9cbc488        281474335753352
x3            0xffffd9cbc488        281474335753352
x4            0x4919e8              4790760
x5            0xc4c3d06c44caa706    -4268338858387921146
x6            0x495a58              4807256
```

```
x7           0x2                    2
x8           0x73                   115
x9           0x2                    2
x10          0x0                    0
x11          0x49a000               4825088
x12          0x46d244               4641348
x13          0x0                    0
x14          0x70                   112
x15          0x0                    0
x16          0x0                    0
x17          0x0                    0
x18          0x0                    0
x19          0x1                    1
x20          0xffffd9cbc718         281474335754008
x21          0x2                    2
x22          0xffffd9cbc728         281474335754024
x23          0x2                    2
x24          0x48f850               4782160
x25          0x18                   24
x26          0x0                    0
x27          0x400280               4194944
x28          0x493030               4796464
x29          0xffffd9cbc4c0         281474335753408
x30          0x400808               4196360
sp           0xffffd9cbc4c0         0xffffd9cbc4c0
pc           0x400808               0x400808 <get_message+56>
cpsr         0x60001000             [ EL=0 BTYPE=0 SSBS C Z ]
fpsr         0x0                    [ ]
fpcr         0x0                    [ RMode=0 ]

(gdb) frame 5
#5  0x00000000004008cc in main ()

(gdb) i r
x0           0x0                    0
x1           0x0                    0
x2           0xffffd9cbc488         281474335753352
x3           0xffffd9cbc488         281474335753352
x4           0x4919e8               4790760
x5           0xc4c3d06c44caa706     -4268338858387921146
x6           0x495a58               4807256
x7           0x2                    2
x8           0x73                   115
x9           0x2                    2
x10          0x0                    0
x11          0x49a000               4825088
x12          0x46d244               4641348
x13          0x0                    0
x14          0x70                   112
x15          0x0                    0
x16          0x0                    0
x17          0x0                    0
x18          0x0                    0
x19          0x1                    1
x20          0xffffd9cbc718         281474335754008
x21          0x2                    2
x22          0xffffd9cbc728         281474335754024
x23          0x2                    2
x24          0x48f850               4782160
```

x25	0x18	24
x26	0x0	0
x27	0x400280	4194944
x28	0x493030	4796464
x29	**0xffffd9cbc500**	**281474335753472**
x30	**0x4008cc**	**4196556**
sp	**0xffffd9cbc500**	**0xffffd9cbc500**
pc	**0x4008cc**	**0x4008cc <main+68>**
cpsr	0x60001000	[EL=0 BTYPE=0 SSBS C Z]
fpsr	0x0	[ ]
fpcr	0x0	[RMode=0]

Note: It also appears that some other registers changed between frames 1, 2, and 3. This is because they were previously saved on the stack, so their value is taken from that location:

```
(gdb) disassemble sleep
Dump of assembler code for function sleep:
   0x0000000000418f50 <+0>:    stp    x29, x30, [sp, #-80]!
   0x0000000000418f54 <+4>:    mov    w2, w0
   0x0000000000418f58 <+8>:    mov    x29, sp
   0x0000000000418f5c <+12>:   stp    x19, x20, [sp, #16]
   0x0000000000418f60 <+16>:   adrp   x19, 0x492000 <tunable_list+1320>
   0x0000000000418f64 <+20>:   adrp   x20, 0x492000 <tunable_list+1320>
   0x0000000000418f68 <+24>:   ldr    x20, [x20, #3552]
   0x0000000000418f6c <+28>:   ldr    x4, [x19, #3056]
   0x0000000000418f70 <+32>:   stp    x21, x22, [sp, #32]
   0x0000000000418f74 <+36>:   mrs    x21, tpidr_el0
   0x0000000000418f78 <+40>:   ldr    x0, [x4]
   0x0000000000418f7c <+44>:   str    x0, [sp, #72]
   0x0000000000418f80 <+48>:   mov    x0, #0x0                    // #0
   0x0000000000418f84 <+52>:   add    x1, sp, #0x38
   0x0000000000418f88 <+56>:   mov    x0, x1
   0x0000000000418f8c <+60>:   stp    x2, xzr, [sp, #56]
   0x0000000000418f90 <+64>:   ldr    w22, [x21, x20]
   0x0000000000418f94 <+68>:   bl     0x418fe0 <nanosleep>
   0x0000000000418f98 <+72>:   tbnz   w0, #31, 0x418fcc <sleep+124>
   0x0000000000418f9c <+76>:   mov    w0, #0x0                    // #0
   0x0000000000418fa0 <+80>:   str    w22, [x21, x20]
   0x0000000000418fa4 <+84>:   ldr    x19, [x19, #3056]
   0x0000000000418fa8 <+88>:   ldr    x1, [sp, #72]
   0x0000000000418fac <+92>:   ldr    x2, [x19]
   0x0000000000418fb0 <+96>:   subs   x1, x1, x2
   0x0000000000418fb4 <+100>:  mov    x2, #0x0                    // #0
   0x0000000000418fb8 <+104>:  b.ne   0x418fd4 <sleep+132>   // b.any
   0x0000000000418fbc <+108>:  ldp    x19, x20, [sp, #16]
   0x0000000000418fc0 <+112>:  ldp    x21, x22, [sp, #32]
   0x0000000000418fc4 <+116>:  ldp    x29, x30, [sp], #80
   0x0000000000418fc8 <+120>:  ret
   0x0000000000418fcc <+124>:  ldr    w0, [sp, #56]
   0x0000000000418fd0 <+128>:  b      0x418fa4 <sleep+84>
   0x0000000000418fd4 <+132>:  bl     0x41c270 <__stack_chk_fail_local>
End of assembler dump.
```

17.   Some CPU registers can be recovered manually, such as PC (saved address in LR when using **bl** instruction) and SP (the stack pointer value before saving LR address). Other register values can be recovered manually, too, if they were not used in called frames or were saved in temporary memory cells (such as on stack, as we saw in the case of some registers above). Let's recover some registers for the first few frames.

```
(gdb) frame 0
#0  0x000000000043a3fc in clock_nanosleep ()
```

Let's disassemble the current function:

```
(gdb) disassemble clock_nanosleep
Dump of assembler code for function clock_nanosleep:
   0x000000000043a380 <+0>:     stp     x29, x30, [sp, #-128]!
   0x000000000043a384 <+4>:     mov     x29, sp
   0x000000000043a388 <+8>:     stp     x19, x20, [sp, #16]
   0x000000000043a38c <+12>:    adrp    x20, 0x492000 <tunable_list+1320>
   0x000000000043a390 <+16>:    ldr     x4, [x20, #3056]
   0x000000000043a394 <+20>:    stp     x21, x22, [sp, #32]
   0x000000000043a398 <+24>:    mov     x22, x2
   0x000000000043a39c <+28>:    stp     x23, x24, [sp, #48]
   0x000000000043a3a0 <+32>:    mov     w24, w1
   0x000000000043a3a4 <+36>:    ldr     x1, [x4]
   0x000000000043a3a8 <+40>:    str     x1, [sp, #120]
   0x000000000043a3ac <+44>:    mov     x1, #0x0                    // #0
   0x000000000043a3b0 <+48>:    cmp     w0, #0x3
   0x000000000043a3b4 <+52>:    b.eq    0x43a494 <clock_nanosleep+276>  // b.none
   0x000000000043a3b8 <+56>:    stp     x25, x26, [sp, #64]
   0x000000000043a3bc <+60>:    mov     x23, x3
   0x000000000043a3c0 <+64>:    cmp     w0, #0x2
   0x000000000043a3c4 <+68>:    b.eq    0x43a448 <clock_nanosleep+200>  // b.none
   0x000000000043a3c8 <+72>:    mrs     x21, tpidr_el0
   0x000000000043a3cc <+76>:    cmp     w0, #0x0
   0x000000000043a3d0 <+80>:    sub     x21, x21, #0x7c0
   0x000000000043a3d4 <+84>:    sxtw    x19, w0
   0x000000000043a3d8 <+88>:    cset    w26, eq  // eq = none
   0x000000000043a3dc <+92>:    sxtw    x25, w24
   0x000000000043a3e0 <+96>:    ldr     w0, [x21]
   0x000000000043a3e4 <+100>:   cbnz    w0, 0x43a464 <clock_nanosleep+228>
   0x000000000043a3e8 <+104>:   mov     x0, x19
   0x000000000043a3ec <+108>:   mov     x1, x25
   0x000000000043a3f0 <+112>:   mov     x2, x22
   0x000000000043a3f4 <+116>:   mov     x3, x23
   0x000000000043a3f8 <+120>:   mov     x8, #0x73                   // #115
=> 0x000000000043a3fc <+124>:   svc     #0x0
   0x000000000043a400 <+128>:   mov     x19, x0
   0x000000000043a404 <+132>:   cmp     w26, #0x0
   0x000000000043a408 <+136>:   ccmn    w19, #0x16, #0x0, ne  // ne = any
   0x000000000043a40c <+140>:   b.eq    0x43a49c <clock_nanosleep+284>  // b.none
   0x000000000043a410 <+144>:   ldp     x25, x26, [sp, #64]
   0x000000000043a414 <+148>:   neg     w19, w19
   0x000000000043a418 <+152>:   ldr     x20, [x20, #3056]
[...]
```

It is a long function, so we provided only disassembly before the *svc* call.

We see that, after entering the *clock_nanosleep* function, the SP pointer is adjusted inside by 128 bytes and assigned to X29, and the current X29 value + 8 should point to the return address of the caller (saved X30 or LR), *nanosleep* function during the execution of the **bl** instruction:

```
(gdb) x/a $x29+8
0xffffd9cbc3c8: 0x418ffc <nanosleep+28>
```

Note: X29 for the caller should be the value before the **bl** instruction was executed. We can get this value from the saved X29, which is pointed to by the current X29 value:

```
(gdb) x/gx $x29
0xffffd9cbc3c0: 0x0000ffffd9cbc440
```

Note: We see that for the next frame PC is `0x418ffc <nanosleep+28>` and X29 is `0xffffd9cbc440`. Let's now find out PC and X29 for the yet another next frame (the caller of the *nanosleep* function). X29 + 8 should point to the return address of the caller, and X29 should point to the caller's X29:

```
(gdb) x/a 0x0000ffffd9cbc440+8
0xffffd9cbc448: 0x418f98 <sleep+72>
```

```
(gdb) x/gx 0x0000ffffd9cbc440
0xffffd9cbc440: 0x0000ffffd9cbc450
```

We repeat this algorithm until we come to the *main* function:

```
(gdb) x/a 0x0000ffffd9cbc450+8
0xffffd9cbc458: 0x4007c4 <internal_get_message+132>
```

```
(gdb) x/gx 0x0000ffffd9cbc450
0xffffd9cbc450: 0x0000ffffd9cbc4a0
```

```
(gdb) x/a 0x0000ffffd9cbc4a0+8
0xffffd9cbc4a8: 0x400808 <get_message+56>
```

```
(gdb) x/gx 0x0000ffffd9cbc4a0
0xffffd9cbc4a0: 0x0000ffffd9cbc4c0
```

```
(gdb) x/a 0x0000ffffd9cbc4c0+8
0xffffd9cbc4c8: 0x4008cc <main+68>
```

Note: We can reconstruct the stack trace like a debugger. Note that we can correctly reconstruct stack trace using this method even if the **disassemble** command fails when function boundaries are not available in symbol files or the start of the function is not available from the image file section. If such information is not available, we would most likely have a truncated or incorrect stack trace using the **bt** command:

```
(gdb) symbol-file
No symbol file now.
```

```
(gdb) bt
#0  0x000000000043a3fc in ?? ()
#1  0x0000000000000030 in ?? ()
Backtrace stopped: previous frame identical to this frame (corrupt stack?)
```

18.   Other registers and memory values are reused and overwritten when we move down the frames, so less and less information can be recovered. We call this ADDR pattern (Inverse) **Context Pyramid**.

19.   We also introduce special **Stack Frame** memory cell diagrams. For example, the case of the stack frame for the *get_message* function before calling *internal_get_message* is illustrated in the MCD-R1.xlsx section D (offsets are hexadecimal), where [SP+8] corresponds to the stored return address of the *get_message* caller, *main*.

Stack Reconstruction (A64)

1. Top frame from the current PC_1, $X29_1$ (**info reg**)
2. Get PC_{n+1} for the next frame (**x/a** $X29_n + 8$)
3. Get $X29_{n+1}$ for the next frame (**x/gx** $X29_n$)
4. ++n
5. goto #2

The slide shows an algorithm for reconstructing thread stack traces on the Linux ARM64 platform.

ADDR: Universal Pointer

- A memory cell value interpreted as a pointer to memory cells
- A memory address that was not specifically designed as a pointer

ADDR: Symbolic Pointer, S^2

- A memory cell value associated with a symbolic value from a symbol file or a binary file (exported symbol)

ADDR: Interpreted Pointer, S³

- Interpretation of a memory cell pointer value and its symbol
- Implemented via a typed structure or debugger (extension) command

ADDR: Context Pyramid

- When we move down stack trace frames, we can recover less and less contextual memory information due to register and memory overwrites

Exercise R2

- **Goal:** Learn how to map source code to disassembly

- **ADDR Patterns:** Function Skeleton, Function Call, Call Path, Local Variable, Static Variable, Pointer Dereference

- **Memory Cell Diagrams:** Pointer Dereference

- \ADDR-Linux\Exercise-R2-x64-GDB.pdf
- \ADDR-Linux\MCD-R2-x64.xlsx

- \ADDR-Linux\Exercise-R2-ARM64-GDB.pdf
- \ADDR-Linux\MCD-R2-ARM64.xlsx

Mapping is essential when we don't have symbol files but source code only.

Exercise R2 (x64, GDB)

Goal: Learn how to map source code to disassembly.

ADDR Patterns: Function Skeleton, Function Call, Call Path, Local Variable, Static Variable, Pointer Dereference.

Memory Cell Diagrams: Pointer Dereference.

1.   Load a core dump *data-types.21* and *data-types* executable from x64/MemoryDumps directory:

```
~/ADDR-Linux/x64/MemoryDumps$ gdb -c data-types.21 -se data-types
GNU gdb (Debian 8.2.1-2+b3) 8.2.1
Copyright (C) 2018 Free Software Foundation, Inc.
License GPLv3+: GNU GPL version 3 or later <http://gnu.org/licenses/gpl.html>
This is free software: you are free to change and redistribute it.
There is NO WARRANTY, to the extent permitted by law.
Type "show copying" and "show warranty" for details.
This GDB was configured as "x86_64-linux-gnu".
Type "show configuration" for configuration details.
For bug reporting instructions, please see:
<http://www.gnu.org/software/gdb/bugs/>.
Find the GDB manual and other documentation resources online at:
    <http://www.gnu.org/software/gdb/documentation/>.

For help, type "help".
Type "apropos word" to search for commands related to "word"...
Reading symbols from data-types...(no debugging symbols found)...done.
[New LWP 21]
Core was generated by `./data-types'.
#0  0x0000000000407629 in raise ()
```

2.   We open a log file:

```
(gdb) set logging on R2.log
Copying output to R2.log.
```

3.   We get this stack trace and disassemble the function that called *debug_break* (its return address is **0x0000000000401bed**):

```
(gdb) bt
#0  0x0000000000407629 in raise ()
#1  0x0000000000401b5b in debug_break ()
#2  0x0000000000401bed in start_modeling ()
#3  0x0000000000401c09 in main ()

(gdb) disassemble 0x0000000000401bed
Dump of assembler code for function start_modeling:
   0x0000000000401b5e <+0>:     push   %rbp
   0x0000000000401b5f <+1>:     mov    %rsp,%rbp
   0x0000000000401b62 <+4>:     sub    $0x40,%rsp
   0x0000000000401b66 <+8>:     lea    -0x1c(%rbp),%rax
   0x0000000000401b6a <+12>:    mov    %rax,-0x8(%rbp)
   0x0000000000401b6e <+16>:    lea    -0x1d(%rbp),%rax
   0x0000000000401b72 <+20>:    mov    %rax,-0x10(%rbp)
   0x0000000000401b76 <+24>:    lea    0x7b49c(%rip),%rax        # 0x47d019
```

```
0x0000000000401b7d <+31>:     mov     %rax,-0x18(%rbp)
0x0000000000401b81 <+35>:     movabs  $0x4441206f6c6c6548,%rax
0x0000000000401b8b <+45>:     movabs  $0x636f4c2820215244,%rdx
0x0000000000401b95 <+55>:     mov     %rax,-0x40(%rbp)
0x0000000000401b99 <+59>:     mov     %rdx,-0x38(%rbp)
0x0000000000401b9d <+63>:     movl    $0x296c61,-0x30(%rbp)
0x0000000000401ba4 <+70>:     movl    $0xabcd,-0x1c(%rbp)
0x0000000000401bab <+77>:     mov     -0x8(%rbp),%rax
0x0000000000401baf <+81>:     movl    $0xdcba,(%rax)
0x0000000000401bb5 <+87>:     movl    $0xabce,0xa57d5(%rip)        # 0x4a7394 <s_dwData>
0x0000000000401bbf <+97>:     mov     0xa3542(%rip),%rax          # 0x4a5108 <s_pdwData>
0x0000000000401bc6 <+104>:    movl    $0xecba,(%rax)
0x0000000000401bcc <+110>:    movl    $0xabcf,0xa682e(%rip)        # 0x4a8404 <g_dwData>
0x0000000000401bd6 <+120>:    mov     0xa355b(%rip),%rax          # 0x4a5138 <g_pdwData>
0x0000000000401bdd <+127>:    movl    $0xfcba,(%rax)
0x0000000000401be3 <+133>:    mov     $0x0,%eax
0x0000000000401be8 <+138>:    callq   0x401b4d <debug_break>
0x0000000000401bed <+143>:    nop
0x0000000000401bee <+144>:    leaveq
0x0000000000401bef <+145>:    retq
End of assembler dump.
```

Note: Understanding any function most of the time starts with checking what other functions it may call. We call this ADDR pattern **Function Skeleton**. In our case, the function skeleton of *start_modeling* consists of just one *debug_break* function because we don't see any other calls.

4.   Let's disassemble the *debug_break* function and follow **Call Path**.

```
(gdb) disassemble debug_break
Dump of assembler code for function debug_break:
   0x0000000000401b4d <+0>:      push    %rbp
   0x0000000000401b4e <+1>:      mov     %rsp,%rbp
   0x0000000000401b51 <+4>:      mov     $0x13,%edi
   0x0000000000401b56 <+9>:      callq   0x407540 <raise>
   0x0000000000401b5b <+14>:     nop
   0x0000000000401b5c <+15>:     pop     %rbp
   0x0000000000401b5d <+16>:     retq
End of assembler dump.
```

Note: We see *debug_break* calls *raise* function without any diversions as we don't see any absolute or conditional jumps. Also, its function skeleton consists of just one call. So let's disassemble the *raise* function:

```
(gdb) disassemble raise
Dump of assembler code for function raise:
   0x0000000000407540 <+0>:      push    %rbx
   0x0000000000407541 <+1>:      mov     $0xffffffffffffffff,%r8
   0x0000000000407548 <+8>:      mov     %edi,%ebx
   0x000000000040754a <+10>:     mov     $0x8,%r10d
   0x0000000000407550 <+16>:     xor     %edi,%edi
   0x0000000000407552 <+18>:     sub     $0x110,%rsp
   0x0000000000407559 <+25>:     mov     %fs:0x28,%rax
   0x0000000000407562 <+34>:     mov     %rax,0x108(%rsp)
   0x000000000040756a <+42>:     xor     %eax,%eax
   0x000000000040756c <+44>:     mov     %rsp,%r9
   0x000000000040756f <+47>:     movabs  $0xfffffffe7ffffffff,%rax
```

```
   0x0000000000407579 <+57>:    mov    %r8,0x88(%rsp)
   0x0000000000407581 <+65>:    mov    %rax,0x80(%rsp)
   0x0000000000407589 <+73>:    mov    %r9,%rdx
   0x000000000040758c <+76>:    lea    0x80(%rsp),%rsi
   0x0000000000407594 <+84>:    mov    $0xe,%eax
   0x0000000000407599 <+89>:    mov    %r8,0x90(%rsp)
   0x00000000004075a1 <+97>:    mov    %r8,0x98(%rsp)
   0x00000000004075a9 <+105>:   mov    %r8,0xa0(%rsp)
   0x00000000004075b1 <+113>:   mov    %r8,0xa8(%rsp)
   0x00000000004075b9 <+121>:   mov    %r8,0xb0(%rsp)
   0x00000000004075c1 <+129>:   mov    %r8,0xb8(%rsp)
   0x00000000004075c9 <+137>:   mov    %r8,0xc0(%rsp)
   0x00000000004075d1 <+145>:   mov    %r8,0xc8(%rsp)
   0x00000000004075d9 <+153>:   mov    %r8,0xd0(%rsp)
   0x00000000004075e1 <+161>:   mov    %r8,0xd8(%rsp)
   0x00000000004075e9 <+169>:   mov    %r8,0xe0(%rsp)
   0x00000000004075f1 <+177>:   mov    %r8,0xe8(%rsp)
   0x00000000004075f9 <+185>:   mov    %r8,0xf0(%rsp)
   0x0000000000407601 <+193>:   mov    %r8,0xf8(%rsp)
   0x0000000000407609 <+201>:   syscall
   0x000000000040760b <+203>:   mov    $0x27,%ecx
   0x0000000000407610 <+208>:   mov    %ecx,%eax
   0x0000000000407612 <+210>:   syscall
   0x0000000000407614 <+212>:   mov    %rax,%rdi
   0x0000000000407617 <+215>:   mov    $0xba,%eax
   0x000000000040761c <+220>:   syscall
   0x000000000040761e <+222>:   mov    %eax,%esi
--Type <RET> for more, q to quit, c to continue without paging--
   0x0000000000407620 <+224>:   mov    %ebx,%edx
   0x0000000000407622 <+226>:   mov    $0xea,%eax
   0x0000000000407627 <+231>:   syscall
=> 0x0000000000407629 <+233>:   cmp    $0xfffffffffffff000,%rax
   0x000000000040762f <+239>:   ja     0x407670 <raise+304>
   0x0000000000407631 <+241>:   mov    %eax,%r8d
   0x0000000000407634 <+244>:   mov    $0x8,%r10d
   0x000000000040763a <+250>:   xor    %edx,%edx
   0x000000000040763c <+252>:   mov    %r9,%rsi
   0x000000000040763f <+255>:   mov    $0x2,%edi
   0x0000000000407644 <+260>:   mov    $0xe,%eax
   0x0000000000407649 <+265>:   syscall
   0x000000000040764b <+267>:   mov    0x108(%rsp),%rcx
   0x0000000000407653 <+275>:   xor    %fs:0x28,%rcx
   0x000000000040765c <+284>:   mov    %r8d,%eax
   0x000000000040765f <+287>:   jne    0x40767e <raise+318>
   0x0000000000407661 <+289>:   add    $0x110,%rsp
   0x0000000000407668 <+296>:   pop    %rbx
   0x0000000000407669 <+297>:   retq
   0x000000000040766a <+298>:   nopw   0x0(%rax,%rax,1)
   0x0000000000407670 <+304>:   mov    $0xffffffffffffffc0,%rdx
   0x0000000000407677 <+311>:   neg    %eax
   0x0000000000407679 <+313>:   mov    %eax,%fs:(%rdx)
   0x000000000040767c <+316>:   jmp    0x407634 <raise+244>
   0x000000000040767e <+318>:   callq  0x43ea80 <__stack_chk_fail_local>
End of assembler dump.
```

Note: We see the *raise* function went through 4 syscalls before the current return address 0x0000000000407629. After that, a conditional jump, another syscall, another conditional jump, and another call. So, a possible continuation of a call path (one of several) would be **syscall** -> **call**.

The *raise* function skeleton is (syscall number is provided in EAX):

```
syscall 0xe
syscall 0x27
syscall 0xba
syscall 0xea
syscall 0xe
callq __stack_chk_fail_local
```

5.   Suppose we only have source code but not the debug info file for the *data-types* module. We search for *debug-break* there and find this function:

```
void start_modeling()
{
        _Bool bData;

        uint32_t dwData;
        uint32_t *pdwData = &dwData;

        char cData;
        char *pcData = &cData;

        const char *pcstrData = "Hello ADDR! (Local)";
        char acData[] = "Hello ADDR! (Local)";

        dwData = 0xABCD;
        *pdwData = 0xDCBA;

        s_dwData = 0xABCE;
        *s_pdwData = 0xECBA;

        g_dwData = 0xABCF;
        *g_pdwData = 0xFCBA;

        debug_break();
}
```

Note: It looks like it corresponds to our previously disassembled code which called *debug_break()* because we see the same constants (marked as green above and as blue below):

```
(gdb) disassemble start_modeling
Dump of assembler code for function start_modeling:
   0x0000000000401b5e <+0>:     push   %rbp
   0x0000000000401b5f <+1>:     mov    %rsp,%rbp
   0x0000000000401b62 <+4>:     sub    $0x40,%rsp
   0x0000000000401b66 <+8>:     lea    -0x1c(%rbp),%rax
   0x0000000000401b6a <+12>:    mov    %rax,-0x8(%rbp)
   0x0000000000401b6e <+16>:    lea    -0x1d(%rbp),%rax
   0x0000000000401b72 <+20>:    mov    %rax,-0x10(%rbp)
   0x0000000000401b76 <+24>:    lea    0x7b49c(%rip),%rax      # 0x47d019
   0x0000000000401b7d <+31>:    mov    %rax,-0x18(%rbp)
   0x0000000000401b81 <+35>:    movabs $0x4441206f6c6c6548,%rax
   0x0000000000401b8b <+45>:    movabs $0x636f4c2820215244,%rdx
   0x0000000000401b95 <+55>:    mov    %rax,-0x40(%rbp)
   0x0000000000401b99 <+59>:    mov    %rdx,-0x38(%rbp)
   0x0000000000401b9d <+63>:    movl   $0x296c61,-0x30(%rbp)
   0x0000000000401ba4 <+70>:    movl   $0xabcd,-0x1c(%rbp)
```

```
   0x0000000000401bab <+77>:    mov     -0x8(%rbp),%rax
   0x0000000000401baf <+81>:    movl    $0xdcba,(%rax)
   0x0000000000401bb5 <+87>:    movl    $0xabce,0xa57d5(%rip)        # 0x4a7394 <s_dwData>
   0x0000000000401bbf <+97>:    mov     0xa3542(%rip),%rax          # 0x4a5108 <s_pdwData>
   0x0000000000401bc6 <+104>:   movl    $0xecba,(%rax)
   0x0000000000401bcc <+110>:   movl    $0xabcf,0xa682e(%rip)        # 0x4a8404 <g_dwData>
   0x0000000000401bd6 <+120>:   mov     0xa355b(%rip),%rax          # 0x4a5138 <g_pdwData>
   0x0000000000401bdd <+127>:   movl    $0xfcba,(%rax)
   0x0000000000401be3 <+133>:   mov     $0x0,%eax
   0x0000000000401be8 <+138>:   callq   0x401b4d <debug_break>
=> 0x0000000000401bed <+143>:   nop
   0x0000000000401bee <+144>:   leaveq
   0x0000000000401bef <+145>:   retq
End of assembler dump.
```

6.   There are 6 different assignments. Let's see their differences and associated memory references and changes. The first two assignments use **Local Variables.** Their storage was allocated in the stack region. We see this because an offset from RBP is used.

```
   0x0000000000401ba4 <+70>:    movl    $0xabcd,-0x1c(%rbp)

   0x0000000000401bab <+77>:    mov     -0x8(%rbp),%rax
   0x0000000000401baf <+81>:    movl    $0xdcba,(%rax)
```

The first assignment directly changes the memory cell located at offset -0x1c from the address in RBP. The second is an example of a **Pointer Dereference**. The memory cell at offset -0x8 contains another memory address. This address is moved into RAX, and then the assigned value 0xDCBA is stored at the memory cell pointed to by that address. Both assignments are illustrated in the MCD-R2-x64.xlsx A section (offsets are hexadecimal). Note that this is a doubleword assignment; only the one doubleword from the full 64-bit cell is affected.

7.   Let's check the results from these memory assignments. We calculate RBP from the backtrace:

```
(gdb) bt
#0  0x0000000000407629 in raise ()
#1  0x0000000000401b5b in debug_break ()
#2  0x0000000000401bed in start_modeling ()
#3  0x0000000000401c09 in main ()

(gdb) disassemble raise, +20
Dump of assembler code from 0x407540 to 0x407554:
   0x0000000000407540 <raise+0>:       push    %rbx
   0x0000000000407541 <raise+1>:       mov     $0xffffffffffffffff,%r8
   0x0000000000407548 <raise+8>:       mov     %edi,%ebx
   0x000000000040754a <raise+10>:      mov     $0x8,%r10d
   0x0000000000407550 <raise+16>:      xor     %edi,%edi
   0x0000000000407552 <raise+18>:      sub     $0x110,%rsp
End of assembler dump.

(gdb) disassemble debug_break, +10
Dump of assembler code from 0x401b4d to 0x401b57:
   0x0000000000401b4d <debug_break+0>: push    %rbp
   0x0000000000401b4e <debug_break+1>: mov     %rsp,%rbp
   0x0000000000401b51 <debug_break+4>: mov     $0x13,%edi
   0x0000000000401b56 <debug_break+9>: callq   0x407540 <raise>
End of assembler dump.
```

```
(gdb) disassemble start_modeling, +10
Dump of assembler code from 0x401b5e to 0x401b68:
   0x0000000000401b5e <start_modeling+0>:      push   %rbp
   0x0000000000401b5f <start_modeling+1>:      mov    %rsp,%rbp
   0x0000000000401b62 <start_modeling+4>:      sub    $0x40,%rsp
   0x0000000000401b66 <start_modeling+8>:      lea    -0x1c(%rbp),%rax
```

```
(gdb) i r $rsp
rsp            0x7ffd92b92050          0x7ffd92b92050
```

We calculate the RSP value for the *start_modeling* function before it called *debug_break* (see the algorithm in Exercise R1, we also add 8 for each saved return address):

```
(gdb) p/x 0x7ffd92b92050 + (8 + 0x110 + 8) + (8 + 8)
$1 = 0x7ffd92b92180
```

We then add $0x40 to get the value of RSP saved in RBP:

```
(gdb) p/x 0x7ffd92b92180 + 0x40
$2 = 0x7ffd92b921c0
```

Finally, we get the doubleword value at the location of the first assignment:

```
(gdb) x/wx 0x7ffd92b921c0 - 0x1c
0x7ffd92b921a4: 0x0000dcba
```

Note: We expect *abcd* instead of *dcba*! Let's check the next local variable (a pointer) involved in the second assignment:

```
(gdb) x/gx 0x7ffd92b921c0 - 0x8
0x7ffd92b921b8: 0x00007ffd92b921a4
```

Note: We see that the pointer value points to the memory cell of the previous assignment variable. This is why the second assignment with pointer dereference overwrites the previously assigned value. Looking at function disassembly, we find this fragment:

```
(gdb) disassemble start_modeling
Dump of assembler code for function start_modeling:
   0x0000000000401b5e <+0>:       push   %rbp
   0x0000000000401b5f <+1>:       mov    %rsp,%rbp
   0x0000000000401b62 <+4>:       sub    $0x40,%rsp
   0x0000000000401b66 <+8>:       lea    -0x1c(%rbp),%rax
   0x0000000000401b6a <+12>:      mov    %rax,-0x8(%rbp)
[...]
```

LEA instruction here puts the address of the memory cell at RBP-0x1c (which is the value of RBP-0x1c) into RAX. Then this value is put into the memory cell located at RBP-0x8. All this is illustrated in the MCD-R2-x64.xlsx B section (offsets are hexadecimal).

Note: This initialization is reflected in the source code:

```
void start_modeling()
{
        _Bool bData;

        uint32_t dwData;
        uint32_t *pdwData = &dwData;
```

8.   The next 4 assignments involve **Static Variables**:

```
0x0000000000401bb5 <+87>:     movl    $0xabce,0xa57d5(%rip)         # 0x4a7394 <s_dwData>

0x0000000000401bbf <+97>:     mov     0xa3542(%rip),%rax       # 0x4a5108 <s_pdwData>
0x0000000000401bc6 <+104>:    movl    $0xecba,(%rax)

0x0000000000401bcc <+110>:    movl    $0xabcf,0xa682e(%rip)         # 0x4a8404 <g_dwData>

0x0000000000401bd6 <+120>:    mov     0xa355b(%rip),%rax       # 0x4a5138 <g_pdwData>
0x0000000000401bdd <+127>:    movl    $0xfcba,(%rax)
```

Note: The first and the third assignments are plain DWORD variables. The 2nd and the 4th assignments involve pointer dereference. When we check the results of the first assignment, we see a different result: instead of *abce,* we see *ecba* from the second assignment:

```
0x0000000000401bb5 <+87>:     movl    $0xabce,0xa57d5(%rip)         # 0x4a7394 <s_dwData>
0x0000000000401bbf <+97>:
```

```
(gdb) x/wx 0x4a7394
0x4a7394 <s_dwData>:      0x0000ecba
```

```
(gdb) x/wx 0x0000000000401bbf + 0xa57d5
0x4a7394 <s_dwData>:      0x0000ecba
```

This is because the pointer from the second assignment points to the memory cell of the first assignment:

```
0x0000000000401bbf <+97>:     mov     0xa3542(%rip),%rax       # 0x4a5108 <s_pdwData>
0x0000000000401bc6 <+104>:
```

```
(gdb) x/gx 0x4a5108
0x4a5108 <s_pdwData>:     0x00000000004a7394
```

```
(gdb) x/gx 0x0000000000401bc6 + 0xa3542
0x4a5108 <s_pdwData>:     0x00000000004a7394
```

The same difference is with the next two assignments:

```
0x0000000000401bcc <+110>:    movl    $0xabcf,0xa682e(%rip)         # 0x4a8404 <g_dwData>
```

```
(gdb) x/wx 0x4a8404
0x4a8404 <g_dwData>:      0x0000fcba
```

```
(gdb) x/wx 0x0000000000401bd6 + 0xa682e
0x4a8404 <g_dwData>:      0x0000fcba
```

```
0x0000000000401bd6 <+120>:    mov     0xa355b(%rip),%rax       # 0x4a5138 <g_pdwData>
```

```
(gdb) x/gx 0x4a5138
0x4a5138 <g_pdwData>:    0x00000000004a8404

(gdb) x/gx 0x0000000000401bdd + 0xa355b
0x4a5138 <g_pdwData>:    0x00000000004a8404

    0x0000000000401bdd <+127>:    movl    $0xfcba,(%rax)
```

Note: All this correlates with the source code that initializes the variables:

```
// data-types.c

extern uint32_t g_dwData;
extern uint32_t *g_pdwData;
...
static uint32_t s_dwData;
static uint32_t *s_pdwData = &s_dwData;


// separate.c

uint32_t g_dwData;
uint32_t *g_pdwData = &g_dwData;
```

The last two assignments are illustrated in the MCD-R2-x64.xlsx C section (offsets are hexadecimal).

9.   The default Clang-generated code is different. Let's look at the core dump differences.

```
~/ADDR-Linux/x64/MemoryDumps$ gdb -c data-types-clang.36 -se data-types-clang
```

```
(gdb) disassemble start_modeling
Dump of assembler code for function start_modeling:
   0x0000000000401b70 <+0>:      push    %rbp
   0x0000000000401b71 <+1>:      mov     %rsp,%rbp
   0x0000000000401b74 <+4>:      sub     $0x40,%rsp
   0x0000000000401b78 <+8>:      lea     -0x8(%rbp),%rax
   0x0000000000401b7c <+12>:     mov     %rax,-0x10(%rbp)
   0x0000000000401b80 <+16>:     lea     -0x11(%rbp),%rax
   0x0000000000401b84 <+20>:     mov     %rax,-0x20(%rbp)
   0x0000000000401b88 <+24>:     movabs  $0x47d004,%rax
   0x0000000000401b92 <+34>:     mov     %rax,-0x28(%rbp)
   0x0000000000401b96 <+38>:     mov     0x47d020,%rax
   0x0000000000401b9e <+46>:     mov     %rax,-0x40(%rbp)
   0x0000000000401ba2 <+50>:     mov     0x47d028,%rax
   0x0000000000401baa <+58>:     mov     %rax,-0x38(%rbp)
   0x0000000000401bae <+62>:     mov     0x47d030,%ecx
   0x0000000000401bb5 <+69>:     mov     %ecx,-0x30(%rbp)
   0x0000000000401bb8 <+72>:     movl    $0xabcd,-0x8(%rbp)
   0x0000000000401bbf <+79>:     mov     -0x10(%rbp),%rax
   0x0000000000401bc3 <+83>:     movl    $0xdcba,(%rax)
   0x0000000000401bc9 <+89>:     movl    $0xabce,0x4a9370
   0x0000000000401bd4 <+100>:    mov     0x4a70f0,%rax
   0x0000000000401bdc <+108>:    movl    $0xecba,(%rax)
   0x0000000000401be2 <+114>:    movl    $0xabcf,0x4aa3e4
   0x0000000000401bed <+125>:    mov     0x4a7100,%rax
   0x0000000000401bf5 <+133>:    movl    $0xfcba,(%rax)
   0x0000000000401bfb <+139>:    callq   0x401b50 <debug_break>
   0x0000000000401c00 <+144>:    add     $0x40,%rsp
```

```
   0x0000000000401c04 <+148>:    pop    %rbp
   0x0000000000401c05 <+149>:    retq
End of assembler dump.
```

Note: The compiler code generator uses direct memory references instead of relative RIP addressing, as in GCC-generated code.

Exercise R2 (A64, GDB)

Goal: Learn how to map source code to disassembly.

ADDR Patterns: Function Skeleton, Function Call, Call Path, Local Variable, Static Variable, Pointer Dereference.

Memory Cell Diagrams: Pointer Dereference.

1. Load a core dump *data-types.50791* and *data-types* executable from A64/MemoryDumps directory:

```
~/ADDR-Linux/A64/MemoryDumps$ gdb -c data-types.50791 -se data-types
GNU gdb (Ubuntu 12.0.90-0ubuntu1) 12.0.90
Copyright (C) 2022 Free Software Foundation, Inc.
License GPLv3+: GNU GPL version 3 or later <http://gnu.org/licenses/gpl.html>
This is free software: you are free to change and redistribute it.
There is NO WARRANTY, to the extent permitted by law.
Type "show copying" and "show warranty" for details.
This GDB was configured as "aarch64-linux-gnu".
Type "show configuration" for configuration details.
For bug reporting instructions, please see:
<https://www.gnu.org/software/gdb/bugs/>.
Find the GDB manual and other documentation resources online at:
    <http://www.gnu.org/software/gdb/documentation/>.

For help, type "help".
Type "apropos word" to search for commands related to "word"...
Reading symbols from data-types...
(No debugging symbols found in data-types)
[New LWP 50791]
Core was generated by `./data-types'.
#0  0x000000000040e750 in __pthread_kill_implementation.constprop.0 ()
```

2. We open a log file and set color highlighting off:

```
(gdb) set logging file R2.log
```

```
(gdb) set logging enabled on
Copying output to R2.log.
Copying debug output to R2.log.
```

```
(gdb) set style enabled off
```

3. We get this stack trace and disassemble the function that called *debug_break* (its return address is 0x00000000004007a8):

```
(gdb) bt
#0  0x000000000040e750 in __pthread_kill_implementation.constprop.0 ()
#1  0x000000000040551c in raise ()
#2  0x00000000004006e4 in debug_break ()
#3  0x00000000004007a8 in start_modeling ()
#4  0x00000000004007e8 in main ()
```

116

```
(gdb) disassemble 0x00000000004007a8
Dump of assembler code for function start_modeling:
   0x00000000004006f0 <+0>:      stp     x29, x30, [sp, #-80]!
   0x00000000004006f4 <+4>:      mov     x29, sp
   0x00000000004006f8 <+8>:      adrp    x0, 0x491000 <tunable_list+1336>
   0x00000000004006fc <+12>:     ldr     x0, [x0, #3040]
   0x0000000000400700 <+16>:     ldr     x1, [x0]
   0x0000000000400704 <+20>:     str     x1, [sp, #72]
   0x0000000000400708 <+24>:     mov     x1, #0x0                      // #0
   0x000000000040070c <+28>:     add     x0, sp, #0x14
   0x0000000000400710 <+32>:     str     x0, [sp, #24]
   0x0000000000400714 <+36>:     add     x0, sp, #0x13
   0x0000000000400718 <+40>:     str     x0, [sp, #32]
   0x000000000040071c <+44>:     adrp    x0, 0x457000 <__getauxval2+80>
   0x0000000000400720 <+48>:     add     x0, x0, #0xd60
   0x0000000000400724 <+52>:     str     x0, [sp, #40]
   0x0000000000400728 <+56>:     adrp    x0, 0x457000 <__getauxval2+80>
   0x000000000040072c <+60>:     add     x0, x0, #0xd60
   0x0000000000400730 <+64>:     add     x2, sp, #0x30
   0x0000000000400734 <+68>:     mov     x3, x0
   0x0000000000400738 <+72>:     ldp     x0, x1, [x3]
   0x000000000040073c <+76>:     stp     x0, x1, [x2]
   0x0000000000400740 <+80>:     ldr     w0, [x3, #16]
   0x0000000000400744 <+84>:     str     w0, [x2, #16]
   0x0000000000400748 <+88>:     mov     w0, #0xabcd                   // #43981
   0x000000000040074c <+92>:     str     w0, [sp, #20]
   0x0000000000400750 <+96>:     ldr     x0, [sp, #24]
   0x0000000000400754 <+100>:    mov     w1, #0xdcba                   // #56506
   0x0000000000400758 <+104>:    str     w1, [x0]
   0x000000000040075c <+108>:    adrp    x0, 0x494000 <_IO_strn_jumps+40>
   0x0000000000400760 <+112>:    add     x0, x0, #0xc4
   0x0000000000400764 <+116>:    mov     w1, #0xabce                   // #43982
   0x0000000000400768 <+120>:    str     w1, [x0]
   0x000000000040076c <+124>:    adrp    x0, 0x492000
   0x0000000000400770 <+128>:    add     x0, x0, #0x60
   0x0000000000400774 <+132>:    ldr     x0, [x0]
--Type <RET> for more, q to quit, c to continue without paging--
   0x0000000000400778 <+136>:    mov     w1, #0xecba                   // #60602
   0x000000000040077c <+140>:    str     w1, [x0]
   0x0000000000400780 <+144>:    adrp    x0, 0x491000 <tunable_list+1336>
   0x0000000000400784 <+148>:    ldr     x0, [x0, #3536]
   0x0000000000400788 <+152>:    mov     w1, #0xabcf                   // #43983
   0x000000000040078c <+156>:    str     w1, [x0]
   0x0000000000400790 <+160>:    adrp    x0, 0x491000 <tunable_list+1336>
   0x0000000000400794 <+164>:    ldr     x0, [x0, #3784]
   0x0000000000400798 <+168>:    ldr     x0, [x0]
   0x000000000040079c <+172>:    mov     w1, #0xfcba                   // #64698
   0x00000000004007a0 <+176>:    str     w1, [x0]
   0x00000000004007a4 <+180>:    bl      0x4006d4 <debug_break>
   0x00000000004007a8 <+184>:    nop
   0x00000000004007ac <+188>:    adrp    x0, 0x491000 <tunable_list+1336>
   0x00000000004007b0 <+192>:    ldr     x0, [x0, #3040]
   0x00000000004007b4 <+196>:    ldr     x2, [sp, #72]
   0x00000000004007b8 <+200>:    ldr     x1, [x0]
   0x00000000004007bc <+204>:    subs    x2, x2, x1
   0x00000000004007c0 <+208>:    mov     x1, #0x0                      // #0
   0x00000000004007c4 <+212>:    b.eq    0x4007cc <start_modeling+220> // b.none
   0x00000000004007c8 <+216>:    bl      0x41c0b0 <__stack_chk_fail_local>
   0x00000000004007cc <+220>:    ldp     x29, x30, [sp], #80
```
117

```
   0x00000000004007d0 <+224>:    ret
End of assembler dump.
```

Note: Understanding any function most of the time starts with checking what other functions it may call. We call this ADDR pattern **Function Skeleton**. In our case, the function skeleton of *start_modeling* consists of just two functions because we don't see any other calls: *debug_break* and *__stack_chk_fail_local*.

4.   Let's disassemble the *debug_break* function and follow **Call Path**.

```
(gdb) disassemble debug_break
Dump of assembler code for function debug_break:
   0x00000000004006d4 <+0>:     stp     x29, x30, [sp, #-16]!
   0x00000000004006d8 <+4>:     mov     x29, sp
   0x00000000004006dc <+8>:     mov     w0, #0x13                          // #19
   0x00000000004006e0 <+12>:    bl      0x405500 <raise>
   0x00000000004006e4 <+16>:    nop
   0x00000000004006e8 <+20>:    ldp     x29, x30, [sp], #16
   0x00000000004006ec <+24>:    ret
End of assembler dump.
```

Note: We see *debug_break* calls *raise* function without any diversions as we don't see any absolute or conditional branches. Also, its function skeleton consists of just one branch and link. So let's disassemble the *raise* function:

```
(gdb) disassemble raise
Dump of assembler code for function raise:
   0x0000000000405500 <+0>:     stp     x29, x30, [sp, #-32]!
   0x0000000000405504 <+4>:     mov     x29, sp
   0x0000000000405508 <+8>:     str     x19, [sp, #16]
   0x000000000040550c <+12>:    mov     w19, w0
   0x0000000000405510 <+16>:    bl      0x40f150 <pthread_self>
   0x0000000000405514 <+20>:    mov     w1, w19
   0x0000000000405518 <+24>:    bl      0x40e784 <pthread_kill>
   0x000000000040551c <+28>:    cbnz    w0, 0x40552c <raise+44>
   0x0000000000405520 <+32>:    ldr     x19, [sp, #16]
   0x0000000000405524 <+36>:    ldp     x29, x30, [sp], #32
   0x0000000000405528 <+40>:    ret
   0x000000000040552c <+44>:    adrp    x1, 0x491000 <tunable_list+1336>
   0x0000000000405530 <+48>:    ldr     x1, [x1, #3544]
   0x0000000000405534 <+52>:    mrs     x2, tpidr_el0
   0x0000000000405538 <+56>:    str     w0, [x2, x1]
   0x000000000040553c <+60>:    mov     w0, #0xffffffff                    // #-1
   0x0000000000405540 <+64>:    b       0x405520 <raise+32>
End of assembler dump.
```

Note: We see the *raise* function calls *pthread_kill,* which we don't see in the backtrace. Let's disassemble it too.

```
(gdb) disassemble pthread_kill
Dump of assembler code for function pthread_kill:
   0x000000000040e784 <+0>:     sub     w2, w1, #0x20
   0x000000000040e788 <+4>:     cmp     w2, #0x1
   0x000000000040e78c <+8>:     b.ls    0x40e794 <pthread_kill+16>  // b.plast
   0x000000000040e790 <+12>:    b       0x40e620 <__pthread_kill_implementation.constprop.0>
   0x000000000040e794 <+16>:    mov     w0, #0x16                          // #22
   0x000000000040e798 <+20>:    ret
End of assembler dump.
```

Note: Since we see __pthread_kill_implementation.constprop.0 in backtrace *b.ls* branch wasn't taken. If we disassemble *b* target, we see a few syscalls:

```
(gdb) disassemble 0x40e620
Dump of assembler code for function __pthread_kill_implementation.constprop.0:
   0x000000000040e620 <+0>:     stp     x29, x30, [sp, #-208]!
   0x000000000040e624 <+4>:     mrs     x3, tpidr_el0
   0x000000000040e628 <+8>:     sub     x3, x3, #0x7c0
   0x000000000040e62c <+12>:    mov     x29, sp
   0x000000000040e630 <+16>:    stp     x19, x20, [sp, #16]
   0x000000000040e634 <+20>:    adrp    x20, 0x491000 <tunable_list+1336>
   0x000000000040e638 <+24>:    mov     x19, x0
   0x000000000040e63c <+28>:    ldr     x0, [x20, #3040]
   0x000000000040e640 <+32>:    stp     x21, x22, [sp, #32]
   0x000000000040e644 <+36>:    sxtw    x21, w1
   0x000000000040e648 <+40>:    ldr     x1, [x0]
   0x000000000040e64c <+44>:    str     x1, [sp, #200]
   0x000000000040e650 <+48>:    mov     x1, #0x0                          // #0
   0x000000000040e654 <+52>:    cmp     x19, x3
   0x000000000040e658 <+56>:    b.eq    0x40e72c
<__pthread_kill_implementation.constprop.0+268>  // b.none
   0x000000000040e65c <+60>:    str     x23, [sp, #48]
   0x000000000040e660 <+64>:    add     x23, sp, #0x48
   0x000000000040e664 <+68>:    mov     x2, x23
   0x000000000040e668 <+72>:    adrp    x1, 0x458000
   0x000000000040e66c <+76>:    mov     x0, #0x0                          // #0
   0x000000000040e670 <+80>:    add     x1, x1, #0x558
   0x000000000040e674 <+84>:    mov     x3, #0x8                          // #8
   0x000000000040e678 <+88>:    mov     x8, #0x87                         // #135
   0x000000000040e67c <+92>:    svc     #0x0
   0x000000000040e680 <+96>:    add     x22, x19, #0x774
   0x000000000040e684 <+100>:   mov     w1, #0x1                          // #1
   0x000000000040e688 <+104>:   mov     x2, x22
   0x000000000040e68c <+108>:   mov     w0, #0x0                          // #0
   0x000000000040e690 <+112>:   bl      0x451c70 <__aarch64_cas4_acq>
   0x000000000040e694 <+116>:   cbnz    w0, 0x40e75c
<__pthread_kill_implementation.constprop.0+316>
   0x000000000040e698 <+120>:   ldrb    w0, [x19, #1907]
   0x000000000040e69c <+124>:   cbz     w0, 0x40e700
<__pthread_kill_implementation.constprop.0+224>
   0x000000000040e6a0 <+128>:   mov     w19, #0x0                         // #0
   0x000000000040e6a4 <+132>:   mov     x1, x22
--Type <RET> for more, q to quit, c to continue without paging--
   0x000000000040e6a8 <+136>:   mov     w0, #0x0                          // #0
   0x000000000040e6ac <+140>:   bl      0x451ec0 <__aarch64_swp4_rel>
   0x000000000040e6b0 <+144>:   cmp     w0, #0x1
   0x000000000040e6b4 <+148>:   b.gt    0x40e768
<__pthread_kill_implementation.constprop.0+328>
   0x000000000040e6b8 <+152>:   mov     x1, x23
   0x000000000040e6bc <+156>:   mov     x0, #0x2                          // #2
   0x000000000040e6c0 <+160>:   mov     x2, #0x0                          // #0
   0x000000000040e6c4 <+164>:   mov     x3, #0x8                          // #8
   0x000000000040e6c8 <+168>:   mov     x8, #0x87                         // #135
   0x000000000040e6cc <+172>:   svc     #0x0
   0x000000000040e6d0 <+176>:   ldr     x23, [sp, #48]
   0x000000000040e6d4 <+180>:   ldr     x20, [x20, #3040]
   0x000000000040e6d8 <+184>:   ldr     x0, [sp, #200]
```

```
   0x000000000040e6dc <+188>:    ldr      x1, [x20]
   0x000000000040e6e0 <+192>:    subs     x0, x0, x1
   0x000000000040e6e4 <+196>:    mov      x1, #0x0                        // #0
   0x000000000040e6e8 <+200>:    b.ne     0x40e774
<__pthread_kill_implementation.constprop.0+340>  // b.any
   0x000000000040e6ec <+204>:    mov      w0, w19
   0x000000000040e6f0 <+208>:    ldp      x19, x20, [sp, #16]
   0x000000000040e6f4 <+212>:    ldp      x21, x22, [sp, #32]
   0x000000000040e6f8 <+216>:    ldp      x29, x30, [sp], #208
   0x000000000040e6fc <+220>:    ret
   0x000000000040e700 <+224>:    ldrsw    x19, [x19, #208]
   0x000000000040e704 <+228>:    bl       0x418f00 <getpid>
   0x000000000040e708 <+232>:    sxtw     x2, w21
   0x000000000040e70c <+236>:    sxtw     x0, w0
   0x000000000040e710 <+240>:    mov      x1, x19
   0x000000000040e714 <+244>:    mov      x8, #0x83                       // #131
   0x000000000040e718 <+248>:    svc      #0x0
   0x000000000040e71c <+252>:    cmn      w0, #0x1, lsl #12
   0x000000000040e720 <+256>:    b.ls     0x40e6a0
<__pthread_kill_implementation.constprop.0+128>  // b.plast
   0x000000000040e724 <+260>:    neg      w19, w0
   0x000000000040e728 <+264>:    b        0x40e6a4
<__pthread_kill_implementation.constprop.0+132>
   0x000000000040e72c <+268>:    mov      x8, #0xb2                       // #178
   0x000000000040e730 <+272>:    svc      #0x0
--Type <RET> for more, q to quit, c to continue without paging--
   0x000000000040e734 <+276>:    sxtw     x19, w0
   0x000000000040e738 <+280>:    bl       0x418f00 <getpid>
   0x000000000040e73c <+284>:    mov      x1, x19
   0x000000000040e740 <+288>:    mov      x2, x21
   0x000000000040e744 <+292>:    sxtw     x0, w0
   0x000000000040e748 <+296>:    mov      x8, #0x83                       // #131
   0x000000000040e74c <+300>:    svc      #0x0
=> 0x000000000040e750 <+304>:    cmn      w0, #0x1, lsl #12
   0x000000000040e754 <+308>:    csneg    w19, wzr, w0, ls   // ls = plast
   0x000000000040e758 <+312>:    b        0x40e6d4
<__pthread_kill_implementation.constprop.0+180>
   0x000000000040e75c <+316>:    mov      x0, x22
   0x000000000040e760 <+320>:    bl       0x40e3a0 <__lll_lock_wait_private>
   0x000000000040e764 <+324>:    b        0x40e698
<__pthread_kill_implementation.constprop.0+120>
   0x000000000040e768 <+328>:    mov      x0, x22
   0x000000000040e76c <+332>:    bl       0x40e4b0 <__lll_lock_wake_private>
   0x000000000040e770 <+336>:    b        0x40e6b8
<__pthread_kill_implementation.constprop.0+152>
   0x000000000040e774 <+340>:    str      x23, [sp, #48]
   0x000000000040e778 <+344>:    bl       0x41c0b0 <__stack_chk_fail_local>
End of assembler dump.
```

The *__pthread_kill_implementation.constprop.0* function skeleton is (syscall number is provided in X8):

```
syscall 0x87
__aarch64_cas4_acq
__aarch64_swp4_rel
syscall 0x87
getpid
syscall 0x83
getpid
```

```
__lll_lock_wait_private
__lll_lock_wake_private
__stack_chk_fail_local
```

5.   Suppose we only have source code but not the debug info file for the *data-types* module. We search for *debug-break* there and find this function:

```
void start_modeling()
{
        _Bool bData;

        uint32_t dwData;
        uint32_t *pdwData = &dwData;

        char cData;
        char *pcData = &cData;

        const char *pcstrData = "Hello ADDR! (Local)";
        char acData[] = "Hello ADDR! (Local)";

        dwData = 0xABCD;
        *pdwData = 0xDCBA;

        s_dwData = 0xABCE;
        *s_pdwData = 0xECBA;

        g_dwData = 0xABCF;
        *g_pdwData = 0xFCBA;

        debug_break();
}
```

Note: It looks like it corresponds to our previously disassembled code which called *debug_break()* because we see the same constants (marked as green above and as blue below):

```
(gdb) disassemble start_modeling
Dump of assembler code for function start_modeling:
   0x00000000004006f0 <+0>:    stp     x29, x30, [sp, #-80]!
   0x00000000004006f4 <+4>:    mov     x29, sp
   0x00000000004006f8 <+8>:    adrp    x0, 0x491000 <tunable_list+1336>
   0x00000000004006fc <+12>:   ldr     x0, [x0, #3040]
   0x0000000000400700 <+16>:   ldr     x1, [x0]
   0x0000000000400704 <+20>:   str     x1, [sp, #72]
   0x0000000000400708 <+24>:   mov     x1, #0x0                         // #0
   0x000000000040070c <+28>:   add     x0, sp, #0x14
   0x0000000000400710 <+32>:   str     x0, [sp, #24]
   0x0000000000400714 <+36>:   add     x0, sp, #0x13
   0x0000000000400718 <+40>:   str     x0, [sp, #32]
   0x000000000040071c <+44>:   adrp    x0, 0x457000 <__getauxval2+80>
   0x0000000000400720 <+48>:   add     x0, x0, #0xd60
   0x0000000000400724 <+52>:   str     x0, [sp, #40]
   0x0000000000400728 <+56>:   adrp    x0, 0x457000 <__getauxval2+80>
   0x000000000040072c <+60>:   add     x0, x0, #0xd60
   0x0000000000400730 <+64>:   add     x2, sp, #0x30
   0x0000000000400734 <+68>:   mov     x3, x0
   0x0000000000400738 <+72>:   ldp     x0, x1, [x3]
   0x000000000040073c <+76>:   stp     x0, x1, [x2]
```

```
0x0000000000400740 <+80>:    ldr     w0, [x3, #16]
0x0000000000400744 <+84>:    str     w0, [x2, #16]
0x0000000000400748 <+88>:    mov     w0, #0xabcd                      // #43981
0x000000000040074c <+92>:    str     w0, [sp, #20]
0x0000000000400750 <+96>:    ldr     x0, [sp, #24]
0x0000000000400754 <+100>:   mov     w1, #0xdcba                      // #56506
0x0000000000400758 <+104>:   str     w1, [x0]
0x000000000040075c <+108>:   adrp    x0, 0x494000 <_IO_strn_jumps+40>
0x0000000000400760 <+112>:   add     x0, x0, #0xc4
0x0000000000400764 <+116>:   mov     w1, #0xabce                      // #43982
0x0000000000400768 <+120>:   str     w1, [x0]
0x000000000040076c <+124>:   adrp    x0, 0x492000
0x0000000000400770 <+128>:   add     x0, x0, #0x60
0x0000000000400774 <+132>:   ldr     x0, [x0]
--Type <RET> for more, q to quit, c to continue without paging--
0x0000000000400778 <+136>:   mov     w1, #0xecba                      // #60602
0x000000000040077c <+140>:   str     w1, [x0]
0x0000000000400780 <+144>:   adrp    x0, 0x491000 <tunable_list+1336>
0x0000000000400784 <+148>:   ldr     x0, [x0, #3536]
0x0000000000400788 <+152>:   mov     w1, #0xabcf                      // #43983
0x000000000040078c <+156>:   str     w1, [x0]
0x0000000000400790 <+160>:   adrp    x0, 0x491000 <tunable_list+1336>
0x0000000000400794 <+164>:   ldr     x0, [x0, #3784]
0x0000000000400798 <+168>:   ldr     x0, [x0]
0x000000000040079c <+172>:   mov     w1, #0xfcba                      // #64698
0x00000000004007a0 <+176>:   str     w1, [x0]
0x00000000004007a4 <+180>:   bl      0x4006d4 <debug_break>
0x00000000004007a8 <+184>:   nop
0x00000000004007ac <+188>:   adrp    x0, 0x491000 <tunable_list+1336>
0x00000000004007b0 <+192>:   ldr     x0, [x0, #3040]
0x00000000004007b4 <+196>:   ldr     x2, [sp, #72]
0x00000000004007b8 <+200>:   ldr     x1, [x0]
0x00000000004007bc <+204>:   subs    x2, x2, x1
0x00000000004007c0 <+208>:   mov     x1, #0x0                         // #0
0x00000000004007c4 <+212>:   b.eq    0x4007cc <start_modeling+220>   // b.none
0x00000000004007c8 <+216>:   bl      0x41c0b0 <__stack_chk_fail_local>
0x00000000004007cc <+220>:   ldp     x29, x30, [sp], #80
0x00000000004007d0 <+224>:   ret
End of assembler dump.
```

6.   There are 6 different assignments. Let's see their differences and associated memory references and changes. The first two assignments use **Local Variables.** Their storage was allocated in the stack region. We see this because an offset from SP is used.

```
0x0000000000400748 <+88>:    mov     w0, #0xabcd                      // #43981
0x000000000040074c <+92>:    str     w0, [sp, #20]
0x0000000000400750 <+96>:    ldr     x0, [sp, #24]
0x0000000000400754 <+100>:   mov     w1, #0xdcba                      // #56506
0x0000000000400758 <+104>:   str     w1, [x0]
```

The first assignment directly changes the memory cell located at offset +20 from the address in SP. The second is an example of a **Pointer Dereference**. The memory cell at offset +24 contains another memory address. This address is moved into X0, and then the assigned value 0xDCBA is stored at the memory cell pointed to by that address. Both assignments are illustrated in the MCD-R2-ARM64.xlsx A section (offsets are hexadecimal). Note that this is a word assignment; only the second word from the full 64-bit cell is affected (32-bit cells are called words in ARM64).

7.   Let's check the results from these memory assignments. We calculate SP for the 3rd frame from the backtrace (and here SP is equal to X29 value). We apply 3 times the algorithm we learned in Exercise R1:

```
(gdb) bt
#0  0x000000000040e750 in __pthread_kill_implementation.constprop.0 ()
#1  0x000000000040551c in raise ()
#2  0x00000000004006e4 in debug_break ()
#3  0x00000000004007a8 in start_modeling ()
#4  0x00000000004007e8 in main ()

(gdb) x/gx $sp
0xffffff99a1920: 0x0000ffffff99a19f0

(gdb) x/gx 0x0000ffffff99a19f0
0xffffff99a19f0: 0x0000ffffff99a1a10

(gdb) x/gx 0x0000ffffff99a1a10
0xffffff99a1a10: 0x0000ffffff99a1a20
```

Finally, we get the doubleword value at the location of the first assignment:

```
(gdb) x/wx 0x0000ffffff99a1a20 + 20
0xffffff99a1a34: 0x0000dcba
```

Note: We expect *abcd* instead of *dcba*! Let's check the next local variable (a pointer) involved in the second assignment:

```
(gdb) x/gx 0x0000ffffff99a1a20 + 24
0xffffff99a1a38: 0xffffff99a1a34
```

Note: We see that the pointer value points to the memory cell of the previous assignment variable. This is why the second assignment with pointer dereference overwrites the previously assigned value. Looking at function disassembly, we find this fragment:

```
(gdb) disassemble start_modeling
Dump of assembler code for function start_modeling:
   0x00000000004006f0 <+0>:     stp     x29, x30, [sp, #-80]!
   0x00000000004006f4 <+4>:     mov     x29, sp
   0x00000000004006f8 <+8>:     adrp    x0, 0x491000 <tunable_list+1336>
   0x00000000004006fc <+12>:    ldr     x0, [x0, #3040]
   0x0000000000400700 <+16>:    ldr     x1, [x0]
   0x0000000000400704 <+20>:    str     x1, [sp, #72]
   0x0000000000400708 <+24>:    mov     x1, #0x0                         // #0
   0x000000000040070c <+28>:    add     x0, sp, #0x14
   0x0000000000400710 <+32>:    str     x0, [sp, #24]
[...]
```

The first *add* instruction puts the address of the memory cell at SP+0x14 (which is the value of SP+20) into X0. Then this value is put into the memory cell located at SP+24. All this is illustrated in the MCD-R2-ARM64.xlsx B section (offsets are hexadecimal).

Note: This initialization is reflected in the source code:

```c
void start_modeling()
{
    _Bool bData;

    uint32_t dwData;
    uint32_t *pdwData = &dwData;
```

8.   The next 4 assignments involve **Static Variables**:

```
0x000000000040075c <+108>:    adrp    x0, 0x494000 <_IO_strn_jumps+40>
0x0000000000400760 <+112>:    add     x0, x0, #0xc4
0x0000000000400764 <+116>:    mov     w1, #0xabce                // #43982
0x0000000000400768 <+120>:    str     w1, [x0]
0x000000000040076c <+124>:    adrp    x0, 0x492000
0x0000000000400770 <+128>:    add     x0, x0, #0x60
0x0000000000400774 <+132>:    ldr     x0, [x0]
--Type <RET> for more, q to quit, c to continue without paging--
0x0000000000400778 <+136>:    mov     w1, #0xecba                // #60602
0x000000000040077c <+140>:    str     w1, [x0]
0x0000000000400780 <+144>:    adrp    x0, 0x491000 <tunable_list+1336>
0x0000000000400784 <+148>:    ldr     x0, [x0, #3536]
0x0000000000400788 <+152>:    mov     w1, #0xabcf                // #43983
0x000000000040078c <+156>:    str     w1, [x0]
0x0000000000400790 <+160>:    adrp    x0, 0x491000 <tunable_list+1336>
0x0000000000400794 <+164>:    ldr     x0, [x0, #3784]
0x0000000000400798 <+168>:    ldr     x0, [x0]
0x000000000040079c <+172>:    mov     w1, #0xfcba                // #64698
0x00000000004007a0 <+176>:    str     w1, [x0]
```

Note: The first and the third assignments are plain 32-bit variables. The 2nd and the 4th assignments involve pointer dereference. When we check the results of the first assignment, we see a different result: instead of *abce,* we see *ecba* from the second assignment:

```
0x000000000040075c <+108>:    adrp    x0, 0x494000 <_IO_strn_jumps+40>
0x0000000000400760 <+112>:    add     x0, x0, #0xc4
```

```
(gdb) x/wx 0x494000 + 0xc4
0x4940c4 <s_dwData>:      0x0000ecba
```

This is because the pointer from the second assignment points to the memory cell of the first assignment:

```
0x000000000040076c <+124>:    adrp    x0, 0x492000
0x0000000000400770 <+128>:    add     x0, x0, #0x60
0x0000000000400774 <+132>:    ldr     x0, [x0]
```

```
(gdb) x/gx 0x492000 + 0x60
0x492060 <s_pdwData>:    0x00000000004940c4
```

The same difference is with the next two assignments (which also involve an additional pointer dereference because of external variables):

```
0x0000000000400780 <+144>:    adrp    x0, 0x491000 <tunable_list+1336>
0x0000000000400784 <+148>:    ldr     x0, [x0, #3536]
```

124

```
    0x0000000000400788 <+152>:    mov    w1, #0xabcf                    // #43983
    0x000000000040078c <+156>:    str    w1, [x0]
```

(gdb) **x/gx** 0x491000 + 3536
0x491dd0:   0x00000000004940d0

(gdb) **x/wx** 0x00000000004940d0
0x4940d0 <g_dwData>:   0x0000fcba

```
    0x0000000000400790 <+160>:    adrp   x0, 0x491000 <tunable_list+1336>
    0x0000000000400794 <+164>:    ldr    x0, [x0, #3784]
    0x0000000000400798 <+168>:    ldr    x0, [x0]
```

(gdb) **x/gx** 0x491000 + 3784
0x491ec8:   0x0000000000492090

(gdb) **x/gx** 0x0000000000492090
0x492090 <g_pdwData>:   0x00000000004940d0

```
    0x000000000040079c <+172>:    mov    w1, #0xfcba                    // #64698
    0x00000000004007a0 <+176>:    str    w1, [x0]
```

Note: All this correlates with the source code that initializes the variables:

```
// data-types.c

extern uint32_t g_dwData;
extern uint32_t *g_pdwData;
...
static uint32_t s_dwData;
static uint32_t *s_pdwData = &s_dwData;

// separate.c

uint32_t g_dwData;
uint32_t *g_pdwData = &g_dwData;
```

The last two assignments are illustrated in the MCD-R2-ARM64.xlsx C section (offsets are hexadecimal).

9.   The default Clang-generated code is different. Let's look at the core dump differences.

~/ADDR-Linux/A64/MemoryDumps$ **gdb -c data-types-clang.918790 -se data-types-clang**

(gdb) **disassemble** start_modeling
Dump of assembler code for function start_modeling:
```
    0x00000000004006ec <+0>:     sub    sp, sp, #0x50
    0x00000000004006f0 <+4>:     stp    x29, x30, [sp, #64]
    0x00000000004006f4 <+8>:     add    x29, sp, #0x40
    0x00000000004006f8 <+12>:    sub    x8, x29, #0x8
    0x00000000004006fc <+16>:    stur   x8, [x29, #-16]
    0x0000000000400700 <+20>:    sub    x8, x29, #0x11
    0x0000000000400704 <+24>:    str    x8, [sp, #32]
    0x0000000000400708 <+28>:    adrp   x8, 0x457000 <getauxval+16>
    0x000000000040070c <+32>:    add    x8, x8, #0xd08
    0x0000000000400710 <+36>:    str    x8, [sp, #24]
    0x0000000000400714 <+40>:    adrp   x8, 0x457000 <getauxval+16>
    0x0000000000400718 <+44>:    add    x8, x8, #0xd08
```
125

```
0x000000000040071c <+48>:    ldr     q0, [x8]
0x0000000000400720 <+52>:    str     q0, [sp]
0x0000000000400724 <+56>:    ldr     w8, [x8, #16]
0x0000000000400728 <+60>:    str     w8, [sp, #16]
0x000000000040072c <+64>:    mov     w8, #0xabcd                    // #43981
0x0000000000400730 <+68>:    stur    w8, [x29, #-8]
0x0000000000400734 <+72>:    ldur    x9, [x29, #-16]
0x0000000000400738 <+76>:    mov     w8, #0xdcba                    // #56506
0x000000000040073c <+80>:    str     w8, [x9]
0x0000000000400740 <+84>:    adrp    x9, 0x495000 <_IO_strn_jumps+80>
0x0000000000400744 <+88>:    mov     w8, #0xabce                    // #43982
0x0000000000400748 <+92>:    str     w8, [x9, #152]
0x000000000040074c <+96>:    adrp    x8, 0x493000
0x0000000000400750 <+100>:   ldr     x9, [x8, #72]
0x0000000000400754 <+104>:   mov     w8, #0xecba                    // #60602
0x0000000000400758 <+108>:   str     w8, [x9]
0x000000000040075c <+112>:   adrp    x9, 0x492000 <tunable_list+1336>
0x0000000000400760 <+116>:   ldr     x9, [x9, #3536]
0x0000000000400764 <+120>:   mov     w8, #0xabcf                    // #43983
0x0000000000400768 <+124>:   str     w8, [x9]
0x000000000040076c <+128>:   adrp    x8, 0x492000 <tunable_list+1336>
0x0000000000400770 <+132>:   ldr     x8, [x8, #3784]
0x0000000000400774 <+136>:   ldr     x9, [x8]
0x0000000000400778 <+140>:   mov     w8, #0xfcba                    // #64698
0x000000000040077c <+144>:   str     w8, [x9]
0x0000000000400780 <+148>:   bl      0x4006d4 <debug_break>
0x0000000000400784 <+152>:   ldp     x29, x30, [sp, #64]
0x0000000000400788 <+156>:   add     sp, sp, #0x50
0x000000000040078c <+160>:   ret
End of assembler dump.
```

Note: We see the compiler code generator uses different general-purpose registers for addressing and negative X29 offsets compared to GCC-generated code.

ADDR: Function Skeleton

- Function calls (or branch and links) inside a function body
- Splits a function body into regions
- Helps in understanding a function

ADDR: Function Call

- Simply the call of (or branch and link to) a function
- Call (bl, blr) or unconditional jmp (b) instructions

ADDR: Call Path

- ◉ Following a sequence of Function Calls
- ◉ Example: call procA, call procC (or bl procA, bl procC)

```
...
call procA
call procB

...


procA:
...
call procC

...
```

```
...
bl procA
bl procB

...


procA:
...
bl procC

...
```

ADDR: Local Variable

- A variable is a memory cell with an address
- A variable with stack region storage
- Usually, a local variable memory cell is referenced by stack pointer or frame pointer registers

ADDR: Static Variable

- A variable is a memory cell with an address
- A variable with non-stack and non-register storage
- Usually, there is a direct memory reference

ADDR: Pointer Dereference

- A pointer is a memory cell that contains the address of (references) another memory cell

- Dereference is a sequence of instructions to get a value from a memory cell referenced by another memory cell

Exercise R3

- **Goal:** Learn a function structure and associated memory operations

- **ADDR Patterns:** Function Prologue, Function Epilogue, Variable Initialization, Memory Copy

- **Memory Cell Diagrams:** Function Prologue, Function Epilogue

- \ADDR-Linux\Exercise-R3-x64-GDB.pdf
- \ADDR-Linux\MCD-R3-x64.xlsx

- \ADDR-Linux\Exercise-R3-ARM64-GDB.pdf
- \ADDR-Linux\MCD-R3-ARM64.xlsx

Exercise R3 (x64, GDB)

Goal: Learn a function structure and associated memory operations.

ADDR Patterns: Function Prologue, Function Epilogue, Variable Initialization, Memory Copy.

Memory Cell Diagrams: Function Prologue, Function Epilogue.

1.   Load a core dump *data-types.93* and *data-types* executable from x64/MemoryDumps directory:

```
~/ADDR-Linux/x64/MemoryDumps$ gdb -c data-types.93 -se data-types
GNU gdb (Debian 8.2.1-2+b3) 8.2.1
Copyright (C) 2018 Free Software Foundation, Inc.
License GPLv3+: GNU GPL version 3 or later <http://gnu.org/licenses/gpl.html>
This is free software: you are free to change and redistribute it.
There is NO WARRANTY, to the extent permitted by law.
Type "show copying" and "show warranty" for details.
This GDB was configured as "x86_64-linux-gnu".
Type "show configuration" for configuration details.
For bug reporting instructions, please see:
<http://www.gnu.org/software/gdb/bugs/>.
Find the GDB manual and other documentation resources online at:
    <http://www.gnu.org/software/gdb/documentation/>.

For help, type "help".
Type "apropos word" to search for commands related to "word"...
Reading symbols from data-types...(no debugging symbols found)...done.

warning: exec file is newer than core file.
[New LWP 93]
Core was generated by `./data-types'.
#0  0x0000000000407629 in raise ()
```

2.   We open a log file:

```
(gdb) set logging on R3.log
Copying output to R3.log.
```

3.   We get this stack trace:

```
(gdb) bt
#0  0x0000000000407629 in raise ()
#1  0x0000000000401b5b in debug_break ()
#2  0x0000000000401bed in start_modeling ()
#3  0x0000000000401c09 in main ()
```

Note: This is a different process from the same *data-types* application from the previous exercise. RSP addresses are different due to ASLR (Address Space Layout Randomization). However, function offsets remain the same because the compiled and linked code didn't change. Return addresses also look the same.

4.   Let's disassemble the function that called *debug_break*:

```
(gdb) disassemble start_modeling
Dump of assembler code for function start_modeling:
   0x0000000000401b5e <+0>:     push   %rbp
   0x0000000000401b5f <+1>:     mov    %rsp,%rbp
   0x0000000000401b62 <+4>:     sub    $0x40,%rsp
   0x0000000000401b66 <+8>:     lea    -0x1c(%rbp),%rax
   0x0000000000401b6a <+12>:    mov    %rax,-0x8(%rbp)
   0x0000000000401b6e <+16>:    lea    -0x1d(%rbp),%rax
   0x0000000000401b72 <+20>:    mov    %rax,-0x10(%rbp)
   0x0000000000401b76 <+24>:    lea    0x7b49c(%rip),%rax        # 0x47d019
   0x0000000000401b7d <+31>:    mov    %rax,-0x18(%rbp)
   0x0000000000401b81 <+35>:    movabs $0x4441206f6c6c6548,%rax
   0x0000000000401b8b <+45>:    movabs $0x636f4c2820215244,%rdx
   0x0000000000401b95 <+55>:    mov    %rax,-0x40(%rbp)
   0x0000000000401b99 <+59>:    mov    %rdx,-0x38(%rbp)
   0x0000000000401b9d <+63>:    movl   $0x296c61,-0x30(%rbp)
   0x0000000000401ba4 <+70>:    movl   $0xabcd,-0x1c(%rbp)
   0x0000000000401bab <+77>:    mov    -0x8(%rbp),%rax
   0x0000000000401baf <+81>:    movl   $0xdcba,(%rax)
   0x0000000000401bb5 <+87>:    movl   $0xabce,0xa57d5(%rip)         # 0x4a7394 <s_dwData>
   0x0000000000401bbf <+97>:    mov    0xa3542(%rip),%rax        # 0x4a5108 <s_pdwData>
   0x0000000000401bc6 <+104>:   movl   $0xecba,(%rax)
   0x0000000000401bcc <+110>:   movl   $0xabcf,0xa682e(%rip)         # 0x4a8404 <g_dwData>
   0x0000000000401bd6 <+120>:   mov    0xa355b(%rip),%rax        # 0x4a5138 <g_pdwData>
   0x0000000000401bdd <+127>:   movl   $0xfcba,(%rax)
   0x0000000000401be3 <+133>:   mov    $0x0,%eax
   0x0000000000401be8 <+138>:   callq  0x401b4d <debug_break>
   0x0000000000401bed <+143>:   nop
   0x0000000000401bee <+144>:   leaveq
   0x0000000000401bef <+145>:   retq
End of assembler dump.
```

Note: We call by **Function Prologue** and **Function Epilogue** the code emitted by a compiler that is necessary to set up the working internals of a function. Such code doesn't have a real counterpart in the actual source code, such as C or C++. For example, allocating memory on the stack for all local variables at once is a part of a function prolog, but initializing an individual local variable is not a part of a function prolog. We highlighted the function prolog above in blue and the function epilog in green colors.

5.   Let's now examine the function prolog from the code above instruction by instruction.

```
   0x0000000000401b5e <+0>:     push   %rbp
```

Note: RBP register is saved because the function uses it later on. Registers such as RAX and RDX are not saved as they are commonly used, so the caller needs to save them before calling a function if it wants to preserve their values.

```
   0x0000000000401b5f <+1>:     mov    %rsp,%rbp
```

Note: RSP stack pointer value is now moved into RBP. The fixed RBP value is used later to address local variables regardless of the current value of RSP.

```
0x0000000000401b62 <+4>:       sub     $0x40,%rsp
```

Note: This instruction allocates 0x40 (**64**) bytes for various local variables. Please recall that the stack grows down in memory, hence *sub* subtraction instruction.

```
(gdb) p/d 0x40
$1 = 64
```

Note: All this prologue code is illustrated in the MCD-R3-x64.xlsx A section (offsets are hexadecimal).

6.   Now we examine the function epilog code instruction by instruction.

The *leave* instruction deallocates the storage for local variables by restoring the previous RSP value saved in RBP and then restores the previous RBP value saved on the stack:

```
0x0000000000401bee <+144>:     leaveq
```

It is equivalent to these two instructions:

```
mov     %rbp,%rsp
pop     %rbp
```

The final epilog instruction gets the saved RIP from the stack and replaces the current value of RIP. It also increments the RSP by 8 bytes (a pointer size):

```
0x0000000000401bef <+145>:     retq
```

Now the caller resumes execution after the *call* instruction:

```
(gdb) bt
#0  0x0000000000407629 in raise ()
#1  0x0000000000401b5b in debug_break ()
#2  0x0000000000401bed in start_modeling ()
#3  0x0000000000401c09 in main ()

(gdb) disassemble /r 0x0000000000401c09
Dump of assembler code for function main:
   0x0000000000401bf0 <+0>:     55            push   %rbp
   0x0000000000401bf1 <+1>:     48 89 e5      mov    %rsp,%rbp
   0x0000000000401bf4 <+4>:     48 83 ec 10   sub    $0x10,%rsp
   0x0000000000401bf8 <+8>:     89 7d fc      mov    %edi,-0x4(%rbp)
   0x0000000000401bfb <+11>:    48 89 75 f0   mov    %rsi,-0x10(%rbp)
   0x0000000000401bff <+15>:    b8 00 00 00 00 mov   $0x0,%eax
   0x0000000000401c04 <+20>:    e8 55 ff ff ff callq 0x401b5e <start_modeling>
   0x0000000000401c09 <+25>:    b8 00 00 00 00 mov   $0x0,%eax
   0x0000000000401c0e <+30>:    c9            leaveq
   0x0000000000401c0f <+31>:    c3            retq
```

Note: All this epilog code is illustrated in the MCD-R3-x64.xlsx B section. We also see that local values remain on the stack unless overwritten by subsequent function calls: the so-called **Execution Residue** memory analysis pattern.

7.   Between function prologue and epilogue lies the function logic. Most functions have local variables whose storage is allocated on a thread stack region (as we saw in the prologue code). Some variables require initialization. This is the next block of instructions after the function prologue:

```
(gdb) disassemble 0x0000000000401bed
Dump of assembler code for function start_modeling:
   0x0000000000401b5e <+0>:     push   %rbp
   0x0000000000401b5f <+1>:     mov    %rsp,%rbp
   0x0000000000401b62 <+4>:     sub    $0x40,%rsp
   0x0000000000401b66 <+8>:     lea    -0x1c(%rbp),%rax
   0x0000000000401b6a <+12>:    mov    %rax,-0x8(%rbp)
   0x0000000000401b6e <+16>:    lea    -0x1d(%rbp),%rax
   0x0000000000401b72 <+20>:    mov    %rax,-0x10(%rbp)
   0x0000000000401b76 <+24>:    lea    0x7b49c(%rip),%rax        # 0x47d019
   0x0000000000401b7d <+31>:    mov    %rax,-0x18(%rbp)
   0x0000000000401b81 <+35>:    movabs $0x4441206f6c6c6548,%rax
   0x0000000000401b8b <+45>:    movabs $0x636f4c2820215244,%rdx
   0x0000000000401b95 <+55>:    mov    %rax,-0x40(%rbp)
   0x0000000000401b99 <+59>:    mov    %rdx,-0x38(%rbp)
   0x0000000000401b9d <+63>:    movl   $0x296c61,-0x30(%rbp)
   0x0000000000401ba4 <+70>:    movl   $0xabcd,-0x1c(%rbp)
   0x0000000000401bab <+77>:    mov    -0x8(%rbp),%rax
   0x0000000000401baf <+81>:    movl   $0xdcba,(%rax)
   0x0000000000401bb5 <+87>:    movl   $0xabce,0xa57d5(%rip)        # 0x4a7394 <s_dwData>
   0x0000000000401bbf <+97>:    mov    0xa3542(%rip),%rax       # 0x4a5108 <s_pdwData>
   0x0000000000401bc6 <+104>:   movl   $0xecba,(%rax)
   0x0000000000401bcc <+110>:   movl   $0xabcf,0xa682e(%rip)        # 0x4a8404 <g_dwData>
   0x0000000000401bd6 <+120>:   mov    0xa355b(%rip),%rax       # 0x4a5138 <g_pdwData>
   0x0000000000401bdd <+127>:   movl   $0xfcba,(%rax)
   0x0000000000401be3 <+133>:   mov    $0x0,%eax
   0x0000000000401be8 <+138>:   callq  0x401b4d <debug_break>
   0x0000000000401bed <+143>:   nop
   0x0000000000401bee <+144>:   leaveq
   0x0000000000401bef <+145>:   retq
End of assembler dump.
```

Note: In general, the offset xxx in -xxx(%rbp) increases. Then we see -0x1c again, as highlighted in green color. We consider it a start of function logic that now uses initialized local variables.

Please also recall that we saw a memory cell diagram for an initialization fragment (the first 2 instructions) in the previous Exercise R2:

```
   0x0000000000401b66 <+8>:     lea    -0x1c(%rbp),%rax
   0x0000000000401b6a <+12>:    mov    %rax,-0x8(%rbp)
```
...

8.   In the past, we only looked at *lea/mov* pointer initialization, where a local pointer pointed to a local variable. What we also see *lea/mov* pointer initialization where a local pointer points to a memory area outside the stack region, such as:

```
   0x0000000000401b76 <+24>:    lea    0x7b49c(%rip),%rax        # 0x47d019
   0x0000000000401b7d <+31>:    mov    %rax,-0x18(%rbp)
   0x0000000000401b81 <+35>:
```

After this pair of instructions **RBP-0x18** memory cell contains the address `0x47d019`, which seems to be a null-terminated ASCII string:

```
(gdb) x/4gx 0x47d019
0x47d019:        0x4441206f6c6c6548       0x636f4c2820215244
0x47d029:        0x6c6c654800296c61       0x202152444441206f
```

```
(gdb) x/20bx 0x47d019
0x47d019:        0x48    0x65    0x6c    0x6c    0x6f    0x20    0x41    0x44
0x47d021:        0x44    0x52    0x21    0x20    0x28    0x4c    0x6f    0x63
0x47d029:        0x61    0x6c    0x29    0x00
```

```
(gdb) x/20c 0x47d019
0x47d019:        72 'H'  101 'e' 108 'l' 108 'l' 111 'o' 32 ' '  65 'A'  68 'D'
0x47d021:        68 'D'  82 'R'  33 '!'  32 ' '  40 '('  76 'L'  111 'o' 99 'c'
0x47d029:        97 'a'  108 'l' 41 ')'  0 '\000'
```

```
(gdb) x/s 0x47d019
0x47d019:        "Hello ADDR! (Local)"
```

Note: Please familiarize yourself with a difference in the output of **gx** and **bx** command modifiers showing Intel's little-endian layout. This fragment above was translated from this C/C++ code:

```
const char *pcstrData = "Hello ADDR! (Local)";
```

Note: String address belongs to read-only pages:

```
(gdb) maintenance info sections
Exec file:
     `/home/coredump/ADDR-Linux/x64/MemoryDumps/data-types', file type elf64-x86-64.
 [0]      0x00400200->0x00400220 at 0x00000200: .note.ABI-tag ALLOC LOAD READONLY DATA HAS_CONTENTS
 [1]      0x00400220->0x00400244 at 0x00000220: .note.gnu.build-id ALLOC LOAD READONLY DATA HAS_CONTENTS
 [2]      0x00400248->0x00400470 at 0x00000248: .rela.plt ALLOC LOAD READONLY DATA HAS_CONTENTS
 [3]      0x00401000->0x00401017 at 0x00001000: .init ALLOC LOAD READONLY CODE HAS_CONTENTS
 [4]      0x00401018->0x004010d0 at 0x00001018: .plt ALLOC LOAD READONLY CODE HAS_CONTENTS
 [5]      0x004010d0->0x0047b620 at 0x000010d0: .text ALLOC LOAD READONLY CODE HAS_CONTENTS
 [6]      0x0047b620->0x0047c0a7 at 0x0007b620: __libc_freeres_fn ALLOC LOAD READONLY CODE HAS_CONTENTS
 [7]      0x0047c0a8->0x0047c0b1 at 0x0007c0a8: .fini ALLOC LOAD READONLY CODE HAS_CONTENTS
 [8]      0x0047d000->0x0049647c at 0x0007d000: .rodata ALLOC LOAD READONLY DATA HAS_CONTENTS
 [9]      0x00496480->0x004a0740 at 0x00096480: .eh_frame ALLOC LOAD READONLY DATA HAS_CONTENTS
 [10]     0x004a0740->0x004a07ec at 0x000a0740: .gcc_except_table ALLOC LOAD READONLY DATA HAS_CONTENTS
 [11]     0x004a20e0->0x004a2100 at 0x000a10e0: .tdata ALLOC LOAD DATA HAS_CONTENTS
 [12]     0x004a2100->0x004a2140 at 0x000a1100: .tbss ALLOC
 [13]     0x004a2100->0x004a2110 at 0x000a1100: .init_array ALLOC LOAD DATA HAS_CONTENTS
 [14]     0x004a2110->0x004a2120 at 0x000a1110: .fini_array ALLOC LOAD DATA HAS_CONTENTS
 [15]     0x004a2120->0x004a4f14 at 0x000a1120: .data.rel.ro ALLOC LOAD DATA HAS_CONTENTS
 [16]     0x004a4f18->0x004a4ff8 at 0x000a3f18: .got ALLOC LOAD DATA HAS_CONTENTS
 [17]     0x004a5000->0x004a50d0 at 0x000a4000: .got.plt ALLOC LOAD DATA HAS_CONTENTS
 [18]     0x004a50e0->0x004a6c30 at 0x000a40e0: .data ALLOC LOAD DATA HAS_CONTENTS
 [19]     0x004a6c30->0x004a6c78 at 0x000a5c30: __libc_subfreeres ALLOC LOAD DATA HAS_CONTENTS
 [20]     0x004a6c80->0x004a7328 at 0x000a5c80: __libc_IO_vtables ALLOC LOAD DATA HAS_CONTENTS
 [21]     0x004a7328->0x004a7330 at 0x000a6328: __libc_atexit ALLOC LOAD DATA HAS_CONTENTS
 [22]     0x004a7340->0x004a8a78 at 0x000a6330: .bss ALLOC
 [23]     0x004a8a78->0x004a8aa0 at 0x000a6330: __libc_freeres_ptrs ALLOC
 [24]     0x00000000->0x0000001c at 0x000a6330: .comment READONLY HAS_CONTENTS
Core file:
     `/home/coredump/ADDR-Linux/x64/MemoryDumps/data-types.93', file type elf64-x86-64.
 [0]      0x00000000->0x00000924 at 0x00000190: note0 READONLY HAS_CONTENTS
 [1]      0x00000000->0x000000d8 at 0x000002b0: .reg/93 HAS_CONTENTS
```

```
[2]      0x00000000->0x000000d8 at 0x000002b0: .reg HAS_CONTENTS
[3]      0x00000000->0x00000200 at 0x000003a4: .reg2/93 HAS_CONTENTS
[4]      0x00000000->0x00000200 at 0x000003a4: .reg2 HAS_CONTENTS
[5]      0x00000000->0x00000340 at 0x000005b8: .reg-xstate/93 HAS_CONTENTS
[6]      0x00000000->0x00000340 at 0x000005b8: .reg-xstate HAS_CONTENTS
[7]      0x00000000->0x00000140 at 0x0000090c: .auxv HAS_CONTENTS
[8]      0x00000000->0x00000054 at 0x00000a60: .note.linuxcore.file/93 HAS_CONTENTS
[9]      0x00000000->0x00000054 at 0x00000a60: .note.linuxcore.file HAS_CONTENTS
--Type <RET> for more, q to quit, c to continue without paging--
[10]     0x004a2000->0x004a8000 at 0x00000ab4: load1 ALLOC LOAD HAS_CONTENTS
[11]     0x004a8000->0x004a9000 at 0x00006ab4: load2 ALLOC LOAD HAS_CONTENTS
[12]     0x01fa0000->0x01fc3000 at 0x00007ab4: load3 ALLOC LOAD HAS_CONTENTS
[13]     0x7ffee2913000->0x7ffee2934000 at 0x0002aab4: load4 ALLOC LOAD HAS_CONTENTS
[14]     0x7ffee296b000->0x7ffee296c000 at 0x0004bab4: load5 ALLOC LOAD READONLY CODE HAS_CONTENTS

(gdb) x/10s 0x47d000
0x47d000 <_IO_stdin_used>:        "\001"
0x47d002 <_IO_stdin_used+2>:      "\002"
0x47d004:        "Hello ADDR! (Static)"
0x47d019:        "Hello ADDR! (Local)"
0x47d02d:        "Hello ADDR! (Global)"
0x47d042:        "xeon_phi"
0x47d04b:        "haswell"
0x47d053:        "../csu/libc-start.c"
0x47d067:        "FATAL: kernel too old\n"
0x47d07e:        ""
```

9.   Among initialization code, we also see the **Memory Copy** pattern via the *movabs* and *movl* instructions:

```
0x0000000000401b81 <+35>:      movabs $0x4441206f6c6c6548,%rax
0x0000000000401b8b <+45>:      movabs $0x636f4c2820215244,%rdx
0x0000000000401b95 <+55>:      mov    %rax,-0x40(%rbp)
0x0000000000401b99 <+59>:      mov    %rdx,-0x38(%rbp)
0x0000000000401b9d <+63>:      movl   $0x296c61,-0x30(%rbp)
```

We see that ASCII-like data is copied into subsequent memory cells starting from RBP-0x40.

```
(gdb) p (char[8])0x4441206f6c6c6548
$2 = "Hello AD"

(gdb) p (char[8])0x636f4c2820215244
$3 = "DR! (Loc"

(gdb) p (char[4])0x296c61
$4 = "al)"
```

In Exercise R2 we calculated the value of RBP:

```
(gdb) p/x $rsp + (8 + 0x110 + 8) + (8 + 8) + 0x40
$5 = 0x7ffee2931c70
```

Now we can check local storage:

```
(gdb) x/s 0x7ffee2931c70-0x40
0x7ffee2931c30: "Hello ADDR! (Local)"
```

The fragment above was translated from the following C/C++ array initialization code:

```
char acData[] = "Hello ADDR! (Local)";
```

10.   The default Clang-generated code is different. Let's look at the core dump differences.

~/ADDR-Linux/x64/MemoryDumps$ gdb -c data-types-clang.36 -se data-types-clang

```
(gdb) disassemble start_modeling
Dump of assembler code for function start_modeling:
   0x0000000000401b70 <+0>:     push   %rbp
   0x0000000000401b71 <+1>:     mov    %rsp,%rbp
   0x0000000000401b74 <+4>:     sub    $0x40,%rsp
   0x0000000000401b78 <+8>:     lea    -0x8(%rbp),%rax
   0x0000000000401b7c <+12>:    mov    %rax,-0x10(%rbp)
   0x0000000000401b80 <+16>:    lea    -0x11(%rbp),%rax
   0x0000000000401b84 <+20>:    mov    %rax,-0x20(%rbp)
   0x0000000000401b88 <+24>:    movabs $0x47d004,%rax
   0x0000000000401b92 <+34>:    mov    %rax,-0x28(%rbp)
   0x0000000000401b96 <+38>:    mov    0x47d020,%rax
   0x0000000000401b9e <+46>:    mov    %rax,-0x40(%rbp)
   0x0000000000401ba2 <+50>:    mov    0x47d028,%rax
   0x0000000000401baa <+58>:    mov    %rax,-0x38(%rbp)
   0x0000000000401bae <+62>:    mov    0x47d030,%ecx
   0x0000000000401bb5 <+69>:    mov    %ecx,-0x30(%rbp)
   0x0000000000401bb8 <+72>:    movl   $0xabcd,-0x8(%rbp)
   0x0000000000401bbf <+79>:    mov    -0x10(%rbp),%rax
   0x0000000000401bc3 <+83>:    movl   $0xdcba,(%rax)
   0x0000000000401bc9 <+89>:    movl   $0xabce,0x4a9370
   0x0000000000401bd4 <+100>:   mov    0x4a70f0,%rax
   0x0000000000401bdc <+108>:   movl   $0xecba,(%rax)
   0x0000000000401be2 <+114>:   movl   $0xabcf,0x4aa3e4
   0x0000000000401bed <+125>:   mov    0x4a7100,%rax
   0x0000000000401bf5 <+133>:   movl   $0xfcba,(%rax)
   0x0000000000401bfb <+139>:   callq  0x401b50 <debug_break>
   0x0000000000401c00 <+144>:   add    $0x40,%rsp
   0x0000000000401c04 <+148>:   pop    %rbp
   0x0000000000401c05 <+149>:   retq
End of assembler dump.
```

Note: The compiler code generator uses repeated memory move instructions that use direct memory addresses for memory copy compared to GCC-generated code, which encodes the constant string in *mov* instructions.

Exercise R3 (A64, GDB)

Goal: Learn a function structure and associated memory operations.

ADDR Patterns: Function Prologue, Function Epilogue, Variable Initialization, Memory Copy.

Memory Cell Diagrams: Function Prologue, Function Epilogue.

1.   Load a core dump *data-types.50817* and *data-types* executable from A64/MemoryDumps directory:

```
~/ADDR-Linux/A64/MemoryDumps$ gdb -c data-types.50817 -se data-types
GNU gdb (Ubuntu 12.0.90-0ubuntu1) 12.0.90
Copyright (C) 2022 Free Software Foundation, Inc.
License GPLv3+: GNU GPL version 3 or later <http://gnu.org/licenses/gpl.html>
This is free software: you are free to change and redistribute it.
There is NO WARRANTY, to the extent permitted by law.
Type "show copying" and "show warranty" for details.
This GDB was configured as "aarch64-linux-gnu".
Type "show configuration" for configuration details.
For bug reporting instructions, please see:
<https://www.gnu.org/software/gdb/bugs/>.
Find the GDB manual and other documentation resources online at:
    <http://www.gnu.org/software/gdb/documentation/>.

For help, type "help".
Type "apropos word" to search for commands related to "word"...
Reading symbols from data-types...
(No debugging symbols found in data-types)
[New LWP 50817]
Core was generated by `./data-types'.
#0  0x000000000040e750 in __pthread_kill_implementation.constprop.0 ()
```

2.   We open a log file and set color highlighting off:

```
(gdb) set logging file R3.log
```

```
(gdb) set logging enabled on
Copying output to R3.log.
Copying debug output to R3.log.
```

```
(gdb) set style enabled off
```

3.   We get this stack trace:

```
(gdb) bt
#0  0x000000000040e750 in __pthread_kill_implementation.constprop.0 ()
#1  0x000000000040551c in raise ()
#2  0x00000000004006e4 in debug_break ()
#3  0x00000000004007a8 in start_modeling ()
#4  0x00000000004007e8 in main ()
```

Note: This is a different process from the same *data-types* application from the previous exercise. SP addresses are different due to ASLR (Address Space Layout Randomization). However, function offsets remain the same because the compiled and linked code didn't change. Return addresses also look the same.

4. Let's disassemble the function that called *debug_break*:

```
(gdb) disassemble start_modeling
Dump of assembler code for function start_modeling:
   0x00000000004006f0 <+0>:     stp     x29, x30, [sp, #-80]!
   0x00000000004006f4 <+4>:     mov     x29, sp
   0x00000000004006f8 <+8>:     adrp    x0, 0x491000 <tunable_list+1336>
   0x00000000004006fc <+12>:    ldr     x0, [x0, #3040]
   0x0000000000400700 <+16>:    ldr     x1, [x0]
   0x0000000000400704 <+20>:    str     x1, [sp, #72]
   0x0000000000400708 <+24>:    mov     x1, #0x0                          // #0
   0x000000000040070c <+28>:    add     x0, sp, #0x14
   0x0000000000400710 <+32>:    str     x0, [sp, #24]
   0x0000000000400714 <+36>:    add     x0, sp, #0x13
   0x0000000000400718 <+40>:    str     x0, [sp, #32]
   0x000000000040071c <+44>:    adrp    x0, 0x457000 <__getauxval2+80>
   0x0000000000400720 <+48>:    add     x0, x0, #0xd60
   0x0000000000400724 <+52>:    str     x0, [sp, #40]
   0x0000000000400728 <+56>:    adrp    x0, 0x457000 <__getauxval2+80>
   0x000000000040072c <+60>:    add     x0, x0, #0xd60
   0x0000000000400730 <+64>:    add     x2, sp, #0x30
   0x0000000000400734 <+68>:    mov     x3, x0
   0x0000000000400738 <+72>:    ldp     x0, x1, [x3]
   0x000000000040073c <+76>:    stp     x0, x1, [x2]
   0x0000000000400740 <+80>:    ldr     w0, [x3, #16]
   0x0000000000400744 <+84>:    str     w0, [x2, #16]
   0x0000000000400748 <+88>:    mov     w0, #0xabcd                       // #43981
   0x000000000040074c <+92>:    str     w0, [sp, #20]
   0x0000000000400750 <+96>:    ldr     x0, [sp, #24]
   0x0000000000400754 <+100>:   mov     w1, #0xdcba                       // #56506
   0x0000000000400758 <+104>:   str     w1, [x0]
   0x000000000040075c <+108>:   adrp    x0, 0x494000 <_IO_strn_jumps+40>
   0x0000000000400760 <+112>:   add     x0, x0, #0xc4
   0x0000000000400764 <+116>:   mov     w1, #0xabce                       // #43982
   0x0000000000400768 <+120>:   str     w1, [x0]
   0x000000000040076c <+124>:   adrp    x0, 0x492000
   0x0000000000400770 <+128>:   add     x0, x0, #0x60
   0x0000000000400774 <+132>:   ldr     x0, [x0]
   0x0000000000400778 <+136>:   mov     w1, #0xecba                       // #60602
   0x000000000040077c <+140>:   str     w1, [x0]
   0x0000000000400780 <+144>:   adrp    x0, 0x491000 <tunable_list+1336>
   0x0000000000400784 <+148>:   ldr     x0, [x0, #3536]
   0x0000000000400788 <+152>:   mov     w1, #0xabcf                       // #43983
   0x000000000040078c <+156>:   str     w1, [x0]
   0x0000000000400790 <+160>:   adrp    x0, 0x491000 <tunable_list+1336>
--Type <RET> for more, q to quit, c to continue without paging--
   0x0000000000400794 <+164>:   ldr     x0, [x0, #3784]
   0x0000000000400798 <+168>:   ldr     x0, [x0]
   0x000000000040079c <+172>:   mov     w1, #0xfcba                       // #64698
   0x00000000004007a0 <+176>:   str     w1, [x0]
   0x00000000004007a4 <+180>:   bl      0x4006d4 <debug_break>
   0x00000000004007a8 <+184>:   nop
   0x00000000004007ac <+188>:   adrp    x0, 0x491000 <tunable_list+1336>
   0x00000000004007b0 <+192>:   ldr     x0, [x0, #3040]
   0x00000000004007b4 <+196>:   ldr     x2, [sp, #72]
   0x00000000004007b8 <+200>:   ldr     x1, [x0]
   0x00000000004007bc <+204>:   subs    x2, x2, x1
   0x00000000004007c0 <+208>:   mov     x1, #0x0                          // #0
```

```
0x00000000004007c4 <+212>:    b.eq    0x4007cc <start_modeling+220>  // b.none
0x00000000004007c8 <+216>:    bl      0x41c0b0 <__stack_chk_fail_local>
0x00000000004007cc <+220>:    ldp     x29, x30, [sp], #80
0x00000000004007d0 <+224>:    ret
End of assembler dump.
```

Note: We call by **Function Prologue** and **Function Epilogue** the code emitted by a compiler that is necessary to set up the working internals of a function. Such code doesn't have a real counterpart in the actual source code, such as C or C++. For example, allocating memory on the stack for all local variables at once is a part of a function prolog, but initializing an individual local variable is not a part of a function prolog. We highlighted the function prolog above in blue and the function epilog in green colors.

5.   Let's now examine the function prolog from the code above instruction by instruction.

```
0x00000000004006f0 <+0>:      stp     x29, x30, [sp, #-80]!
```

Note: SP is decremented by 80 to allocate space for local variables, then FP (X29) register is saved, and then LR (X30). Registers such as X0 and X1 are not saved as they are commonly used, so the caller needs to save them before calling a function if it wants to preserve their values.

```
0x00000000004006f4 <+4>:      mov     x29, sp
```

Note: SP stack pointer value is now moved into FP (X29) to be saved in callees. The fixed SP value is used later to address local variables.

```
0x00000000004006f8 <+8>:      adrp    x0, 0x491000 <tunable_list+1336>
0x00000000004006fc <+12>:     ldr     x0, [x0, #3040]
0x0000000000400700 <+16>:     ldr     x1, [x0]
0x0000000000400704 <+20>:     str     x1, [sp, #72]
0x0000000000400708 <+24>:     mov     x1, #0x0                        // #0
```

Note: These 5 instructions are related to security checks (such as for buffer overruns).

The first 3 instructions copy a security cookie into X1 via a double pointer dereference. The value of the cookie for this dump is:

```
(gdb) x/gx 0x491000+3040
0x491be0:       0x00000000004909d8

(gdb) x/gx 0x00000000004909d8
0x4909d8 <__stack_chk_guard>:   0xa57ac84793315f00
```

The last two instructions store the cookie in X1 in a local variable with address SP+72 and then clear X1. We can check the stored value by calculating SP in the same way as we did in the previous Exercise R2:

```
(gdb) x/gx $sp
0xffffde8e0ec0: 0x0000ffffde8e0f90

(gdb) x/gx 0x0000ffffde8e0f90
0xffffde8e0f90: 0x0000ffffde8e0fb0

(gdb) x/gx 0x0000ffffde8e0fb0
0xffffde8e0fb0: 0x0000ffffde8e0fc0
```

```
(gdb) x/gx 0x0000ffffde8e0fc0+72
0xffffde8e1008:    0xa57ac84793315f00
```

Note: All this prologue code is illustrated in the MCD-R3-ARM64.xlsx A section (offsets are hexadecimal).

6.   Now we examine the function epilog code instruction by instruction.

```
0x00000000004007ac <+188>:   adrp   x0, 0x491000 <tunable_list+1336>
0x00000000004007b0 <+192>:   ldr    x0, [x0, #3040]
0x00000000004007b4 <+196>:   ldr    x2, [sp, #72]
0x00000000004007b8 <+200>:   ldr    x1, [x0]
0x00000000004007bc <+204>:   subs   x2, x2, x1
0x00000000004007c0 <+208>:   mov    x1, #0x0                      // #0
0x00000000004007c4 <+212>:   b.eq   0x4007cc <start_modeling+220>  // b.none
0x00000000004007c8 <+216>:   bl     0x41c0b0 <__stack_chk_fail_local>
0x00000000004007cc <+220>:
```

Note: The first eight instructions test the previously saved security cookie on the stack to see whether it was overwritten.

The next instruction restores the previous FP (X29) and LR (X30) values from the stack, and then deallocates the storage for local variables by adding 80 to SP:

```
0x00000000004007cc <+220>:   ldp    x29, x30, [sp], #80
```

The final epilog instruction gets the saved PC value from LR (X30) and replaces the current value of PC:

```
0x00000000004007d0 <+224>:   ret
```

Now the caller resumes execution after the *bl* instruction:

```
(gdb) bt
#0  0x000000000040e750 in __pthread_kill_implementation.constprop.0 ()
#1  0x000000000040551c in raise ()
#2  0x00000000004006e4 in debug_break ()
#3  0x00000000004007a8 in start_modeling ()
#4  0x00000000004007e8 in main ()

(gdb) disassemble /r 0x00000000004007e8
Dump of assembler code for function main:
   0x00000000004007d4 <+0>:    fd 7b be a9   stp    x29, x30, [sp, #-32]!
   0x00000000004007d8 <+4>:    fd 03 00 91   mov    x29, sp
   0x00000000004007dc <+8>:    e0 1f 00 b9   str    w0, [sp, #28]
   0x00000000004007e0 <+12>:   e1 0b 00 f9   str    x1, [sp, #16]
   0x00000000004007e4 <+16>:   c3 ff ff 97   bl     0x4006f0 <start_modeling>
   0x00000000004007e8 <+20>:   00 00 80 52   mov    w0, #0x0                      // #0
   0x00000000004007ec <+24>:   fd 7b c2 a8   ldp    x29, x30, [sp], #32
   0x00000000004007f0 <+28>:   c0 03 5f d6   ret
```

Note: All this epilog code is illustrated in the MCD-R3-ARM64.xlsx B section (offsets are hexadecimal). We also see that local values remain on the stack unless overwritten by subsequent function calls: the so-called **Execution Residue** memory analysis pattern.

7.	Between function prologue and epilogue lies the function logic. Most functions have local variables whose storage is allocated on a thread stack region (as we saw in the prologue code). Some variables require initialization. This is the next block of instructions after the function prologue:

```
(gdb) disassemble 0x00000000004007a8
Dump of assembler code for function start_modeling:
   0x00000000004006f0 <+0>:     stp     x29, x30, [sp, #-80]!
   0x00000000004006f4 <+4>:     mov     x29, sp
   0x00000000004006f8 <+8>:     adrp    x0, 0x491000 <tunable_list+1336>
   0x00000000004006fc <+12>:    ldr     x0, [x0, #3040]
   0x0000000000400700 <+16>:    ldr     x1, [x0]
   0x0000000000400704 <+20>:    str     x1, [sp, #72]
   0x0000000000400708 <+24>:    mov     x1, #0x0                         // #0
   0x000000000040070c <+28>:    add     x0, sp, #0x14
   0x0000000000400710 <+32>:    str     x0, [sp, #24]
   0x0000000000400714 <+36>:    add     x0, sp, #0x13
   0x0000000000400718 <+40>:    str     x0, [sp, #32]
   0x000000000040071c <+44>:    adrp    x0, 0x457000 <__getauxval2+80>
   0x0000000000400720 <+48>:    add     x0, x0, #0xd60
   0x0000000000400724 <+52>:    str     x0, [sp, #40]
   0x0000000000400728 <+56>:    adrp    x0, 0x457000 <__getauxval2+80>
   0x000000000040072c <+60>:    add     x0, x0, #0xd60
   0x0000000000400730 <+64>:    add     x2, sp, #0x30
   0x0000000000400734 <+68>:    mov     x3, x0
   0x0000000000400738 <+72>:    ldp     x0, x1, [x3]
   0x000000000040073c <+76>:    stp     x0, x1, [x2]
   0x0000000000400740 <+80>:    ldr     w0, [x3, #16]
   0x0000000000400744 <+84>:    str     w0, [x2, #16]
   0x0000000000400748 <+88>:    mov     w0, #0xabcd                      // #43981
   0x000000000040074c <+92>:    str     w0, [sp, #20]
   0x0000000000400750 <+96>:    ldr     x0, [sp, #24]
   0x0000000000400754 <+100>:   mov     w1, #0xdcba                      // #56506
   0x0000000000400758 <+104>:   str     w1, [x0]
   0x000000000040075c <+108>:   adrp    x0, 0x494000 <_IO_strn_jumps+40>
   0x0000000000400760 <+112>:   add     x0, x0, #0xc4
   0x0000000000400764 <+116>:   mov     w1, #0xabce                      // #43982
   0x0000000000400768 <+120>:   str     w1, [x0]
   0x000000000040076c <+124>:   adrp    x0, 0x492000
   0x0000000000400770 <+128>:   add     x0, x0, #0x60
   0x0000000000400774 <+132>:   ldr     x0, [x0]
   0x0000000000400778 <+136>:   mov     w1, #0xecba                      // #60602
   0x000000000040077c <+140>:   str     w1, [x0]
   0x0000000000400780 <+144>:   adrp    x0, 0x491000 <tunable_list+1336>
   0x0000000000400784 <+148>:   ldr     x0, [x0, #3536]
   0x0000000000400788 <+152>:   mov     w1, #0xabcf                      // #43983
   0x000000000040078c <+156>:   str     w1, [x0]
   0x0000000000400790 <+160>:   adrp    x0, 0x491000 <tunable_list+1336>
--Type <RET> for more, q to quit, c to continue without paging--
   0x0000000000400794 <+164>:   ldr     x0, [x0, #3784]
   0x0000000000400798 <+168>:   ldr     x0, [x0]
   0x000000000040079c <+172>:   mov     w1, #0xfcba                      // #64698
   0x00000000004007a0 <+176>:   str     w1, [x0]
   0x00000000004007a4 <+180>:   bl      0x4006d4 <debug_break>
   0x00000000004007a8 <+184>:   nop
   0x00000000004007ac <+188>:   adrp    x0, 0x491000 <tunable_list+1336>
   0x00000000004007b0 <+192>:   ldr     x0, [x0, #3040]
   0x00000000004007b4 <+196>:   ldr     x2, [sp, #72]
```

```
0x00000000004007b8 <+200>:    ldr     x1, [x0]
0x00000000004007bc <+204>:    subs    x2, x2, x1
0x00000000004007c0 <+208>:    mov     x1, #0x0                        // #0
0x00000000004007c4 <+212>:    b.eq    0x4007cc <start_modeling+220>  // b.none
0x00000000004007c8 <+216>:    bl      0x41c0b0 <__stack_chk_fail_local>
0x00000000004007cc <+220>:    ldp     x29, x30, [sp], #80
0x00000000004007d0 <+224>:    ret
End of assembler dump.
```

Note: In general, the offset xxx in [sp, #xxx] increases. Then we see it reset again, as highlighted in green color. We consider it a start of function logic that now uses initialized local variables.

Please also recall that we saw a memory cell diagram for an initialization fragment (the first 2 instructions) in the previous Exercise R2:

```
0x000000000040070c <+28>:    add     x0, sp, #0x14
0x0000000000400710 <+32>:    str     x0, [sp, #24]
...
```

8.   In the past, we only looked at *add/str* pointer initialization, where a local pointer pointed to a local variable. What we also see *add/str* pointer initialization where a local pointer points to a memory area outside the stack region, such as:

```
0x000000000040071c <+44>:    adrp    x0, 0x457000 <__getauxval2+80>
0x0000000000400720 <+48>:    add     x0, x0, #0xd60
0x0000000000400724 <+52>:    str     x0, [sp, #40]
```

After this pair of instructions SP+40 memory cell contains the address 0x457000+0xd60, which seems to be a null-terminated ASCII string:

```
(gdb) x/4gx 0x457000+0xd60
0x457d60:        0x4441206f6c6c6548        0x636f4c2820215244
0x457d70:        0x0000000000296c61        0x4441206f6c6c6548

(gdb) x/20bx 0x457000+0xd60
0x457d60:        0x48    0x65    0x6c    0x6c    0x6f    0x20    0x41    0x44
0x457d68:        0x44    0x52    0x21    0x20    0x28    0x4c    0x6f    0x63
0x457d70:        0x61    0x6c    0x29    0x00

(gdb) x/20c 0x457000+0xd60
0x457d60:        72 'H'  101 'e' 108 'l' 108 'l' 111 'o' 32 ' '  65 'A'  68 'D'
0x457d68:        68 'D'  82 'R'  33 '!'  32 ' '  40 '('  76 'L'  111 'o' 99 'c'
0x457d70:        97 'a'  108 'l' 41 ')'  0 '\000'

(gdb) x/s 0x457000+0xd60
0x457d60:        "Hello ADDR! (Local)"
```

Note: Please familiarize yourself with a difference in the output of **gx** and **bx** command modifiers showing Intel's little-endian layout. This fragment above was translated from this C/C++ code:

```
const char *pcstrData = "Hello ADDR! (Local)";
```

Note: String address belongs to read-only pages:

```
(gdb) maintenance info sections
Exec file: `/home/ubuntu/ADDR-Linux/A64/MemoryDumps/data-types', file type elf64-littleaarch64.
 [0]      0x00400190->0x004001b4 at 0x00000190: .note.gnu.build-id ALLOC LOAD READONLY DATA HAS_CONTENTS
 [1]      0x004001b4->0x004001d4 at 0x000001b4: .note.ABI-tag ALLOC LOAD READONLY DATA HAS_CONTENTS
 [2]      0x004001d8->0x00400280 at 0x000001d8: .rela.plt ALLOC LOAD READONLY DATA HAS_CONTENTS
 [3]      0x00400280->0x00400298 at 0x00000280: .init ALLOC LOAD READONLY CODE HAS_CONTENTS
 [4]      0x004002a0->0x00400310 at 0x000002a0: .plt ALLOC LOAD READONLY CODE HAS_CONTENTS
 [5]      0x00400340->0x004571d4 at 0x00000340: .text ALLOC LOAD READONLY CODE HAS_CONTENTS
 [6]      0x004571e0->0x00457d04 at 0x000571e0: __libc_freeres_fn ALLOC LOAD READONLY CODE HAS_CONTENTS
 [7]      0x00457d04->0x00457d18 at 0x00057d04: .fini ALLOC LOAD READONLY CODE HAS_CONTENTS
 [8]      0x00457d20->0x00471e28 at 0x00057d20: .rodata ALLOC LOAD READONLY DATA HAS_CONTENTS
 [9]      0x00471e28->0x00471e29 at 0x00071e28: .stapsdt.base ALLOC LOAD READONLY DATA HAS_CONTENTS
 [10]     0x00471e30->0x0047d73c at 0x00071e30: .eh_frame ALLOC LOAD READONLY DATA HAS_CONTENTS
 [11]     0x0047d73c->0x0047d82a at 0x0007d73c: .gcc_except_table ALLOC LOAD READONLY DATA HAS_CONTENTS
 [12]     0x0048e820->0x0048e840 at 0x0007e820: .tdata ALLOC LOAD DATA HAS_CONTENTS
 [13]     0x0048e840->0x0048e888 at 0x0007e840: .tbss ALLOC
 [14]     0x0048e840->0x0048e850 at 0x0007e840: .init_array ALLOC LOAD DATA HAS_CONTENTS
 [15]     0x0048e850->0x0048e858 at 0x0007e850: .fini_array ALLOC LOAD DATA HAS_CONTENTS
 [16]     0x0048e858->0x00491ba0 at 0x0007e858: .data.rel.ro ALLOC LOAD DATA HAS_CONTENTS
 [17]     0x00491ba0->0x00491fe8 at 0x00081ba0: .got ALLOC LOAD DATA HAS_CONTENTS
 [18]     0x00491fe8->0x00492038 at 0x00081fe8: .got.plt ALLOC LOAD DATA HAS_CONTENTS
 [19]     0x00492038->0x004939a8 at 0x00082038: .data ALLOC LOAD DATA HAS_CONTENTS
 [20]     0x004939a8->0x004939f0 at 0x000839a8: __libc_subfreeres ALLOC LOAD DATA HAS_CONTENTS
 [21]     0x004939f0->0x00494080 at 0x000839f0: __libc_IO_vtables ALLOC LOAD DATA HAS_CONTENTS
 [22]     0x00494080->0x00494088 at 0x00084080: __libc_atexit ALLOC LOAD DATA HAS_CONTENTS
 [23]     0x00494088->0x00499720 at 0x00084088: .bss ALLOC
 [24]     0x00499720->0x00499740 at 0x00084088: __libc_freeres_ptrs ALLOC
 [25]     0x00000000->0x00000026 at 0x00084088: .comment READONLY HAS_CONTENTS
 [26]     0x00000000->0x000013a4 at 0x000840b0: .note.stapsdt READONLY HAS_CONTENTS
Core file: `/home/ubuntu/ADDR-Linux/A64/MemoryDumps/data-types.50817', file type elf64-littleaarch64.
 [0]      0x00000000->0x00002858 at 0x000ce200: note0 READONLY HAS_CONTENTS
 [1]      0x00000000->0x00000110 at 0x000ce320: .reg/50817 HAS_CONTENTS
 [2]      0x00000000->0x00000110 at 0x000ce320: .reg HAS_CONTENTS
 [3]      0x00000000->0x00000210 at 0x000ce44c: .reg2/50817 HAS_CONTENTS
 [4]      0x00000000->0x00000210 at 0x000ce44c: .reg2 HAS_CONTENTS
 [5]      0x00000000->0x00000150 at 0x000ce670: .auxv HAS_CONTENTS
 [6]      0x00000000->0x000000f1 at 0x000ce7d4: .note.linuxcore.file/50817 HAS_CONTENTS
 [7]      0x00000000->0x000000f1 at 0x000ce7d4: .note.linuxcore.file HAS_CONTENTS
 [8]      0x00000000->0x0000217f at 0x000ce8d8: .gdb-tdesc/50817 HAS_CONTENTS
 [9]      0x00000000->0x0000217f at 0x000ce8d8: .gdb-tdesc HAS_CONTENTS
 [10]     0x00400000->0x0047e000 at 0x00000200: load1 ALLOC LOAD READONLY CODE HAS_CONTENTS
 [11]     0x0048e000->0x00492000 at 0x0007e200: load2 ALLOC LOAD READONLY HAS_CONTENTS
 [12]     0x00492000->0x00495000 at 0x00082200: load3 ALLOC LOAD HAS_CONTENTS
--Type <RET> for more, q to quit, c to continue without paging--
 [13]     0x00495000->0x0049a000 at 0x00085200: load4 ALLOC LOAD HAS_CONTENTS
 [14]     0x2446f000->0x24491000 at 0x0008a200: load5 ALLOC LOAD HAS_CONTENTS
 [15]     0xffff8a886000->0xffff8a887000 at 0x000ac200: load6 ALLOC LOAD READONLY CODE HAS_CONTENTS
 [16]     0xffffde8c1000->0xffffde8e2000 at 0x000ad200: load7 ALLOC LOAD HAS_CONTENTS

(gdb) x/60s 0x00457d20
0x457d20 <_IO_stdin_used>:        "\001"
0x457d22 <_IO_stdin_used+2>:      "\002"
0x457d24:          ""
0x457d25:          ""
0x457d26:          ""
0x457d27:          ""
0x457d28:          ""
0x457d29:          ""
0x457d2a:          ""
0x457d2b:          ""
0x457d2c:          ""
```

```
0x457d2d:          ""
0x457d2e:          ""
0x457d2f:          ""
0x457d30:          ""
0x457d31:          ""
0x457d32:          ""
0x457d33:          ""
0x457d34:          ""
0x457d35:          ""
0x457d36:          ""
0x457d37:          ""
0x457d38:          "\224hE"
0x457d3c:          ""
0x457d3d:          ""
0x457d3e:          ""
0x457d3f:          ""
0x457d40:          "pdE"
0x457d44:          ""
0x457d45:          ""
0x457d46:          ""
0x457d47:          ""
0x457d48:          "Hello ADDR! (Static)"
0x457d5d:          ""
0x457d5e:          ""
0x457d5f:          ""
0x457d60:          "Hello ADDR! (Local)"
0x457d74:          ""
0x457d75:          ""
0x457d76:          ""
0x457d77:          ""
0x457d78:          "Hello ADDR! (Global)"
--Type <RET> for more, q to quit, c to continue without paging--
0x457d8d:          ""
0x457d8e:          ""
0x457d8f:          ""
0x457d90:          "../csu/libc-start.c"
0x457da4:          ""
0x457da5:          ""
0x457da6:          ""
0x457da7:          ""
0x457da8:          "__ehdr_start.e_phentsize == sizeof *GL(dl_phdr)"
0x457dd8:          "Unexpected reloc type in static binary.\n"
0x457e01:          ""
0x457e02:          ""
0x457e03:          ""
0x457e04:          ""
0x457e05:          ""
0x457e06:          ""
0x457e07:          ""
0x457e08:          "FATAL: kernel too old\n"
```

9.   Among initialization code, we also see **Memory Copy** pattern via the *ldp/ldr* and *stp/str* instructions:

```
0x0000000000400728 <+56>:       adrp    x0, 0x457000 <__getauxval2+80>
0x000000000040072c <+60>:       add     x0, x0, #0xd60
0x0000000000400730 <+64>:       add     x2, sp, #0x30
0x0000000000400734 <+68>:       mov     x3, x0
0x0000000000400738 <+72>:       ldp     x0, x1, [x3]
```

148

```
0x000000000040073c <+76>:    stp    x0, x1, [x2]
0x0000000000400740 <+80>:    ldr    w0, [x3, #16]
0x0000000000400744 <+84>:    str    w0, [x2, #16]
```

We see that ASCII-like data is copied into subsequent memory cells starting from **SP+0x30**. First, two 64-bit values are copied from `0x457000+0xd60` address stored in X3 (ldp/stp). Then, a word 16-bit value is copied that contains a null byte (ldr/str). The source is the same read-only string as in the previous initialization.

```
Previously, we calculated the value of SP in this exercise:
```

```
(gdb) x/gx $sp
0xffffde8e0ec0: 0x0000ffffde8e0f90

(gdb) x/gx 0x0000ffffde8e0f90
0xffffde8e0f90: 0x0000ffffde8e0fb0

(gdb) x/gx 0x0000ffffde8e0fb0
0xffffde8e0fb0: 0x0000ffffde8e0fc0
```

Now we can check local storage:

```
(gdb) x/s 0x0000ffffde8e0fc0+0x30
0xffffde8e0ff0: "Hello ADDR! (Local)"
```

The fragment above was translated from the following C/C++ array initialization code:

```
char acData[] = "Hello ADDR! (Local)";
```

10.   The default Clang-generated code is different. Let's look at the core dump differences.

~/ADDR-Linux/A64/MemoryDumps$ **gdb -c data-types-clang.918790 -se data-types-clang**

```
(gdb) disassemble start_modeling
Dump of assembler code for function start_modeling:
   0x00000000004006ec <+0>:     sub    sp, sp, #0x50
   0x00000000004006f0 <+4>:     stp    x29, x30, [sp, #64]
   0x00000000004006f4 <+8>:     add    x29, sp, #0x40
   0x00000000004006f8 <+12>:    sub    x8, x29, #0x8
   0x00000000004006fc <+16>:    stur   x8, [x29, #-16]
   0x0000000000400700 <+20>:    sub    x8, x29, #0x11
   0x0000000000400704 <+24>:    str    x8, [sp, #32]
   0x0000000000400708 <+28>:    adrp   x8, 0x457000 <getauxval+16>
   0x000000000040070c <+32>:    add    x8, x8, #0xd08
   0x0000000000400710 <+36>:    str    x8, [sp, #24]
   0x0000000000400714 <+40>:    adrp   x8, 0x457000 <getauxval+16>
   0x0000000000400718 <+44>:    add    x8, x8, #0xd08
   0x000000000040071c <+48>:    ldr    q0, [x8]
   0x0000000000400720 <+52>:    str    q0, [sp]
   0x0000000000400724 <+56>:    ldr    w8, [x8, #16]
   0x0000000000400728 <+60>:    str    w8, [sp, #16]
   0x000000000040072c <+64>:    mov    w8, #0xabcd              // #43981
   0x0000000000400730 <+68>:    stur   w8, [x29, #-8]
```

```
0x0000000000400734 <+72>:    ldur    x9, [x29, #-16]
0x0000000000400738 <+76>:    mov     w8, #0xdcba                        // #56506
0x000000000040073c <+80>:    str     w8, [x9]
0x0000000000400740 <+84>:    adrp    x9, 0x495000 <_IO_strn_jumps+80>
0x0000000000400744 <+88>:    mov     w8, #0xabce                        // #43982
0x0000000000400748 <+92>:    str     w8, [x9, #152]
0x000000000040074c <+96>:    adrp    x8, 0x493000
0x0000000000400750 <+100>:   ldr     x9, [x8, #72]
0x0000000000400754 <+104>:   mov     w8, #0xecba                        // #60602
0x0000000000400758 <+108>:   str     w8, [x9]
0x000000000040075c <+112>:   adrp    x9, 0x492000 <tunable_list+1336>
0x0000000000400760 <+116>:   ldr     x9, [x9, #3536]
0x0000000000400764 <+120>:   mov     w8, #0xabcf                        // #43983
0x0000000000400768 <+124>:   str     w8, [x9]
0x000000000040076c <+128>:   adrp    x8, 0x492000 <tunable_list+1336>
0x0000000000400770 <+132>:   ldr     x8, [x8, #3784]
0x0000000000400774 <+136>:   ldr     x9, [x8]
0x0000000000400778 <+140>:   mov     w8, #0xfcba                        // #64698
0x000000000040077c <+144>:   str     w8, [x9]
0x0000000000400780 <+148>:   bl      0x4006d4 <debug_break>
0x0000000000400784 <+152>:   ldp     x29, x30, [sp, #64]
0x0000000000400788 <+156>:   add     sp, sp, #0x50
0x000000000040078c <+160>:   ret
End of assembler dump.
```

Note: We see the compiler code generator uses 128-bit Q0 register for memory copy compared to GCC-generated code, which uses *ldp/stp* instructions.

ADDR: Function Prologue

- The code emitted by a compiler that is necessary to set up the working internals of a function
- Such code doesn't have a real counterpart in actual source code
- Example: allocating memory on the stack for all local variables

ADDR: Function Epilogue

- The code emitted by a compiler that is necessary to finish the working internals of a function
- Such code doesn't have a real counterpart in actual source code
- Example: deallocating memory on the stack for all local variables

ADDR: Variable Initialization

- ◎ Code to initialize an individual local variable
- ◎ Not part of a function prologue

ADDR: Memory Copy

- Repeated memory move instructions

Exercise R4

- **Goal:** Learn how to recognize call and function parameters and track their data flow

- **ADDR Patterns:** Call Prologue, Call Parameter, Call Epilogue, Call Result, Control Path, Function Parameter

- \ADDR-Linux\Exercise-R4-x64-GDB.pdf

- \ADDR-Linux\Exercise-R4-ARM64-GDB.pdf

Exercise R4 (x64, GDB)

Goal: Learn how to recognize call and function parameters and track their data flow.

ADDR Patterns: Call Prologue, Call Parameter, Call Epilogue, Call Result, Control Path, Function Parameter.

1.   Load a core dump *notepad.61* and *notepad* executable from x64/MemoryDumps directory:

```
~/ADDR-Linux/x64/MemoryDumps$ gdb -c notepad.61 -se notepad
GNU gdb (Debian 8.2.1-2+b3) 8.2.1
Copyright (C) 2018 Free Software Foundation, Inc.
License GPLv3+: GNU GPL version 3 or later <http://gnu.org/licenses/gpl.html>
This is free software: you are free to change and redistribute it.
There is NO WARRANTY, to the extent permitted by law.
Type "show copying" and "show warranty" for details.
This GDB was configured as "x86_64-linux-gnu".
Type "show configuration" for configuration details.
For bug reporting instructions, please see:
<http://www.gnu.org/software/gdb/bugs/>.
Find the GDB manual and other documentation resources online at:
    <http://www.gnu.org/software/gdb/documentation/>.

For help, type "help".
Type "apropos word" to search for commands related to "word"...
Reading symbols from notepad...(no debugging symbols found)...done.
[New LWP 61]
Core was generated by `./notepad'.
#0  0x000000000043c4e1 in nanosleep ()
```

2.   We open a log file:

```
(gdb) set logging on R4.log
Copying output to R4.log.
```

3.   We get this stack trace:

```
(gdb) bt
#0  0x000000000043c4e1 in nanosleep ()
#1  0x000000000043c49a in sleep ()
#2  0x0000000000401c17 in internal_get_message ()
#3  0x0000000000401c57 in get_message ()
#4  0x0000000000401cea in main ()
```

4.   We analyzed this memory dump in Exercise R1, where we could recognize the *msg_t* structure on the stack. Let's now see how the *internal_get_message* function was called in the context of the *get_message* caller. The latter disassembly and **Function Skeleton** are these:

```
(gdb) disassemble get_message
Dump of assembler code for function get_message:
   0x0000000000401c1e <+0>:     push   %rbp
   0x0000000000401c1f <+1>:     mov    %rsp,%rbp
   0x0000000000401c22 <+4>:     sub    $0x30,%rsp
   0x0000000000401c26 <+8>:     mov    %rdi,-0x18(%rbp)
   0x0000000000401c2a <+12>:    mov    %rsi,-0x20(%rbp)
   0x0000000000401c2e <+16>:    mov    %rdx,-0x28(%rbp)
   0x0000000000401c32 <+20>:    mov    %rcx,-0x30(%rbp)
   0x0000000000401c36 <+24>:    movl   $0xffffffff,-0x4(%rbp)
   0x0000000000401c3d <+31>:    cmpq   $0x0,-0x18(%rbp)
   0x0000000000401c42 <+36>:    je     0x401c5a <get_message+60>
   0x0000000000401c44 <+38>:    mov    -0x20(%rbp),%rdx
   0x0000000000401c48 <+42>:    mov    -0x18(%rbp),%rax
   0x0000000000401c4c <+46>:    mov    %rdx,%rsi
   0x0000000000401c4f <+49>:    mov    %rax,%rdi
   0x0000000000401c52 <+52>:    callq  0x401b97 <internal_get_message>
   0x0000000000401c57 <+57>:    mov    %eax,-0x4(%rbp)
   0x0000000000401c5a <+60>:    cmpl   $0x0,-0x4(%rbp)
   0x0000000000401c5e <+64>:    je     0x401c6c <get_message+78>
   0x0000000000401c60 <+66>:    mov    -0x4(%rbp),%eax
   0x0000000000401c63 <+69>:    mov    %eax,%edi
   0x0000000000401c65 <+71>:    callq  0x401b58 <set_last_ui_error>
   0x0000000000401c6a <+76>:    jmp    0x401c7b <get_message+93>
   0x0000000000401c6c <+78>:    mov    -0x20(%rbp),%rax
   0x0000000000401c70 <+82>:    mov    %rax,%rdi
   0x0000000000401c73 <+85>:    callq  0x401b6b <call_ui_hooks>
   0x0000000000401c78 <+90>:    mov    %eax,-0x4(%rbp)
   0x0000000000401c7b <+93>:    cmpl   $0x0,-0x4(%rbp)
   0x0000000000401c7f <+97>:    sete   %al
   0x0000000000401c82 <+100>:   movzbl %al,%eax
   0x0000000000401c85 <+103>:   leaveq
   0x0000000000401c86 <+104>:   retq
End of assembler dump.

# internal_get_message
# set_last_ui_error
# call_ui_hooks
```

Note: The standard x64 calling convention passes the first 6 parameters via RDI, RSI, RDX, RCX, R8, and R9 registers or their subregisters, such as ECX or R9D. Here in **Call Prologue**, we only see that some value of RAX is assigned to RDI (the 1st **Call Parameter**), and some value of RDX is assigned to RSI (the 2nd **Call Parameter**). Before that, there were no assignments to other calling convention registers. However, we can track call parameters to **Function Parameters**. If data passed to a function before a function call is called **Call Parameter**, then inside a function (on the receiver side), it is called **Function Parameter**. Such a parameter can be translated to a local variable if passed by a stack or copied to a stack location if passed by a register and referenced as RBP or RSP offset, or it can still be an original register or copied to another register.

Call Epilogue only consists of saving **Call Result** in the local variable RBP-4, which seems to be later reused in calculations before the **Function Epilogue** (highlighted in green. We also see that a function body has several **Control Paths** as there are conditional and direct jumps.

5.   Let's now study control paths after the *internal_get_message* function call:

```
0x0000000000401c52 <+52>:    callq    0x401b97 <internal_get_message>
0x0000000000401c57 <+57>:    mov      %eax,-0x4(%rbp)
0x0000000000401c5a <+60>:    cmpl     $0x0,-0x4(%rbp)
0x0000000000401c5e <+64>:    je       0x401c6c <get_message+78>
0x0000000000401c60 <+66>:    mov      -0x4(%rbp),%eax
0x0000000000401c63 <+69>:    mov      %eax,%edi
0x0000000000401c65 <+71>:    callq    0x401b58 <set_last_ui_error>
0x0000000000401c6a <+76>:    jmp      0x401c7b <get_message+93>
0x0000000000401c6c <+78>:    mov      -0x20(%rbp),%rax
0x0000000000401c70 <+82>:    mov      %rax,%rdi
0x0000000000401c73 <+85>:    callq    0x401b6b <call_ui_hooks>
0x0000000000401c78 <+90>:    mov      %eax,-0x4(%rbp)
0x0000000000401c7b <+93>:    cmpl     $0x0,-0x4(%rbp)
0x0000000000401c7f <+97>:    sete     %al
0x0000000000401c82 <+100>:   movzbl   %al,%eax
0x0000000000401c85 <+103>:   leaveq
0x0000000000401c86 <+104>:   retq
```

6.   Let's now see **Call Parameters** for the *get_message* function. We now need to either disassemble its caller or disassemble the caller's return address. We do the latter:

```
(gdb) bt
#0  0x000000000043c4e1 in nanosleep ()
#1  0x000000000043c49a in sleep ()
#2  0x0000000000401c17 in internal_get_message ()
#3  0x0000000000401c57 in get_message ()
#4  0x0000000000401cea in main ()

(gdb) disassemble 0x0000000000401cea
Dump of assembler code for function main:
   0x0000000000401cb2 <+0>:     push     %rbp
   0x0000000000401cb3 <+1>:     mov      %rsp,%rbp
   0x0000000000401cb6 <+4>:     sub      $0x40,%rsp
   0x0000000000401cba <+8>:     mov      %edi,-0x34(%rbp)
   0x0000000000401cbd <+11>:    mov      %rsi,-0x40(%rbp)
   0x0000000000401cc1 <+15>:    jmp      0x401ccf <main+29>
   0x0000000000401cc3 <+17>:    lea      -0x30(%rbp),%rax
   0x0000000000401cc7 <+21>:    mov      %rax,%rdi
   0x0000000000401cca <+24>:    callq    0x401c87 <dispatch_message>
   0x0000000000401ccf <+29>:    lea      -0x30(%rbp),%rax
   0x0000000000401cd3 <+33>:    mov      $0x0,%ecx
   0x0000000000401cd8 <+38>:    mov      $0x0,%edx
   0x0000000000401cdd <+43>:    mov      $0x0,%esi
   0x0000000000401ce2 <+48>:    mov      %rax,%rdi
   0x0000000000401ce5 <+51>:    callq    0x401c1e <get_message>
   0x0000000000401cea <+56>:    test     %eax,%eax
   0x0000000000401cec <+58>:    jne      0x401cc3 <main+17>
   0x0000000000401cee <+60>:    mov      $0x0,%eax
   0x0000000000401cf3 <+65>:    leaveq
   0x0000000000401cf4 <+66>:    retq
End of assembler dump.
```

Note: We see that in the *main*, the *msg_t* structure was allocated as a local variable on the stack and referenced by RBP-0x30. Also, all remaining call parameters are zeroed by *mov* instruction. That corresponds to the following C or C++ code:

```
{
    msg_t msg;

    // ...

    get_message(&msg, 0, 0, 0);
}
```

7.   Let's now look at the contents of that structure. First, we need to calculate the value of RBP, but this time we do it differently than we did in exercises R2 and R3. Since the RBP value is saved in the *get_message* function prolog after the *main* return address (before in stack memory), we try to find that return address in the stack region.

```
(gdb) bt
#0  0x000000000043c4e1 in nanosleep ()
#1  0x000000000043c49a in sleep ()
#2  0x0000000000401c17 in internal_get_message ()
#3  0x0000000000401c57 in get_message ()
#4  0x0000000000401cea in main ()

(gdb) find/g $rsp, $rsp+200, 0x0000000000401cea
0x7ffffe512a68
1 pattern found.

(gdb) x/a 0x7ffffe512a68
0x7ffffe512a68: 0x401cea <main+56>

(gdb) x/gx 0x7ffffe512a68-8
0x7ffffe512a60: 0x00007ffffe512ab0

(gdb) x/10gx 0x00007ffffe512ab0-0x30
0x7ffffe512a80: 0x0000000000000000    0x0000000000000113
0x7ffffe512a90: 0x0000000000000001    0x0000000000401b4d
0x7ffffe512aa0: 0x0000009c04578350    0x0000000000000147
0x7ffffe512ab0: 0x0000000000402930    0x0000000000402331
0x7ffffe512ac0: 0x0000000000000000    0x0000000100000000

(gdb) x/20wx 0x00007ffffe512ab0-0x30
0x7ffffe512a80: 0x00000000    0x00000000    0x00000113    0x00000000
0x7ffffe512a90: 0x00000001    0x00000000    0x00401b4d    0x00000000
0x7ffffe512aa0: 0x04578350    0x0000009c    0x00000147    0x00000000
0x7ffffe512ab0: 0x00402930    0x00000000    0x00402331    0x00000000
0x7ffffe512ac0: 0x00000000    0x00000000    0x00000000    0x00000001

(gdb) x/10a 0x00007ffffe512ab0-0x30
0x7ffffe512a80: 0x0        0x113
0x7ffffe512a90: 0x1        0x401b4d <time_proc>
0x7ffffe512aa0: 0x9c04578350        0x147
0x7ffffe512ab0: 0x402930 <__libc_csu_init>        0x402331 <__libc_start_main+977>
0x7ffffe512ac0: 0x0        0x100000000
```

8.   The default Clang-generated code is different. Let's look at the core dump differences.

```
~/ADDR-Linux/x64/MemoryDumps$ gdb -c notepad-clang.88 -se notepad-clang
```

```
(gdb) disassemble main
Dump of assembler code for function main:
   0x0000000000401d20 <+0>:     push   %rbp
   0x0000000000401d21 <+1>:     mov    %rsp,%rbp
   0x0000000000401d24 <+4>:     sub    $0x40,%rsp
   0x0000000000401d28 <+8>:     movl   $0x0,-0x4(%rbp)
   0x0000000000401d2f <+15>:    mov    %edi,-0x8(%rbp)
   0x0000000000401d32 <+18>:    mov    %rsi,-0x10(%rbp)
   0x0000000000401d36 <+22>:    xor    %eax,%eax
   0x0000000000401d38 <+24>:    mov    %eax,%ecx
   0x0000000000401d3a <+26>:    lea    -0x40(%rbp),%rdi
   0x0000000000401d3e <+30>:    mov    %rcx,%rsi
   0x0000000000401d41 <+33>:    mov    %rcx,%rdx
   0x0000000000401d44 <+36>:    callq  0x401c70 <get_message>
   0x0000000000401d49 <+41>:    cmp    $0x0,%eax
   0x0000000000401d4c <+44>:    je     0x401d60 <main+64>
   0x0000000000401d52 <+50>:    lea    -0x40(%rbp),%rdi
   0x0000000000401d56 <+54>:    callq  0x401cf0 <dispatch_message>
   0x0000000000401d5b <+59>:    jmpq   0x401d36 <main+22>
   0x0000000000401d60 <+64>:    xor    %eax,%eax
   0x0000000000401d62 <+66>:    add    $0x40,%rsp
   0x0000000000401d66 <+70>:    pop    %rbp
   0x0000000000401d67 <+71>:    retq
End of assembler dump.
```

Note: The Clang compiler code generator uses the *xor* instruction to generate a zero parameter.

Exercise R4 (A64, GDB)

Goal: Learn how to recognize call and function parameters and track their data flow.

ADDR Patterns: Call Prologue, Call Parameter, Call Epilogue, Call Result, Control Path, Function Parameter.

1.   Load a core dump *notepad.12315* and *notepad* executable from A64/MemoryDumps directory:

```
~/ADDR-Linux/A64/MemoryDumps$ gdb -c notepad.12315 -se notepad
GNU gdb (Ubuntu 12.0.90-0ubuntu1) 12.0.90
Copyright (C) 2022 Free Software Foundation, Inc.
License GPLv3+: GNU GPL version 3 or later <http://gnu.org/licenses/gpl.html>
This is free software: you are free to change and redistribute it.
There is NO WARRANTY, to the extent permitted by law.
Type "show copying" and "show warranty" for details.
This GDB was configured as "aarch64-linux-gnu".
Type "show configuration" for configuration details.
For bug reporting instructions, please see:
<https://www.gnu.org/software/gdb/bugs/>.
Find the GDB manual and other documentation resources online at:
    <http://www.gnu.org/software/gdb/documentation/>.

For help, type "help".
Type "apropos word" to search for commands related to "word"...
Reading symbols from notepad...
(No debugging symbols found in notepad)

warning: Can't open file /home/ubuntu/notepad during file-backed mapping note processing
[New LWP 12315]
Core was generated by `./notepad'.
#0  0x000000000043a3fc in clock_nanosleep ()
```

2.   We open a log file and set color highlighting off:

```
(gdb) set logging file R4.log
```

```
(gdb) set logging enabled on
Copying output to R4.log.
Copying debug output to R4.log.
```

```
(gdb) set style enabled off
```

3.   We get this stack trace:

```
(gdb) bt
#0  0x000000000043a3fc in clock_nanosleep ()
#1  0x0000000000418ffc in nanosleep ()
#2  0x0000000000418f98 in sleep ()
#3  0x00000000004007c4 in internal_get_message ()
#4  0x0000000000400808 in get_message ()
#5  0x00000000004008cc in main ()
```

4.   We analyzed this memory dump in Exercise R1, where we could recognize the *msg_t* structure on the stack. Let's now see how the *internal_get_message* function was called in the context of the *get_message* caller. The latter disassembly and **Function Skeleton** are these:

```
(gdb) disassemble get_message
Dump of assembler code for function get_message:
   0x00000000004007d0 <+0>:      stp     x29, x30, [sp, #-64]!
   0x00000000004007d4 <+4>:      mov     x29, sp
   0x00000000004007d8 <+8>:      str     x0, [sp, #40]
   0x00000000004007dc <+12>:     str     x1, [sp, #32]
   0x00000000004007e0 <+16>:     str     x2, [sp, #24]
   0x00000000004007e4 <+20>:     str     x3, [sp, #16]
   0x00000000004007e8 <+24>:     mov     w0, #0xffffffff                    // #-1
   0x00000000004007ec <+28>:     str     w0, [sp, #60]
   0x00000000004007f0 <+32>:     ldr     x0, [sp, #40]
   0x00000000004007f4 <+36>:     cmp     x0, #0x0
   0x00000000004007f8 <+40>:     b.eq    0x40080c <get_message+60>  // b.none
   0x00000000004007fc <+44>:     ldr     x1, [sp, #32]
   0x0000000000400800 <+48>:     ldr     x0, [sp, #40]
   0x0000000000400804 <+52>:     bl      0x400740 <internal_get_message>
   0x0000000000400808 <+56>:     str     w0, [sp, #60]
   0x000000000040080c <+60>:     ldr     w0, [sp, #60]
   0x0000000000400810 <+64>:     cmp     w0, #0x0
   0x0000000000400814 <+68>:     b.eq    0x400824 <get_message+84>  // b.none
   0x0000000000400818 <+72>:     ldr     w0, [sp, #60]
   0x000000000040081c <+76>:     bl      0x4006dc <set_last_ui_error>
   0x0000000000400820 <+80>:     b       0x400830 <get_message+96>
   0x0000000000400824 <+84>:     ldr     x0, [sp, #32]
   0x0000000000400828 <+88>:     bl      0x400700 <call_ui_hooks>
   0x000000000040082c <+92>:     str     w0, [sp, #60]
   0x0000000000400830 <+96>:     ldr     w0, [sp, #60]
   0x0000000000400834 <+100>:    cmp     w0, #0x0
   0x0000000000400838 <+104>:    cset    w0, eq  // eq = none
   0x000000000040083c <+108>:    and     w0, w0, #0xff
   0x0000000000400840 <+112>:    ldp     x29, x30, [sp], #64
   0x0000000000400844 <+116>:    ret
End of assembler dump.
```

```
# internal_get_message
# set_last_ui_error
# call_ui_hooks
```

Note: The standard ARM64 calling convention passes the first 8 parameters via X0-X7 registers or their subregisters W0-W7. Here in **Call Prologue**, we only see that some value of SP+40 is assigned to X0 (the 1st **Call Parameter**), and some value of SP+32 is assigned to X1 (the 2nd **Call Parameter**). Before that, there were no assignments to other calling convention registers. However, we can track call parameters to **Function Parameters**. If data passed to a function before a function call is called **Call Parameter**, then inside a function (on the receiver side), it is called **Function Parameter**. Such a parameter can be translated to a local variable if passed by stack or copied to stack location if passed by a register and referenced as SP or X29 (FP) offset, or it can still be an original register or copied to another register.

Call Epilogue only consists of saving **Call Result** in the local variable SP+60, which seems to be later reused in calculations before the **Function Epilogue** (highlighted in green. We also see that a function body has several **Control Paths** because there are conditional and direct branches.

162

5. Let's now study control paths after the *internal_get_message* function call:

```
0x0000000000400804 <+52>:    bl      0x400740 <internal_get_message>
0x0000000000400808 <+56>:    str     w0, [sp, #60]
0x000000000040080c <+60>:    ldr     w0, [sp, #60]
0x0000000000400810 <+64>:    cmp     w0, #0x0
0x0000000000400814 <+68>:    b.eq    0x400824 <get_message+84>   // b.none
0x0000000000400818 <+72>:    ldr     w0, [sp, #60]
0x000000000040081c <+76>:    bl      0x4006dc <set_last_ui_error>
0x0000000000400820 <+80>:    b       0x400830 <get_message+96>
0x0000000000400824 <+84>:    ldr     x0, [sp, #32]
0x0000000000400828 <+88>:    bl      0x400700 <call_ui_hooks>
0x000000000040082c <+92>:    str     w0, [sp, #60]
0x0000000000400830 <+96>:    ldr     w0, [sp, #60]
0x0000000000400834 <+100>:   cmp     w0, #0x0
0x0000000000400838 <+104>:   cset    w0, eq  // eq = none
0x000000000040083c <+108>:   and     w0, w0, #0xff
0x0000000000400840 <+112>:   ldp     x29, x30, [sp], #64
0x0000000000400844 <+116>:   ret
```

6. Let's now see **Call Parameters** for the *get_message* function. We now need to either disassemble its caller or disassemble the caller's return address. We do the latter:

```
(gdb) bt
#0  0x000000000043a3fc in clock_nanosleep ()
#1  0x0000000000418ffc in nanosleep ()
#2  0x0000000000418f98 in sleep ()
#3  0x00000000004007c4 in internal_get_message ()
#4  0x0000000000400808 in get_message ()
#5  0x00000000004008cc in main ()

(gdb) disassemble 0x00000000004008cc
Dump of assembler code for function main:
   0x0000000000400888 <+0>:     stp     x29, x30, [sp, #-96]!
   0x000000000040088c <+4>:     mov     x29, sp
   0x0000000000400890 <+8>:     str     w0, [sp, #28]
   0x0000000000400894 <+12>:    str     x1, [sp, #16]
   0x0000000000400898 <+16>:    adrp    x0, 0x492000 <tunable_list+1320>
   0x000000000040089c <+20>:    ldr     x0, [x0, #3056]
   0x00000000004008a0 <+24>:    ldr     x1, [x0]
   0x00000000004008a4 <+28>:    str     x1, [sp, #88]
   0x00000000004008a8 <+32>:    mov     x1, #0x0                              // #0
   0x00000000004008ac <+36>:    b       0x4008b8 <main+48>
   0x00000000004008b0 <+40>:    add     x0, sp, #0x28
   0x00000000004008b4 <+44>:    bl      0x400848 <dispatch_message>
   0x00000000004008b8 <+48>:    add     x0, sp, #0x28
   0x00000000004008bc <+52>:    mov     x3, #0x0                              // #0
   0x00000000004008c0 <+56>:    mov     x2, #0x0                              // #0
   0x00000000004008c4 <+60>:    mov     x1, #0x0                              // #0
   0x00000000004008c8 <+64>:    bl      0x4007d0 <get_message>
   0x00000000004008cc <+68>:    cmp     w0, #0x0
   0x00000000004008d0 <+72>:    b.ne    0x4008b0 <main+40>  // b.any
   0x00000000004008d4 <+76>:    mov     w0, #0x0                              // #0
   0x00000000004008d8 <+80>:    mov     w1, w0
   0x00000000004008dc <+84>:    adrp    x0, 0x492000 <tunable_list+1320>
   0x00000000004008e0 <+88>:    ldr     x0, [x0, #3056]
   0x00000000004008e4 <+92>:    ldr     x3, [sp, #88]
   0x00000000004008e8 <+96>:    ldr     x2, [x0]
```

163

```
0x00000000004008ec <+100>:    subs    x3, x3, x2
0x00000000004008f0 <+104>:    mov     x2, #0x0                              // #0
0x00000000004008f4 <+108>:    b.eq    0x4008fc <main+116>  // b.none
0x00000000004008f8 <+112>:    bl      0x41c270 <__stack_chk_fail_local>
0x00000000004008fc <+116>:    mov     w0, w1
0x0000000000400900 <+120>:    ldp     x29, x30, [sp], #96
0x0000000000400904 <+124>:    ret
End of assembler dump.
```

Note: We see that in the *main*, the *msg_t* structure was allocated as a local variable on the stack and referenced by SP+0x28. Also, all remaining call parameters are zeroed by *mov* instruction. That corresponds to the following C or C++ code:

```
{
    msg_t msg;

    // ...

    get_message(&msg, 0, 0, 0);
}
```

7.   Let's now look at the contents of that structure. We need to calculate the value of SP, but this time we do it differently than we did in exercises R2 and R3. Since the X29 value is saved in the *get_message* function prolog before the *main* return address in memory (and it is equal to SP), we try to find that return address in the stack region.

```
(gdb) bt
#0  0x000000000043a3fc in clock_nanosleep ()
#1  0x0000000000418ffc in nanosleep ()
#2  0x0000000000418f98 in sleep ()
#3  0x00000000004007c4 in internal_get_message ()
#4  0x0000000000400808 in get_message ()
#5  0x00000000004008cc in main ()

(gdb) find/g $sp, $sp+300, 0x00000000004008cc
0xffffd9cbc4c8
1 pattern found.

(gdb) x/a 0xffffd9cbc4c8
0xffffd9cbc4c8: 0x4008cc <main+68>

(gdb) x/gx 0xffffd9cbc4c8-8
0xffffd9cbc4c0: 0x0000ffffd9cbc500

(gdb) x/10gx 0x0000ffffd9cbc500+0x28
0xffffd9cbc528: 0x0000000000000000    0x0000000000000113
0xffffd9cbc538: 0x0000000000000001    0x00000000004006d4
0xffffd9cbc548: 0x0000009c04578350    0x0000000000000147
0xffffd9cbc558: 0xca3b4bf9224d6b00    0x0000ffffd9cbc670
0xffffd9cbc568: 0x0000000000400d34    0x0000ffffd9cbc5a0

(gdb) x/20wx 0x0000ffffd9cbc500+0x28
0xffffd9cbc528: 0x00000000    0x00000000    0x00000113    0x00000000
0xffffd9cbc538: 0x00000001    0x00000000    0x004006d4    0x00000000
0xffffd9cbc548: 0x04578350    0x0000009c    0x00000147    0x00000000
0xffffd9cbc558: 0x224d6b00    0xca3b4bf9    0xd9cbc670    0x0000ffff
0xffffd9cbc568: 0x00400d34    0x00000000    0xd9cbc5a0    0x0000ffff
```

```
(gdb) x/10a 0x0000ffffd9cbc500+0x28
0xffffd9cbc528: 0x0        0x113
0xffffd9cbc538: 0x1        0x4006d4 <time_proc>
0xffffd9cbc548: 0x9c04578350      0x147
0xffffd9cbc558: 0xca3b4bf9224d6b00        0xffffd9cbc670
0xffffd9cbc568: 0x400d34 <__libc_start_main_impl+836>    0xffffd9cbc5a0
```

8.   The default Clang-generated code is different. Let's look at the core dump differences.

```
~/ADDR-Linux/A64/MemoryDumps$ gdb -c notepead-clang.901591 -se notepad-clang

(gdb) disassemble main
Dump of assembler code for function main:
   0x00000000004008b4 <+0>:     sub     sp, sp, #0x50
   0x00000000004008b8 <+4>:     stp     x29, x30, [sp, #64]
   0x00000000004008bc <+8>:     add     x29, sp, #0x40
   0x00000000004008c0 <+12>:    stur    wzr, [x29, #-4]
   0x00000000004008c4 <+16>:    stur    w0, [x29, #-8]
   0x00000000004008c8 <+20>:    stur    x1, [x29, #-16]
   0x00000000004008cc <+24>:    b       0x4008d0 <main+28>
   0x00000000004008d0 <+28>:    mov     x0, sp
   0x00000000004008d4 <+32>:    mov     x3, xzr
   0x00000000004008d8 <+36>:    mov     x1, x3
   0x00000000004008dc <+40>:    mov     x2, x3
   0x00000000004008e0 <+44>:    bl      0x4007ec <get_message>
   0x00000000004008e4 <+48>:    cbz     w0, 0x4008f8 <main+68>
   0x00000000004008e8 <+52>:    b       0x4008ec <main+56>
   0x00000000004008ec <+56>:    mov     x0, sp
   0x00000000004008f0 <+60>:    bl      0x400874 <dispatch_message>
   0x00000000004008f4 <+64>:    b       0x4008d0 <main+28>
   0x00000000004008f8 <+68>:    mov     w0, wzr
   0x00000000004008fc <+72>:    ldp     x29, x30, [sp, #64]
   0x0000000000400900 <+76>:    add     sp, sp, #0x50
   0x0000000000400904 <+80>:    ret
End of assembler dump.
```

Note: The Clang compiler code generator uses the XZR register to generate a zero parameter.

ADDR: Call Prologue

- The code emitted by a compiler that is necessary to set up a function call (or branch and link) and its parameters

ADDR: Call Parameter

- Data passed to a function before a function call (or branch and link)

ADDR: Call Epilogue

- The code emitted by a compiler to finish a function call (or branch and link) and processing of its return results

ADDR: Call Result

- Data returned by a function

ADDR: Control Path

- A possible execution path inside a function consisting of direct and conditional jumps or branches

ADDR: Function Parameter

- Data passed to a function inside a function (on the receiver side)
- Such a parameter can be translated to a local variable if passed by stack or copied to a stack location

Exercise R5

- **Goal:** Master memory cell diagrams as an aid to understanding complex disassembly logic

- **ADDR Patterns:** Last Call, Loop, Memory Copy

- **Memory Cell Diagrams:** Memory Copy

- \ADDR-Linux\Exercise-R5-x64-GDB.pdf
- \ADDR-Linux\MCD-R5-x64.xlsx

- \ADDR-Linux\Exercise-R5-ARM64-GDB.pdf
- \ADDR-Linux\MCD-R5-ARM64.xlsx

Exercise R5 (x64, GDB)

Goal: Master memory cell diagrams as an aid in understanding complex disassembly logic.

ADDR Patterns: Last Call, Loop, Memory Copy.

Memory Cell Diagrams: Memory Copy.

1.   Load a core dump *core.cpu* and *cpu* executable from x64/MemoryDumps directory:

```
~/ADDR-Linux/x64/MemoryDumps$ gdb -c core.cpu -se cpu
GNU gdb (Debian 8.2.1-2+b3) 8.2.1
Copyright (C) 2018 Free Software Foundation, Inc.
License GPLv3+: GNU GPL version 3 or later <http://gnu.org/licenses/gpl.html>
This is free software: you are free to change and redistribute it.
There is NO WARRANTY, to the extent permitted by law.
Type "show copying" and "show warranty" for details.
This GDB was configured as "x86_64-linux-gnu".
Type "show configuration" for configuration details.
For bug reporting instructions, please see:
<http://www.gnu.org/software/gdb/bugs/>.
Find the GDB manual and other documentation resources online at:
    <http://www.gnu.org/software/gdb/documentation/>.

For help, type "help".
Type "apropos word" to search for commands related to "word"...
Reading symbols from cpu...(no debugging symbols found)...done.
[New LWP 432]
Core was generated by `./cpu'.
Program terminated with signal SIGSEGV, Segmentation fault.
#0  0x0000000000401bcc in start_modeling ()
```

2.   We open a log file:

```
(gdb) set logging on R5.log
Copying output to R5.log.
```

3.   We get the following stack trace:

```
(gdb) bt
#0  0x0000000000401bcc in start_modeling ()
#1  0x0000000000401bfc in main ()
```

4.   Since there was definitely an exception, let's check the exception address:

```
(gdb) x/i 0x0000000000401bcc
=> 0x401bcc <start_modeling+127>:       mov     %rdx,(%rax)

(gdb) i r rax
rax            0x7f1a503d3fff           139750992068607

(gdb) x/gx 0x7f1a503d3fff
0x7f1a503d3fff: Cannot access memory at address 0x7f1a503d4000

(gdb) x/bx 0x7f1a503d3fff
```

173

```
0x7f1a503d3fff: 0x00

(gdb) x/bx 0x7f1a503d3fff+1
0x7f1a503d4000: Cannot access memory at address 0x7f1a503d4000

(gdb) i r rdx
rdx             0x6f57206f6c6c6548    8022916924116329800

(gdb) p (char[8])0x6f57206f6c6c6548
$1 = "Hello Wo"

(gdb) x/100c 0x7f1a503d3fff-100
0x7f1a503d3f9b: 111 'o' 32 ' '  87 'W'  111 'o' 114 'r' 108 'l' 100 'd' 33 '!'
0x7f1a503d3fa3: 0 '\000'        72 'H'  101 'e' 108 'l' 108 'l' 111 'o' 32 ' '  87 'W'
0x7f1a503d3fab: 111 'o' 114 'r' 108 'l' 100 'd' 33 '!'   0 '\000'        72 'H'  101 'e'
0x7f1a503d3fb3: 108 'l' 108 'l' 111 'o' 32 ' '  87 'W'  111 'o' 114 'r' 108 'l'
0x7f1a503d3fbb: 100 'd' 33 '!'   0 '\000'        72 'H'  101 'e' 108 'l' 108 'l' 111 'o'
0x7f1a503d3fc3: 32 ' '  87 'W'  111 'o' 114 'r' 108 'l' 100 'd' 33 '!'   0 '\000'
0x7f1a503d3fcb: 72 'H'  101 'e' 108 'l' 108 'l' 111 'o' 32 ' '  87 'W'  111 'o'
0x7f1a503d3fd3: 114 'r' 108 'l' 100 'd' 33 '!'   0 '\000'        72 'H'  101 'e' 108 'l'
0x7f1a503d3fdb: 108 'l' 111 'o' 32 ' '  87 'W'  111 'o' 114 'r' 108 'l' 100 'd'
0x7f1a503d3fe3: 33 '!'   0 '\000'        72 'H'  101 'e' 108 'l' 108 'l' 111 'o' 32 ' '
0x7f1a503d3feb: 87 'W'  111 'o' 114 'r' 108 'l' 100 'd' 33 '!'   0 '\000'        72 'H'
0x7f1a503d3ff3: 101 'e' 108 'l' 108 'l' 111 'o' 32 ' '  87 'W'  111 'o' 114 'r'
0x7f1a503d3ffb: 108 'l' 100 'd' 33 '!'   0 '\000'
```

Note: If we look at the section map, we notice that the second byte of the full 64-bit doubleword belongs to a read-only section, and this also explains an exception during memory write:

```
(gdb) maintenance info sections
Exec file:
    `/home/coredump/ADDR-Linux/x64/MemoryDumps/cpu', file type elf64-x86-64.
 [0]     0x00400200->0x00400220 at 0x00000200: .note.ABI-tag ALLOC LOAD READONLY DATA HAS_CONTENTS
 [1]     0x00400220->0x00400244 at 0x00000220: .note.gnu.build-id ALLOC LOAD READONLY DATA HAS_CONTENTS
 [2]     0x00400248->0x00400470 at 0x00000248: .rela.plt ALLOC LOAD READONLY DATA HAS_CONTENTS
 [3]     0x00401000->0x00401017 at 0x00001000: .init ALLOC LOAD READONLY CODE HAS_CONTENTS
 [4]     0x00401018->0x004010d0 at 0x00001018: .plt ALLOC LOAD READONLY CODE HAS_CONTENTS
 [5]     0x004010d0->0x0047b620 at 0x000010d0: .text ALLOC LOAD READONLY CODE HAS_CONTENTS
 [6]     0x0047b620->0x0047c0a7 at 0x0007b620: __libc_freeres_fn ALLOC LOAD READONLY CODE HAS_CONTENTS
 [7]     0x0047c0a8->0x0047c0b1 at 0x0007c0a8: .fini ALLOC LOAD READONLY CODE HAS_CONTENTS
 [8]     0x0047d000->0x0049643c at 0x0007d000: .rodata ALLOC LOAD READONLY DATA HAS_CONTENTS
 [9]     0x00496440->0x004a06e0 at 0x00096440: .eh_frame ALLOC LOAD READONLY DATA HAS_CONTENTS
 [10]    0x004a06e0->0x004a078c at 0x000a06e0: .gcc_except_table ALLOC LOAD READONLY DATA HAS_CONTENTS
 [11]    0x004a20e0->0x004a2100 at 0x000a10e0: .tdata ALLOC LOAD DATA HAS_CONTENTS
 [12]    0x004a2100->0x004a2140 at 0x000a1100: .tbss ALLOC
 [13]    0x004a2100->0x004a2110 at 0x000a1100: .init_array ALLOC LOAD DATA HAS_CONTENTS
 [14]    0x004a2110->0x004a2120 at 0x000a1110: .fini_array ALLOC LOAD DATA HAS_CONTENTS
 [15]    0x004a2120->0x004a4f14 at 0x000a1120: .data.rel.ro ALLOC LOAD DATA HAS_CONTENTS
 [16]    0x004a4f18->0x004a4ff8 at 0x000a3f18: .got ALLOC LOAD DATA HAS_CONTENTS
 [17]    0x004a5000->0x004a50d0 at 0x000a4000: .got.plt ALLOC LOAD DATA HAS_CONTENTS
 [18]    0x004a50e0->0x004a6bd0 at 0x000a40e0: .data ALLOC LOAD DATA HAS_CONTENTS
 [19]    0x004a6bd0->0x004a6c18 at 0x000a5bd0: __libc_subfreres ALLOC LOAD DATA HAS_CONTENTS
 [20]    0x004a6c20->0x004a72c8 at 0x000a5c20: __libc_IO_vtables ALLOC LOAD DATA HAS_CONTENTS
 [21]    0x004a72c8->0x004a72d0 at 0x000a62c8: __libc_atexit ALLOC LOAD DATA HAS_CONTENTS
 [22]    0x004a72e0->0x004a89f8 at 0x000a62d0: .bss ALLOC
 [23]    0x004a89f8->0x004a8a20 at 0x000a62d0: __libc_freeres_ptrs ALLOC
 [24]    0x00000000->0x0000001c at 0x000a62d0: .comment READONLY HAS_CONTENTS
Core file:
    `/home/coredump/ADDR-Linux/x64/MemoryDumps/core.cpu', file type elf64-x86-64.
 [0]     0x00000000->0x00000a68 at 0x000002e0: note0 READONLY HAS_CONTENTS
 [1]     0x00000000->0x000000d8 at 0x00000364: .reg/432 HAS_CONTENTS
```

```
[2]      0x00000000->0x000000d8 at 0x00000364: .reg HAS_CONTENTS
[3]      0x00000000->0x00000080 at 0x000004f4: .note.linuxcore.siginfo/432 HAS_CONTENTS
[4]      0x00000000->0x00000080 at 0x000004f4: .note.linuxcore.siginfo HAS_CONTENTS
[5]      0x00000000->0x00000140 at 0x00000588: .auxv HAS_CONTENTS
[6]      0x00000000->0x00000104 at 0x000006dc: .note.linuxcore.file/432 HAS_CONTENTS
[7]      0x00000000->0x00000104 at 0x000006dc: .note.linuxcore.file HAS_CONTENTS
[8]      0x00000000->0x00000200 at 0x000007f4: .reg2/432 HAS_CONTENTS
[9]      0x00000000->0x00000200 at 0x000007f4: .reg2 HAS_CONTENTS
[10]     0x00000000->0x00000340 at 0x00000a08: .reg-xstate/432 HAS_CONTENTS
[11]     0x00000000->0x00000340 at 0x00000a08: .reg-xstate HAS_CONTENTS
[12]     0x00400000->0x00401000 at 0x00001000: load1 ALLOC LOAD READONLY HAS_CONTENTS
[13]     0x00401000->0x00401000 at 0x00002000: load2 ALLOC READONLY CODE
[14]     0x0047d000->0x0047d000 at 0x00002000: load3 ALLOC READONLY
--Type <RET> for more, q to quit, c to continue without paging--
[15]     0x004a2000->0x004a8000 at 0x00002000: load4 ALLOC LOAD HAS_CONTENTS
[16]     0x004a8000->0x004a9000 at 0x00008000: load5 ALLOC LOAD HAS_CONTENTS
[17]     0x008c3000->0x008e6000 at 0x00009000: load6 ALLOC LOAD HAS_CONTENTS
[18]     0x7f1a503d3000->0x7f1a503d4000 at 0x0002c000: load7 ALLOC LOAD HAS_CONTENTS
[19]     0x7f1a503d4000->0x7f1a503d4000 at 0x0002d000: load8 ALLOC READONLY
[20]     0x7ffe7b1c4000->0x7ffe7b1e5000 at 0x0002d000: load9 ALLOC LOAD HAS_CONTENTS
[21]     0x7ffe7b1fb000->0x7ffe7b1ff000 at 0x0004e000: load10 ALLOC LOAD READONLY HAS_CONTENTS
[22]     0x7ffe7b1ff000->0x7ffe7b200000 at 0x00052000: load11 ALLOC LOAD READONLY CODE HAS_CONTENTS
```

Note: We got the stack trace prior to the exception. From the instruction, we see that memory pointed to by RAX is not valid: only one byte from the full 64-bit memory cell is accessible when we assign a 64-bit RDX value to it. However, before that, the memory is valid with regular ASCII-like data. Perhaps that was a string copy that hit the page boundary, and the next page is not in memory (not committed) or read-only.

Note: The memory layout for the RAX pointer is illustrated in the MCD-R5-x64.xlsx A section.

5.   Sometimes we are interested in the last function called. This is not a caller because, since the start of the callee execution, many functions could have been executed. In the case of no functions, we search for the last function call in the caller's function body, and so on. We call this pattern **Last Call**. In our case, it might be the call *mmap64*:

```
(gdb) disassemble 0x0000000000401bcc
Dump of assembler code for function start_modeling:
   0x0000000000401b4d <+0>:     push   %rbp
   0x0000000000401b4e <+1>:     mov    %rsp,%rbp
   0x0000000000401b51 <+4>:     sub    $0x20,%rsp
   0x0000000000401b55 <+8>:     mov    $0x0,%r9d
   0x0000000000401b5b <+14>:    mov    $0x0,%r8d
   0x0000000000401b61 <+20>:    mov    $0x22,%ecx
   0x0000000000401b66 <+25>:    mov    $0x2,%edx
   0x0000000000401b6b <+30>:    mov    $0x1000,%esi
   0x0000000000401b70 <+35>:    mov    $0x0,%edi
   0x0000000000401b75 <+40>:    callq  0x43d650 <mmap64>
   0x0000000000401b7a <+45>:    mov    %rax,-0x8(%rbp)
   0x0000000000401b7e <+49>:    mov    -0x8(%rbp),%rax
   0x0000000000401b82 <+53>:    add    $0x1000,%rax
   0x0000000000401b88 <+59>:    mov    $0x0,%r9d
   0x0000000000401b8e <+65>:    mov    $0x0,%r8d
   0x0000000000401b94 <+71>:    mov    $0x32,%ecx
   0x0000000000401b99 <+76>:    mov    $0x1,%edx
   0x0000000000401b9e <+81>:    mov    $0x1000,%esi
   0x0000000000401ba3 <+86>:    mov    %rax,%rdi
   0x0000000000401ba6 <+89>:    callq  0x43d650 <mmap64>
```

```
   0x0000000000401bab <+94>:    movabs $0x6f57206f6c6c6548,%rax
   0x0000000000401bb5 <+104>:   mov    %rax,-0x15(%rbp)
   0x0000000000401bb9 <+108>:   movl   $0x21646c72,-0xd(%rbp)
   0x0000000000401bc0 <+115>:   movb   $0x0,-0x9(%rbp)
   0x0000000000401bc4 <+119>:   mov    -0x8(%rbp),%rax
   0x0000000000401bc8 <+123>:   mov    -0x15(%rbp),%rdx
=> 0x0000000000401bcc <+127>:   mov    %rdx,(%rax)
   0x0000000000401bcf <+130>:   mov    -0xd(%rbp),%edx
   0x0000000000401bd2 <+133>:   mov    %edx,0x8(%rax)
   0x0000000000401bd5 <+136>:   movzbl -0x9(%rbp),%edx
   0x0000000000401bd9 <+140>:   mov    %dl,0xc(%rax)
   0x0000000000401bdc <+143>:   addq   $0xd,-0x8(%rbp)
   0x0000000000401be1 <+148>:   jmp    0x401bc4 <start_modeling+119>
End of assembler dump.
```

Note: If unconditional jumps (**jmp**) are present before the current instruction for which we want to find the last call, then more flow analysis is required to find the right **Last Call**. Here we don't see such unconditional jumps. We can also find a possible **Last Call** for it too. It is again *mmap64*, and we don't see even conditional jumps, so the call was the definite **Last Call**.

6.   Let's now check **Call Parameters** and **Call Results**. We look at disassembly forward from the second **Last Call**:

```
   0x0000000000401b66 <+25>:    mov    $0x2,%edx
   0x0000000000401b6b <+30>:    mov    $0x1000,%esi
   0x0000000000401b70 <+35>:    mov    $0x0,%edi
   0x0000000000401b75 <+40>:    callq  0x43d650 <mmap64>
   0x0000000000401b7a <+45>:    mov    %rax,-0x8(%rbp)
   0x0000000000401b7e <+49>:    mov    -0x8(%rbp),%rax
   0x0000000000401b82 <+53>:    add    $0x1000,%rax
   0x0000000000401b88 <+59>:    mov    $0x0,%r9d
   0x0000000000401b8e <+65>:    mov    $0x0,%r8d
   0x0000000000401b94 <+71>:    mov    $0x32,%ecx
   0x0000000000401b99 <+76>:    mov    $0x1,%edx
   0x0000000000401b9e <+81>:    mov    $0x1000,%esi
   0x0000000000401ba3 <+86>:    mov    %rax,%rdi
   0x0000000000401ba6 <+89>:    callq  0x43d650 <mmap64>
   0x0000000000401bab <+94>:    movabs $0x6f57206f6c6c6548,%rax
```

Note: From man pages, we can check that the first parameter is the optional starting address to allocate. For the first call, we see it is NULL (RDI), and the 3rd parameter is allocation protection type, which is 2 (PROT_WRITE). The size of the allocation is the second parameter and 1 page (0x1000 in ESI). The resulting allocated address is copied from RAX into a memory cell pointed to by RBP-8. The second call allocates another page after the first (add 0x1000 to RAX) because the same address is copied from the memory cell pointed by RBP-8 into RAX and then to RDI (first call parameter). The new protection type is 1 (PROT_READ). The call result is discarded because the next instruction (*movabs*) overwrites RAX.

7. Let's now look at full function disassembly:

```
(gdb) disassemble start_modeling
Dump of assembler code for function start_modeling:
   0x0000000000401b4d <+0>:     push   %rbp
   0x0000000000401b4e <+1>:     mov    %rsp,%rbp
   0x0000000000401b51 <+4>:     sub    $0x20,%rsp
   0x0000000000401b55 <+8>:     mov    $0x0,%r9d
   0x0000000000401b5b <+14>:    mov    $0x0,%r8d
   0x0000000000401b61 <+20>:    mov    $0x22,%ecx
   0x0000000000401b66 <+25>:    mov    $0x2,%edx
   0x0000000000401b6b <+30>:    mov    $0x1000,%esi
   0x0000000000401b70 <+35>:    mov    $0x0,%edi
   0x0000000000401b75 <+40>:    callq  0x43d650 <mmap64>
   0x0000000000401b7a <+45>:    mov    %rax,-0x8(%rbp)
   0x0000000000401b7e <+49>:    mov    -0x8(%rbp),%rax
   0x0000000000401b82 <+53>:    add    $0x1000,%rax
   0x0000000000401b88 <+59>:    mov    $0x0,%r9d
   0x0000000000401b8e <+65>:    mov    $0x0,%r8d
   0x0000000000401b94 <+71>:    mov    $0x32,%ecx
   0x0000000000401b99 <+76>:    mov    $0x1,%edx
   0x0000000000401b9e <+81>:    mov    $0x1000,%esi
   0x0000000000401ba3 <+86>:    mov    %rax,%rdi
   0x0000000000401ba6 <+89>:    callq  0x43d650 <mmap64>
   0x0000000000401bab <+94>:    movabs $0x6f57206f6c6c6548,%rax
   0x0000000000401bb5 <+104>:   mov    %rax,-0x15(%rbp)
   0x0000000000401bb9 <+108>:   movl   $0x21646c72,-0xd(%rbp)
   0x0000000000401bc0 <+115>:   movb   $0x0,-0x9(%rbp)
   0x0000000000401bc4 <+119>:   mov    -0x8(%rbp),%rax
   0x0000000000401bc8 <+123>:   mov    -0x15(%rbp),%rdx
=> 0x0000000000401bcc <+127>:   mov    %rdx,(%rax)
   0x0000000000401bcf <+130>:   mov    -0xd(%rbp),%edx
   0x0000000000401bd2 <+133>:   mov    %edx,0x8(%rax)
   0x0000000000401bd5 <+136>:   movzbl -0x9(%rbp),%edx
   0x0000000000401bd9 <+140>:   mov    %dl,0xc(%rax)
   0x0000000000401bdc <+143>:   addq   $0xd,-0x8(%rbp)
   0x0000000000401be1 <+148>:   jmp    0x401bc4 <start_modeling+119>
End of assembler dump.
```

Note: After the function prolog and two *mmap64* calls, we see something that looks like an ASCII string copy (highlighted in green above). The destination address starts from RBP-0x15, 8 bytes are copied, then another 4 to RBP-0x15+8 (RBP-0xd), and then a null-terminating byte to RBP-0xd+4 (RBP-9). In our case, the RBP value is RSP+0x20:

```
(gdb) x/s $rsp+0x20-0x15
0x7ffe7b1e35ab: "Hello World!"
```

Note: By the time the crash dump was saved, the copy had already happened.

8.   Next, we see a loop fragment:

```
0x0000000000401bc4 <+119>:    mov     -0x8(%rbp),%rax
0x0000000000401bc8 <+123>:    mov     -0x15(%rbp),%rdx
=> 0x0000000000401bcc <+127>:    mov     %rdx,(%rax)
0x0000000000401bcf <+130>:    mov     -0xd(%rbp),%edx
0x0000000000401bd2 <+133>:    mov     %edx,0x8(%rax)
0x0000000000401bd5 <+136>:    movzbl  -0x9(%rbp),%edx
0x0000000000401bd9 <+140>:    mov     %dl,0xc(%rax)
0x0000000000401bdc <+143>:    addq    $0xd,-0x8(%rbp)
0x0000000000401be1 <+148>:    jmp     0x401bc4 <start_modeling+119>
```

Note: It looks like at the beginning of the loop, we have the first 8 bytes from the string address RBP-0x15 copied to RDX and then copied to the memory pointed by RAX. The value of RAX comes from memory pointed by RBP-8 (destination address). Then we see the next 4 bytes copied to the memory pointed by RAX+8, and finally, a null-terminating byte in DL is copied to a byte pointed by RAX+0xc. Then we add the length of the string (0xd) to the destination address stored in RBP-8 and repeat the loop iteration.

Note: If it's challenging to comprehend what all this code is doing, then memory cell diagrams should help here. Please look at section B in the MCD-R5-x64.xlsx file.

Now I show you the source code fragment:

```
void start_modeling()
{
    char *paddr = (char *)mmap(NULL, 0x1000, PROT_WRITE, MAP_PRIVATE|MAP_ANONYMOUS, 0, 0);
    mmap(paddr+0x1000, 0x1000, PROT_READ, MAP_PRIVATE|MAP_ANONYMOUS|MAP_FIXED, 0, 0);

    const char str[] = "Hello World!";

    while (true)
    {
        memcpy((char *)paddr, str, sizeof(str));
        paddr += sizeof(str);
    }
}
```

9.   The default Clang-generated code is different. Let's look at the core dump differences.

```
~/ADDR-Linux/x64/MemoryDumps$ gdb -c core.cpu-clang -se cpu-clang
```

```
(gdb) disassemble start_modeling
Dump of assembler code for function start_modeling:
   0x0000000000401b50 <+0>:     push    %rbp
   0x0000000000401b51 <+1>:     mov     %rsp,%rbp
   0x0000000000401b54 <+4>:     sub     $0x30,%rsp
   0x0000000000401b58 <+8>:     xor     %eax,%eax
   0x0000000000401b5a <+10>:    mov     %eax,%ecx
   0x0000000000401b5c <+12>:    mov     $0x1000,%eax
   0x0000000000401b61 <+17>:    mov     %eax,%esi
   0x0000000000401b63 <+19>:    xor     %r8d,%r8d
   0x0000000000401b66 <+22>:    mov     %rcx,%rdi
   0x0000000000401b69 <+25>:    mov     $0x2,%edx
   0x0000000000401b6e <+30>:    mov     $0x22,%eax
   0x0000000000401b73 <+35>:    mov     %rcx,-0x20(%rbp)
```

```
0x0000000000401b77 <+39>:    mov    %eax,%ecx
0x0000000000401b79 <+41>:    mov    -0x20(%rbp),%r9
0x0000000000401b7d <+45>:    callq  0x43d6f0 <mmap64>
0x0000000000401b82 <+50>:    mov    $0x1000,%ecx
0x0000000000401b87 <+55>:    mov    %ecx,%esi
0x0000000000401b89 <+57>:    xor    %r8d,%r8d
0x0000000000401b8c <+60>:    xor    %ecx,%ecx
0x0000000000401b8e <+62>:    mov    %ecx,%r9d
0x0000000000401b91 <+65>:    mov    %rax,-0x8(%rbp)
0x0000000000401b95 <+69>:    mov    -0x8(%rbp),%rax
0x0000000000401b99 <+73>:    add    $0x1000,%rax
0x0000000000401b9f <+79>:    mov    %rax,%rdi
0x0000000000401ba2 <+82>:    mov    $0x1,%edx
0x0000000000401ba7 <+87>:    mov    $0x32,%ecx
0x0000000000401bac <+92>:    callq  0x43d6f0 <mmap64>
0x0000000000401bb1 <+97>:    mov    0x47d004,%rsi
0x0000000000401bb9 <+105>:   mov    %rsi,-0x15(%rbp)
0x0000000000401bbd <+109>:   mov    0x47d00c,%ecx
0x0000000000401bc4 <+116>:   mov    %ecx,-0xd(%rbp)
0x0000000000401bc7 <+119>:   mov    0x47d010,%r10b
0x0000000000401bcf <+127>:   mov    %r10b,-0x9(%rbp)
0x0000000000401bd3 <+131>:   mov    %rax,-0x28(%rbp)
0x0000000000401bd7 <+135>:   mov    -0x8(%rbp),%rax
0x0000000000401bdb <+139>:   mov    -0x15(%rbp),%rcx
=> 0x0000000000401bdf <+143>:   mov    %rcx,(%rax)
0x0000000000401be2 <+146>:   mov    -0xd(%rbp),%edx
0x0000000000401be5 <+149>:   mov    %edx,0x8(%rax)
0x0000000000401be8 <+152>:   mov    -0x9(%rbp),%sil
0x0000000000401bec <+156>:   mov    %sil,0xc(%rax)
0x0000000000401bf0 <+160>:   mov    -0x8(%rbp),%rax
0x0000000000401bf4 <+164>:   add    $0xd,%rax
0x0000000000401bf8 <+168>:   mov    %rax,-0x8(%rbp)
0x0000000000401bfc <+172>:   jmpq   0x401bd7 <start_modeling+135>
End of assembler dump.
```

Note: The compiler code generator uses repeated memory move instructions that use direct memory addresses for memory copy compared to GCC-generated code, which encodes the constant string in *mov* instructions. Memory copy loop uses SIL instead of DL for the byte *mov* instruction.

Exercise R5 (A64, GDB)

Goal: Master memory cell diagrams as an aid in understanding complex disassembly logic.

ADDR Patterns: Last Call, Loop, Memory Copy.

Memory Cell Diagrams: Memory Copy.

1.   Load a core dump *cpu.71385* and *cpu* executable from A64/MemoryDumps directory:

```
~/ADDR-Linux/A64/MemoryDumps$ gdb -c cpu.71385 -se cpu
GNU gdb (Ubuntu 12.0.90-0ubuntu1) 12.0.90
Copyright (C) 2022 Free Software Foundation, Inc.
License GPLv3+: GNU GPL version 3 or later <http://gnu.org/licenses/gpl.html>
This is free software: you are free to change and redistribute it.
There is NO WARRANTY, to the extent permitted by law.
Type "show copying" and "show warranty" for details.
This GDB was configured as "aarch64-linux-gnu".
Type "show configuration" for configuration details.
For bug reporting instructions, please see:
<https://www.gnu.org/software/gdb/bugs/>.
Find the GDB manual and other documentation resources online at:
    <http://www.gnu.org/software/gdb/documentation/>.

For help, type "help".
Type "apropos word" to search for commands related to "word"...
Reading symbols from cpu...
(No debugging symbols found in cpu)

warning: Can't open file /home/ubuntu/ADDR-Linux/Source/cpu during file-backed mapping note
processing
[New LWP 71385]
Core was generated by `./cpu'.
Program terminated with signal SIGSEGV, Segmentation fault.
#0  0x000000000040075c in start_modeling ()
```

10. We open a log file and set color highlighting off:

```
(gdb) set logging file R5.log
```

```
(gdb) set logging enabled on
Copying output to R5.log.
Copying debug output to R5.log.
```

```
(gdb) set style enabled off
```

2.   We get the following stack trace:

```
(gdb) bt
#0  0x000000000040075c in start_modeling ()
#1  0x000000000040078c in main ()
```

3. Since there was definitely an exception, let's check the exception address:

```
(gdb) x/i 0x000000000040075c
=> 0x40075c <start_modeling+136>:        str     x2, [x1]

(gdb) i r x1
x1              0xffffbe272fff         281473871982591

(gdb) x/gx 0xffffbe272fff
0xffffbe272fff: 0x0000000000000000

(gdb) i r x2
x2              0x6f57206f6c6c6548     8022916924116329800

(gdb) p (char[8])0x6f57206f6c6c6548
$1 = "Hello Wo"

(gdb) x/100c 0xffffbe272fff-100
0xffffbe272f9b: 111 'o' 32 ' '  87 'W'  111 'o' 114 'r' 108 'l' 100 'd' 33 '!'
0xffffbe272fa3: 0 '\000'        72 'H'  101 'e' 108 'l' 108 'l' 111 'o' 32 ' '  87 'W'
0xffffbe272fab: 111 'o' 114 'r' 108 'l' 100 'd' 33 '!'  0 '\000'        72 'H'  101 'e'
0xffffbe272fb3: 108 'l' 108 'l' 111 'o' 32 ' '  87 'W'  111 'o' 114 'r' 108 'l'
0xffffbe272fbb: 100 'd' 33 '!'  0 '\000'        72 'H'  101 'e' 108 'l' 108 'l' 111 'o'
0xffffbe272fc3: 32 ' '  87 'W'  111 'o' 114 'r' 108 'l' 100 'd' 33 '!'  0 '\000'
0xffffbe272fcb: 72 'H'  101 'e' 108 'l' 108 'l' 111 'o' 32 ' '  87 'W'  111 'o'
0xffffbe272fd3: 114 'r' 108 'l' 100 'd' 33 '!'  0 '\000'        72 'H'  101 'e' 108 'l'
0xffffbe272fdb: 108 'l' 111 'o' 32 ' '  87 'W'  111 'o' 114 'r' 108 'l' 100 'd'
0xffffbe272fe3: 33 '!'  0 '\000'        72 'H'  101 'e' 108 'l' 108 'l' 111 'o' 32 ' '
0xffffbe272feb: 87 'W'  111 'o' 114 'r' 108 'l' 100 'd' 33 '!'  0 '\000'        72 'H'
0xffffbe272ff3: 101 'e' 108 'l' 108 'l' 111 'o' 32 ' '  87 'W'  111 'o' 114 'r'
0xffffbe272ffb: 108 'l' 100 'd' 33 '!'  0 '\000'
```

Note: The address looks valid from the perspective of reading memory. However, if we look at the section map, we notice that the second byte of the full 64-bit doubleword belongs to a read-only section, and this explains an exception during memory write:

```
(gdb) maintenance info sections
Exec file: `/home/ubuntu/ADDR-Linux/A64/MemoryDumps/cpu', file type elf64-littleaarch64.
 [0]        0x00400190->0x004001b4 at 0x00000190: .note.gnu.build-id ALLOC LOAD READONLY DATA HAS_CONTENTS
 [1]        0x004001b4->0x004001d4 at 0x000001b4: .note.ABI-tag ALLOC LOAD READONLY DATA HAS_CONTENTS
 [2]        0x004001d8->0x00400280 at 0x000001d8: .rela.plt ALLOC LOAD READONLY DATA HAS_CONTENTS
 [3]        0x00400280->0x00400298 at 0x00000280: .init ALLOC LOAD READONLY CODE HAS_CONTENTS
 [4]        0x004002a0->0x00400310 at 0x000002a0: .plt ALLOC LOAD READONLY CODE HAS_CONTENTS
 [5]        0x00400340->0x00457154 at 0x00000340: .text ALLOC LOAD READONLY CODE HAS_CONTENTS
 [6]        0x00457160->0x00457c84 at 0x00057160: __libc_freeres_fn ALLOC LOAD READONLY CODE HAS_CONTENTS
 [7]        0x00457c84->0x00457c98 at 0x00057c84: .fini ALLOC LOAD READONLY CODE HAS_CONTENTS
 [8]        0x00457ca0->0x00471d78 at 0x00057ca0: .rodata ALLOC LOAD READONLY DATA HAS_CONTENTS
 [9]        0x00471d78->0x00471d79 at 0x00071d78: .stapsdt.base ALLOC LOAD READONLY DATA HAS_CONTENTS
 [10]       0x00471d80->0x0047d664 at 0x00071d80: .eh_frame ALLOC LOAD READONLY DATA HAS_CONTENTS
 [11]       0x0047d664->0x0047d752 at 0x0007d664: .gcc_except_table ALLOC LOAD READONLY DATA HAS_CONTENTS
 [12]       0x0048d830->0x0048d850 at 0x0007d830: .tdata ALLOC LOAD DATA HAS_CONTENTS
 [13]       0x0048d850->0x0048d898 at 0x0007d850: .tbss ALLOC
 [14]       0x0048d850->0x0048d860 at 0x0007d850: .init_array ALLOC LOAD DATA HAS_CONTENTS
 [15]       0x0048d860->0x0048d868 at 0x0007d860: .fini_array ALLOC LOAD DATA HAS_CONTENTS
 [16]       0x0048d868->0x00490bb0 at 0x0007d868: .data.rel.ro ALLOC LOAD DATA HAS_CONTENTS
 [17]       0x00490bb0->0x00490fe8 at 0x00080bb0: .got ALLOC LOAD DATA HAS_CONTENTS
 [18]       0x00490fe8->0x00491038 at 0x00080fe8: .got.plt ALLOC LOAD DATA HAS_CONTENTS
 [19]       0x00491038->0x00492948 at 0x00081038: .data ALLOC LOAD DATA HAS_CONTENTS
 [20]       0x00492948->0x00492990 at 0x00082948: __libc_subfreeres ALLOC LOAD DATA HAS_CONTENTS
```

```
[21]     0x00492990->0x00493020 at 0x00082990: __libc_IO_vtables ALLOC LOAD DATA HAS_CONTENTS
[22]     0x00493020->0x00493028 at 0x00083020: __libc_atexit ALLOC LOAD DATA HAS_CONTENTS
[23]     0x00493028->0x004986a8 at 0x00083028: .bss ALLOC
[24]     0x004986a8->0x004986c8 at 0x00083028: __libc_freeres_ptrs ALLOC
[25]     0x00000000->0x00000026 at 0x00083028: .comment READONLY HAS_CONTENTS
[26]     0x00000000->0x000013a4 at 0x00083050: .note.stapsdt READONLY HAS_CONTENTS
Core file: `/home/ubuntu/ADDR-Linux/A64/MemoryDumps/cpu.71385', file type elf64-littleaarch64.
[0]      0x00000000->0x000009b4 at 0x00000270: note0 READONLY HAS_CONTENTS
[1]      0x00000000->0x00000110 at 0x000002f4: .reg/71385 HAS_CONTENTS
[2]      0x00000000->0x00000110 at 0x000002f4: .reg HAS_CONTENTS
[3]      0x00000000->0x00000080 at 0x000004bc: .note.linuxcore.siginfo/71385 HAS_CONTENTS
[4]      0x00000000->0x00000080 at 0x000004bc: .note.linuxcore.siginfo HAS_CONTENTS
[5]      0x00000000->0x00000150 at 0x00000550: .auxv HAS_CONTENTS
[6]      0x00000000->0x000000c1 at 0x000006b4: .note.linuxcore.file/71385 HAS_CONTENTS
[7]      0x00000000->0x000000c1 at 0x000006b4: .note.linuxcore.file HAS_CONTENTS
[8]      0x00000000->0x00000210 at 0x0000078c: .reg2/71385 HAS_CONTENTS
[9]      0x00000000->0x00000210 at 0x0000078c: .reg2 HAS_CONTENTS
[10]     0x00000000->0x00000008 at 0x000009b0: .reg-aarch-tls/71385 HAS_CONTENTS
[11]     0x00000000->0x00000008 at 0x000009b0: .reg-aarch-tls HAS_CONTENTS
[12]     0x00000000->0x00000108 at 0x000009cc: .reg-aarch-hw-break/71385 HAS_CONTENTS
--Type <RET> for more, q to quit, c to continue without paging--
[13]     0x00000000->0x00000108 at 0x000009cc: .reg-aarch-hw-break HAS_CONTENTS
[14]     0x00000000->0x00000108 at 0x00000ae8: .reg-aarch-hw-watch/71385 HAS_CONTENTS
[15]     0x00000000->0x00000108 at 0x00000ae8: .reg-aarch-hw-watch HAS_CONTENTS
[16]     0x00000000->0x00000008 at 0x00000c1c: .reg-aarch-mte/71385 HAS_CONTENTS
[17]     0x00000000->0x00000008 at 0x00000c1c: .reg-aarch-mte HAS_CONTENTS
[18]     0x00400000->0x00401000 at 0x00001000: load1a ALLOC LOAD READONLY CODE HAS_CONTENTS
[19]     0x00401000->0x0047e000 at 0x00002000: load1b ALLOC LOAD READONLY CODE
[20]     0x0048d000->0x00491000 at 0x00002000: load2 ALLOC LOAD READONLY HAS_CONTENTS
[21]     0x00491000->0x00494000 at 0x00006000: load3 ALLOC LOAD HAS_CONTENTS
[22]     0x00494000->0x00499000 at 0x00009000: load4 ALLOC LOAD HAS_CONTENTS
[23]     0x10e6a000->0x10e8c000 at 0x0000e000: load5 ALLOC LOAD HAS_CONTENTS
[24]     0xffffbe272000->0xffffbe273000 at 0x00030000: load6 ALLOC LOAD HAS_CONTENTS
[25]     0xffffbe273000->0xffffbe275000 at 0x00031000: load7 ALLOC LOAD READONLY HAS_CONTENTS
[26]     0xffffbe275000->0xffffbe276000 at 0x00033000: load8 ALLOC LOAD READONLY CODE HAS_CONTENTS
[27]     0xfffffe845000->0xfffffe866000 at 0x00034000: load9 ALLOC LOAD HAS_CONTENTS
```

Note: We got the stack trace prior to the exception. From the instruction, we see that memory pointed to by X1 is not valid for writing: only one byte from the full 64-bit memory cell is valid when we assign a 64-bit X2 value to it. However, before that, the memory is valid with regular ASCII-like data. Perhaps that was a string copy that hit the page boundary, and the next page is read-only.

Note: The memory layout for the X1 pointer is illustrated in the MCD-R5-ARM64.xlsx A section.

4.   Sometimes we are interested in the last function called. This is not a caller because, since the start of the callee execution, many functions could have been executed. In the case of no functions, we search for the last function call in the caller's function body, and so on. We call this pattern **Last Call**. In our case, it might be the call *mmap64*:

```
(gdb) disassemble 0x000000000040075c
Dump of assembler code for function start_modeling:
   0x00000000004006d4 <+0>:     stp     x29, x30, [sp, #-48]!
   0x00000000004006d8 <+4>:     mov     x29, sp
   0x00000000004006dc <+8>:     adrp    x0, 0x490000 <tunable_list+1320>
   0x00000000004006e0 <+12>:    ldr     x0, [x0, #3056]
   0x00000000004006e4 <+16>:    ldr     x1, [x0]
   0x00000000004006e8 <+20>:    str     x1, [sp, #40]
   0x00000000004006ec <+24>:    mov     x1, #0x0                        // #0
```

```
   0x00000000004006f0 <+28>:    mov     x5, #0x0              // #0
   0x00000000004006f4 <+32>:    mov     w4, #0x0              // #0
   0x00000000004006f8 <+36>:    mov     w3, #0x22             // #34
   0x00000000004006fc <+40>:    mov     w2, #0x2              // #2
   0x0000000000400700 <+44>:    mov     x1, #0x1000           // #4096
   0x0000000000400704 <+48>:    mov     x0, #0x0              // #0
   0x0000000000400708 <+52>:    bl      0x41a590 <mmap64>
   0x000000000040070c <+56>:    str     x0, [sp, #16]
   0x0000000000400710 <+60>:    ldr     x0, [sp, #16]
   0x0000000000400714 <+64>:    add     x0, x0, #0x1, lsl #12
   0x0000000000400718 <+68>:    mov     x5, #0x0              // #0
   0x000000000040071c <+72>:    mov     w4, #0x0              // #0
   0x0000000000400720 <+76>:    mov     w3, #0x32             // #50
   0x0000000000400724 <+80>:    mov     w2, #0x1              // #1
   0x0000000000400728 <+84>:    mov     x1, #0x1000           // #4096
   0x000000000040072c <+88>:    bl      0x41a590 <mmap64>
   0x0000000000400730 <+92>:    adrp    x0, 0x457000 <getauxval+80>
   0x0000000000400734 <+96>:    add     x1, x0, #0xcc8
   0x0000000000400738 <+100>:   add     x0, sp, #0x18
   0x000000000040073c <+104>:   ldr     x2, [x1]
   0x0000000000400740 <+108>:   str     x2, [x0]
   0x0000000000400744 <+112>:   ldur    x1, [x1, #5]
   0x0000000000400748 <+116>:   stur    x1, [x0, #5]
   0x000000000040074c <+120>:   ldr     x0, [sp, #16]
   0x0000000000400750 <+124>:   mov     x1, x0
   0x0000000000400754 <+128>:   add     x0, sp, #0x18
   0x0000000000400758 <+132>:   ldr     x2, [x0]
=> 0x000000000040075c <+136>:   str     x2, [x1]
   0x0000000000400760 <+140>:   ldur    x0, [x0, #5]
   0x0000000000400764 <+144>:   stur    x0, [x1, #5]
   0x0000000000400768 <+148>:   ldr     x0, [sp, #16]
   0x000000000040076c <+152>:   add     x0, x0, #0xd
   0x0000000000400770 <+156>:   str     x0, [sp, #16]
   0x0000000000400774 <+160>:   b       0x40074c <start_modeling+120>
--Type <RET> for more, q to quit, c to continue without paging--
End of assembler dump.
```

Note: If unconditional branches (**b**) are present before the current instruction for which we want to find the last call, then more flow analysis is required to find the right **Last Call**. Here we don't see such unconditional branches. We can also find a possible **Last Call** for it too. It is again *mmap64*, and we don't see even conditional branches, so the call was the definite **Last Call**.

5.   Let's now check **Call Parameters** and **Call Results**. We look at disassembly forward from the second **Last Call**:

```
   0x00000000004006fc <+40>:    mov     w2, #0x2              // #2
   0x0000000000400700 <+44>:    mov     x1, #0x1000           // #4096
   0x0000000000400704 <+48>:    mov     x0, #0x0              // #0
   0x0000000000400708 <+52>:    bl      0x41a590 <mmap64>
   0x000000000040070c <+56>:    str     x0, [sp, #16]
   0x0000000000400710 <+60>:    ldr     x0, [sp, #16]
   0x0000000000400714 <+64>:    add     x0, x0, #0x1, lsl #12
   0x0000000000400718 <+68>:    mov     x5, #0x0              // #0
   0x000000000040071c <+72>:    mov     w4, #0x0              // #0
   0x0000000000400720 <+76>:    mov     w3, #0x32             // #50
   0x0000000000400724 <+80>:    mov     w2, #0x1              // #1
   0x0000000000400728 <+84>:    mov     x1, #0x1000           // #4096
```

```
0x000000000040072c <+88>:     bl      0x41a590 <mmap64>
0x0000000000400730 <+92>:     adrp    x0, 0x457000 <getauxval+80>
```

Note: From man pages, we can check that the first parameter is the optional starting address to allocate. For the first call, we see it is NULL (X0), and the 3rd parameter is allocation protection type, which is 2 (PROT_WRITE). The size of the allocation is the second parameter and 1 page (0x1000 in X1). The resulting allocated address is copied from X0 into a memory cell pointed to by SP+16. The second call allocates another page after the first (add 0x1000 to X0 via 1 << 12) because the same address is copied from the memory cell pointed by SP+16 into X0 (first call parameter). The new protection type is 1 (PROT_READ). The call result is discarded because the next instruction (*adrp*) overwrites RAX.

6.   Let's now look at full function disassembly:

```
(gdb) disassemble start_modeling
Dump of assembler code for function start_modeling:
   0x00000000004006d4 <+0>:     stp     x29, x30, [sp, #-48]!
   0x00000000004006d8 <+4>:     mov     x29, sp
   0x00000000004006dc <+8>:     adrp    x0, 0x490000 <tunable_list+1320>
   0x00000000004006e0 <+12>:    ldr     x0, [x0, #3056]
   0x00000000004006e4 <+16>:    ldr     x1, [x0]
   0x00000000004006e8 <+20>:    str     x1, [sp, #40]
   0x00000000004006ec <+24>:    mov     x1, #0x0                    // #0
   0x00000000004006f0 <+28>:    mov     x5, #0x0                    // #0
   0x00000000004006f4 <+32>:    mov     w4, #0x0                    // #0
   0x00000000004006f8 <+36>:    mov     w3, #0x22                   // #34
   0x00000000004006fc <+40>:    mov     w2, #0x2                    // #2
   0x0000000000400700 <+44>:    mov     x1, #0x1000                 // #4096
   0x0000000000400704 <+48>:    mov     x0, #0x0                    // #0
   0x0000000000400708 <+52>:    bl      0x41a590 <mmap64>
   0x000000000040070c <+56>:    str     x0, [sp, #16]
   0x0000000000400710 <+60>:    ldr     x0, [sp, #16]
   0x0000000000400714 <+64>:    add     x0, x0, #0x1, lsl #12
   0x0000000000400718 <+68>:    mov     x5, #0x0                    // #0
   0x000000000040071c <+72>:    mov     w4, #0x0                    // #0
   0x0000000000400720 <+76>:    mov     w3, #0x32                   // #50
   0x0000000000400724 <+80>:    mov     w2, #0x1                    // #1
   0x0000000000400728 <+84>:    mov     x1, #0x1000                 // #4096
   0x000000000040072c <+88>:    bl      0x41a590 <mmap64>
   0x0000000000400730 <+92>:    adrp    x0, 0x457000 <getauxval+80>
   0x0000000000400734 <+96>:    add     x1, x0, #0xcc8
   0x0000000000400738 <+100>:   add     x0, sp, #0x18
   0x000000000040073c <+104>:   ldr     x2, [x1]
   0x0000000000400740 <+108>:   str     x2, [x0]
   0x0000000000400744 <+112>:   ldur    x1, [x1, #5]
   0x0000000000400748 <+116>:   stur    x1, [x0, #5]
   0x000000000040074c <+120>:   ldr     x0, [sp, #16]
   0x0000000000400750 <+124>:   mov     x1, x0
   0x0000000000400754 <+128>:   add     x0, sp, #0x18
   0x0000000000400758 <+132>:   ldr     x2, [x0]
=> 0x000000000040075c <+136>:   str     x2, [x1]
   0x0000000000400760 <+140>:   ldur    x0, [x0, #5]
   0x0000000000400764 <+144>:   stur    x0, [x1, #5]
   0x0000000000400768 <+148>:   ldr     x0, [sp, #16]
   0x000000000040076c <+152>:   add     x0, x0, #0xd
   0x0000000000400770 <+156>:   str     x0, [sp, #16]
   0x0000000000400774 <+160>:   b       0x40074c <start_modeling+120>
```

```
--Type <RET> for more, q to quit, c to continue without paging--
End of assembler dump.
```

Note: After the function prolog and two *mmap64* calls, we see something that looks like an ASCII string copy (highlighted in green above). The destination address starts from SP+0x18, 8 bytes are copied, then another 8 to SP+0x18+5 (overwriting the previous 3 so only 13 are copied in total, including a null-terminating byte):

```
(gdb) x/s $sp+0x18
0xfffffe864b58: "Hello World!"
```

Note: By the time the crash dump was saved, the copy had already happened.

7.   Next, we see a loop fragment:

```
   0x000000000040074c <+120>:    ldr     x0, [sp, #16]
   0x0000000000400750 <+124>:    mov     x1, x0
   0x0000000000400754 <+128>:    add     x0, sp, #0x18
   0x0000000000400758 <+132>:    ldr     x2, [x0]
=> 0x000000000040075c <+136>:    str     x2, [x1]
   0x0000000000400760 <+140>:    ldur    x0, [x0, #5]
   0x0000000000400764 <+144>:    stur    x0, [x1, #5]
   0x0000000000400768 <+148>:    ldr     x0, [sp, #16]
   0x000000000040076c <+152>:    add     x0, x0, #0xd
   0x0000000000400770 <+156>:    str     x0, [sp, #16]
   0x0000000000400774 <+160>:    b       0x40074c <start_modeling+120>
```

Note: It looks like at the beginning of the loop, we have the first 8 bytes from the string address SP+0x18 copied to X2 and then copied to the memory pointed by X1. The value of X1 comes from memory pointed by SP+16 (destination address). Then we see the next 8 bytes copied to the memory pointed by X1+5. Then we add the length of the string (0xd) to the destination address stored in SP+16 and repeat the loop iteration.

Note: If it's challenging to comprehend what all this code is doing, then memory cell diagrams should help here. Please look at section B in the MCD-R5-ARM64.xlsx file (offsets are hexadecimal).

Now I show you the source code fragment:

```
void start_modeling()
{
    char *paddr = (char *)mmap(NULL, 0x1000, PROT_WRITE, MAP_PRIVATE|MAP_ANONYMOUS, 0, 0);
    mmap(paddr+0x1000, 0x1000, PROT_READ, MAP_PRIVATE|MAP_ANONYMOUS|MAP_FIXED, 0, 0);

    const char str[] = "Hello World!";

    while (true)
    {
        memcpy((char *)paddr, str, sizeof(str));
        paddr += sizeof(str);
    }
}
```

8.   The default Clang-generated code is different. Let's look at the core dump differences.

```
~/ADDR-Linux/A64/MemoryDumps$ gdb -c cpu-clang.918917 -se cpu-clang
```

```
(gdb) disassemble start_modeling
Dump of assembler code for function start_modeling:
   0x00000000004006d4 <+0>:      sub     sp, sp, #0x40
   0x00000000004006d8 <+4>:      stp     x29, x30, [sp, #48]
   0x00000000004006dc <+8>:      add     x29, sp, #0x30
   0x00000000004006e0 <+12>:     mov     x0, xzr
   0x00000000004006e4 <+16>:     mov     x1, #0x1000                     // #4096
   0x00000000004006e8 <+20>:     str     x1, [sp]
   0x00000000004006ec <+24>:     mov     w2, #0x2                        // #2
   0x00000000004006f0 <+28>:     mov     w3, #0x22                       // #34
   0x00000000004006f4 <+32>:     mov     w4, wzr
   0x00000000004006f8 <+36>:     str     w4, [sp, #12]
   0x00000000004006fc <+40>:     mov     x5, xzr
   0x0000000000400700 <+44>:     str     x5, [sp, #16]
   0x0000000000400704 <+48>:     bl      0x41a590 <mmap64>
   0x0000000000400708 <+52>:     ldr     x1, [sp]
   0x000000000040070c <+56>:     ldr     w4, [sp, #12]
   0x0000000000400710 <+60>:     ldr     x5, [sp, #16]
   0x0000000000400714 <+64>:     stur    x0, [x29, #-8]
   0x0000000000400718 <+68>:     ldur    x8, [x29, #-8]
   0x000000000040071c <+72>:     add     x0, x8, #0x1, lsl #12
   0x0000000000400720 <+76>:     mov     w2, #0x1                        // #1
   0x0000000000400724 <+80>:     mov     w3, #0x32                       // #50
   0x0000000000400728 <+84>:     bl      0x41a590 <mmap64>
   0x000000000040072c <+88>:     adrp    x8, 0x457000 <getauxval+80>
   0x0000000000400730 <+92>:     add     x8, x8, #0xcc8
   0x0000000000400734 <+96>:     ldr     x10, [x8]
   0x0000000000400738 <+100>:    add     x9, sp, #0x18
   0x000000000040073c <+104>:    str     x10, [sp, #24]
   0x0000000000400740 <+108>:    ldur    x8, [x8, #5]
   0x0000000000400744 <+112>:    stur    x8, [x9, #5]
   0x0000000000400748 <+116>:    b       0x40074c <start_modeling+120>
   0x000000000040074c <+120>:    ldur    x9, [x29, #-8]
   0x0000000000400750 <+124>:    add     x8, sp, #0x18
   0x0000000000400754 <+128>:    ldr     x10, [sp, #24]
=> 0x0000000000400758 <+132>:    str     x10, [x9]
   0x000000000040075c <+136>:    ldur    x8, [x8, #5]
   0x0000000000400760 <+140>:    stur    x8, [x9, #5]
   0x0000000000400764 <+144>:    ldur    x8, [x29, #-8]
   0x0000000000400768 <+148>:    add     x8, x8, #0xd
   0x000000000040076c <+152>:    stur    x8, [x29, #-8]
   0x0000000000400770 <+156>:    b       0x40074c <start_modeling+120>
End of assembler dump.
```

Note: We see the compiler code generator uses different general-purpose registers for addressing and negative X29 offsets compared to GCC-generated code.

ADDR: Last Call

- A function possibly called (or branched and linked to) before the current instruction pointer

ADDR: Loop

- An unconditional jump or branch to the previous code address

Exercise R6

- **Goal:** Learn how to map code to execution residue and reconstruct past behaviour; recognise previously introduced ADDR patterns in the context of compiled classic C++ code

- **ADDR Patterns:** Virtual Call

- **Memory Cell Diagrams:** Virtual Call

- \ADDR-Linux\Exercise-R6-x64-GDB.pdf
- \ADDR-Linux\MCD-R6-x64.xlsx

- \ADDR-Linux\Exercise-R6-ARM64-GDB.pdf
- \ADDR-Linux\MCD-R6-ARM64.xlsx

Exercise R6 (x64, GDB)

Goal: Learn how to map code to execution residue and reconstruct past behavior; recognize previously introduced ADDR patterns in the context of compiled C++ code.

ADDR Patterns: Virtual Call.

Memory Cell Diagrams: Virtual Call.

1.   Load a core dump *cpp.151* and *cpp* executable from x64/MemoryDumps directory:

```
~/ADDR-Linux/x64/MemoryDumps$ gdb -c cpp.151 -se cpp
GNU gdb (Debian 8.2.1-2+b3) 8.2.1
Copyright (C) 2018 Free Software Foundation, Inc.
License GPLv3+: GNU GPL version 3 or later <http://gnu.org/licenses/gpl.html>
This is free software: you are free to change and redistribute it.
There is NO WARRANTY, to the extent permitted by law.
Type "show copying" and "show warranty" for details.
This GDB was configured as "x86_64-linux-gnu".
Type "show configuration" for configuration details.
For bug reporting instructions, please see:
<http://www.gnu.org/software/gdb/bugs/>.
Find the GDB manual and other documentation resources online at:
    <http://www.gnu.org/software/gdb/documentation/>.

For help, type "help".
Type "apropos word" to search for commands related to "word"...
Reading symbols from cpp...(no debugging symbols found)...done.
[New LWP 151]
Core was generated by `./cpp'.
#0  0x000000000049d2f9 in raise ()
```

2.   We open a log file:

```
(gdb) set logging on R6.log
Copying output to R6.log.
```

3.   We get the following stack trace:

```
(gdb) bt
#0  0x000000000049d2f9 in raise ()
#1  0x0000000000404113 in message_box(void*, char const*, char const*, unsigned int) ()
#2  0x0000000000404201 in start_modeling() ()
#3  0x0000000000404236 in main ()
```

4.   We now check **Call Parameters** for the *message_box* function:

```
(gdb) disassemble 0x0000000000404201
Dump of assembler code for function _Z14start_modelingv:
   0x0000000000404116 <+0>:     push   %rbp
   0x0000000000404117 <+1>:     mov    %rsp,%rbp
   0x000000000040411a <+4>:     push   %rbx
   0x000000000040411b <+5>:     sub    $0x38,%rsp
   0x000000000040411f <+9>:     lea    -0x30(%rbp),%rax
```

190

```
0x0000000000404123 <+13>:    mov     %rax,%rdi
0x0000000000404126 <+16>:    callq   0x40449c <_ZN8CDerivedC2Ev>
0x000000000040412b <+21>:    movl    $0x1,-0x34(%rbp)
0x0000000000404132 <+28>:    lea     -0x34(%rbp),%rax
0x0000000000404136 <+32>:    mov     %rax,-0x40(%rbp)
0x000000000040413a <+36>:    lea     -0x40(%rbp),%rcx
0x000000000040413e <+40>:    lea     -0x34(%rbp),%rdx
0x0000000000404142 <+44>:    lea     -0x30(%rbp),%rax
0x0000000000404146 <+48>:    mov     $0x5,%esi
0x000000000040414b <+53>:    mov     %rax,%rdi
0x000000000040414e <+56>:    callq   0x40430e <_ZN5CBase6m_ProcEiPiPS0_>
0x0000000000404153 <+61>:    lea     -0x40(%rbp),%rcx
0x0000000000404157 <+65>:    lea     -0x34(%rbp),%rdx
0x000000000040415b <+69>:    lea     -0x30(%rbp),%rax
0x000000000040415f <+73>:    mov     $0xa,%esi
0x0000000000404164 <+78>:    mov     %rax,%rdi
0x0000000000404167 <+81>:    callq   0x404388 <_ZN5CBase7m_vProcEiPiPS0_>
0x000000000040416c <+86>:    lea     -0x30(%rbp),%rax
0x0000000000404170 <+90>:    mov     %rax,-0x18(%rbp)
0x0000000000404174 <+94>:    mov     -0x18(%rbp),%rax
0x0000000000404178 <+98>:    lea     -0x40(%rbp),%rcx
0x000000000040417c <+102>:   lea     -0x34(%rbp),%rdx
0x0000000000404180 <+106>:   mov     $0xf,%esi
0x0000000000404185 <+111>:   mov     %rax,%rdi
0x0000000000404188 <+114>:   callq   0x40430e <_ZN5CBase6m_ProcEiPiPS0_>
0x000000000040418d <+119>:   mov     -0x18(%rbp),%rdi
0x0000000000404191 <+123>:   mov     -0x18(%rbp),%rax
0x0000000000404195 <+127>:   mov     (%rax),%rax
0x0000000000404198 <+130>:   add     $0x8,%rax
0x000000000040419c <+134>:   mov     (%rax),%rax
0x000000000040419f <+137>:   lea     -0x40(%rbp),%rcx
0x00000000004041a3 <+141>:   lea     -0x34(%rbp),%rdx
0x00000000004041a7 <+145>:   mov     $0x14,%esi
0x00000000004041ac <+150>:   callq   *%rax
0x00000000004041ae <+152>:   lea     -0x30(%rbp),%rax
0x00000000004041b2 <+156>:   mov     %rax,%rdi
0x00000000004041b5 <+159>:   callq   0x40444a <_ZN8CDerived5m_TryEv>
0x00000000004041ba <+164>:   lea     -0x30(%rbp),%rax
0x00000000004041be <+168>:   mov     %rax,%rdi
--Type <RET> for more, q to quit, c to continue without paging--
0x00000000004041c1 <+171>:   callq   0x4044c6 <_ZN8CDerivedD2Ev>
0x00000000004041c6 <+176>:   jmp     0x40421b <_Z14start_modelingv+261>
0x00000000004041c8 <+178>:   mov     %rax,%rbx
0x00000000004041cb <+181>:   lea     -0x30(%rbp),%rax
0x00000000004041cf <+185>:   mov     %rax,%rdi
0x00000000004041d2 <+188>:   callq   0x4044c6 <_ZN8CDerivedD2Ev>
0x00000000004041d7 <+193>:   mov     %rbx,%rax
0x00000000004041da <+196>:   jmp     0x4041dc <_Z14start_modelingv+198>
0x00000000004041dc <+198>:   mov     %rax,%rdi
0x00000000004041df <+201>:   callq   0x405590 <__cxa_begin_catch>
0x00000000004041e4 <+206>:   mov     $0x100,%ecx
0x00000000004041e9 <+211>:   lea     0x137e18(%rip),%rdx        # 0x53c008
0x00000000004041f0 <+218>:   lea     0x137e27(%rip),%rsi        # 0x53c01e
0x00000000004041f7 <+225>:   mov     $0x0,%edi
0x00000000004041fc <+230>:   callq   0x40409d <_Z11message_boxPvPKcS1_j>
0x0000000000404201 <+235>:   callq   0x405600 <__cxa_end_catch>
0x0000000000404206 <+240>:   jmp     0x40421b <_Z14start_modelingv+261>
0x0000000000404208 <+242>:   mov     %rax,%rbx
0x000000000040420b <+245>:   callq   0x405600 <__cxa_end_catch>
```

```
0x0000000000404210 <+250>:    mov     %rbx,%rax
0x0000000000404213 <+253>:    mov     %rax,%rdi
0x0000000000404216 <+256>:    callq   0x492910 <_Unwind_Resume>
0x000000000040421b <+261>:    add     $0x38,%rsp
0x000000000040421f <+265>:    pop     %rbx
0x0000000000404220 <+266>:    pop     %rbp
0x0000000000404221 <+267>:    retq
End of assembler dump.
```

Note: We set C++ name de-mangling on and disassemble again:

(gdb) **set print asm-demangle on**

(gdb) **disassemble** 0x0000000000404201
```
Dump of assembler code for function _Z14start_modelingv:
0x0000000000404116 <+0>:      push    %rbp
0x0000000000404117 <+1>:      mov     %rsp,%rbp
0x000000000040411a <+4>:      push    %rbx
0x000000000040411b <+5>:      sub     $0x38,%rsp
0x000000000040411f <+9>:      lea     -0x30(%rbp),%rax
0x0000000000404123 <+13>:     mov     %rax,%rdi
0x0000000000404126 <+16>:     callq   0x40449c <CDerived::CDerived()>
0x000000000040412b <+21>:     movl    $0x1,-0x34(%rbp)
0x0000000000404132 <+28>:     lea     -0x34(%rbp),%rax
0x0000000000404136 <+32>:     mov     %rax,-0x40(%rbp)
0x000000000040413a <+36>:     lea     -0x40(%rbp),%rcx
0x000000000040413e <+40>:     lea     -0x34(%rbp),%rdx
0x0000000000404142 <+44>:     lea     -0x30(%rbp),%rax
0x0000000000404146 <+48>:     mov     $0x5,%esi
0x000000000040414b <+53>:     mov     %rax,%rdi
0x000000000040414e <+56>:     callq   0x40430e <CBase::m_Proc(int, int*, int**)>
0x0000000000404153 <+61>:     lea     -0x40(%rbp),%rcx
0x0000000000404157 <+65>:     lea     -0x34(%rbp),%rdx
0x000000000040415b <+69>:     lea     -0x30(%rbp),%rax
0x000000000040415f <+73>:     mov     $0xa,%esi
0x0000000000404164 <+78>:     mov     %rax,%rdi
0x0000000000404167 <+81>:     callq   0x404388 <CBase::m_vProc(int, int*, int**)>
0x000000000040416c <+86>:     lea     -0x30(%rbp),%rax
0x0000000000404170 <+90>:     mov     %rax,-0x18(%rbp)
0x0000000000404174 <+94>:     mov     -0x18(%rbp),%rax
0x0000000000404178 <+98>:     lea     -0x40(%rbp),%rcx
0x000000000040417c <+102>:    lea     -0x34(%rbp),%rdx
0x0000000000404180 <+106>:    mov     $0xf,%esi
0x0000000000404185 <+111>:    mov     %rax,%rdi
0x0000000000404188 <+114>:    callq   0x40430e <CBase::m_Proc(int, int*, int**)>
0x000000000040418d <+119>:    mov     -0x18(%rbp),%rdi
0x0000000000404191 <+123>:    mov     -0x18(%rbp),%rax
0x0000000000404195 <+127>:    mov     (%rax),%rax
0x0000000000404198 <+130>:    add     $0x8,%rax
0x000000000040419c <+134>:    mov     (%rax),%rax
0x000000000040419f <+137>:    lea     -0x40(%rbp),%rcx
0x00000000004041a3 <+141>:    lea     -0x34(%rbp),%rdx
0x00000000004041a7 <+145>:    mov     $0x14,%esi
0x00000000004041ac <+150>:    callq   *%rax
0x00000000004041ae <+152>:    lea     -0x30(%rbp),%rax
0x00000000004041b2 <+156>:    mov     %rax,%rdi
0x00000000004041b5 <+159>:    callq   0x40444a <CDerived::m_Try()>
0x00000000004041ba <+164>:    lea     -0x30(%rbp),%rax
```

```
   0x00000000004041be <+168>:    mov     %rax,%rdi
--Type <RET> for more, q to quit, c to continue without paging--
   0x00000000004041c1 <+171>:    callq   0x4044c6 <CDerived::~CDerived()>
   0x00000000004041c6 <+176>:    jmp     0x40421b <start_modeling()+261>
   0x00000000004041c8 <+178>:    mov     %rax,%rbx
   0x00000000004041cb <+181>:    lea     -0x30(%rbp),%rax
   0x00000000004041cf <+185>:    mov     %rax,%rdi
   0x00000000004041d2 <+188>:    callq   0x4044c6 <CDerived::~CDerived()>
   0x00000000004041d7 <+193>:    mov     %rbx,%rax
   0x00000000004041da <+196>:    jmp     0x4041dc <start_modeling()+198>
   0x00000000004041dc <+198>:    mov     %rax,%rdi
   0x00000000004041df <+201>:    callq   0x405590 <__cxa_begin_catch>
   0x00000000004041e4 <+206>:    mov     $0x100,%ecx
   0x00000000004041e9 <+211>:    lea     0x137e18(%rip),%rdx        # 0x53c008
   0x00000000004041f0 <+218>:    lea     0x137e27(%rip),%rsi        # 0x53c01e
   0x00000000004041f7 <+225>:    mov     $0x0,%edi
   0x00000000004041fc <+230>:    callq   0x40409d <message_box(void*, char const*, char const*,
unsigned int)>
   0x0000000000404201 <+235>:    callq   0x405600 <__cxa_end_catch>
   0x0000000000404206 <+240>:    jmp     0x40421b <start_modeling()+261>
   0x0000000000404208 <+242>:    mov     %rax,%rbx
   0x000000000040420b <+245>:    callq   0x405600 <__cxa_end_catch>
   0x0000000000404210 <+250>:    mov     %rbx,%rax
   0x0000000000404213 <+253>:    mov     %rax,%rdi
   0x0000000000404216 <+256>:    callq   0x492910 <_Unwind_Resume>
   0x000000000040421b <+261>:    add     $0x38,%rsp
   0x000000000040421f <+265>:    pop     %rbx
   0x0000000000404220 <+266>:    pop     %rbp
   0x0000000000404221 <+267>:    retq
End of assembler dump.
```

Note: This function has 4 call parameters:

```
void message_box (void *window, const char *title, const char *message, unsigned int type);
```

We see that *window* is NULL (RDI), *type* is 0x100 (ECX), *title* and *message* are **Static Variables** whose addresses are loaded to RSI and RDX:

```
(gdb) x/s 0x53c01e
0x53c01e:        "Error"
```

```
(gdb) x/s 0x53c008
0x53c008:        "Exception was caught!"
```

Note: We see that we are actually in the catch block. Let's look at the previous **Last Calls**:

```
   0x00000000004041ae <+152>:    lea     -0x30(%rbp),%rax
   0x00000000004041b2 <+156>:    mov     %rax,%rdi
   0x00000000004041b5 <+159>:    callq   0x40444a <CDerived::m_Try()>
   0x00000000004041ba <+164>:    lea     -0x30(%rbp),%rax
   0x00000000004041be <+168>:    mov     %rax,%rdi
--Type <RET> for more, q to quit, c to continue without paging--
   0x00000000004041c1 <+171>:    callq   0x4044c6 <CDerived::~CDerived()>
   0x00000000004041c6 <+176>:    jmp     0x40421b <start_modeling()+261>
   0x00000000004041c8 <+178>:    mov     %rax,%rbx
   0x00000000004041cb <+181>:    lea     -0x30(%rbp),%rax
   0x00000000004041cf <+185>:    mov     %rax,%rdi
```

```
0x00000000004041d2 <+188>:    callq   0x4044c6 <CDerived::~CDerived()>
0x00000000004041d7 <+193>:    mov     %rbx,%rax
0x00000000004041da <+196>:    jmp     0x4041dc <start_modeling()+198>
0x00000000004041dc <+198>:    mov     %rax,%rdi
0x00000000004041df <+201>:    callq   0x405590 <__cxa_begin_catch>
```

Note: The class object is a **Local Variable**, and its address in RBP-0x30 is loaded into RDI. We don't see any other **Call Parameters** so that the member function may have a *void* parameter list. Let's look at execution residue, past survived addresses in the raw stack region just before the current RSP address, and try to find those last calls:

```
(gdb) x/256a $rsp-0x800
0x7ffdb673e7d0: 0x0      0x7ffd0000000b
0x7ffdb673e7e0: 0x7ffdb673f098  0x7ffdb673f0a0
0x7ffdb673e7f0: 0x0      0x40444a <CDerived::m_Try()>
0x7ffdb673e800: 0x51     0x404d6f <parse_lsda_header(_Unwind_Context*, unsigned char const*,
lsda_header_info*)+31>
0x7ffdb673e810: 0x7ffdb673f0d0  0x7ffdb673ebe0
0x7ffdb673e820: 0x0      0x14d5830
0x7ffdb673e830: 0x7ffdb673e930  0x404f08 <__gxx_personality_v0+184>
0x7ffdb673e840: 0x404487 <CDerived::m_Try()+61> 0x14d5830
0x7ffdb673e850: 0x20140444a     0x0
0x7ffdb673e860: 0x586758        0x7ffdb673e800
0x7ffdb673e870: 0x7ffdb673e8c0  0x7ffdb673ebe0
0x7ffdb673e880: 0x0      0x55ba3d
0x7ffdb673e890: 0x55ba3d        0xb673ebe0
0x7ffdb673e8a0: 0x0      0x39
0x7ffdb673e8b0: 0x5      0x3e
0x7ffdb673e8c0: 0x40444a <CDerived::m_Try()>    0x40444a <CDerived::m_Try()>
0x7ffdb673e8d0: 0x0      0x586770
0x7ffdb673e8e0: 0x586769        0x58019b
0x7ffdb673e8f0: 0x7ffdb673e930  0x7ffdb673ebe0
0x7ffdb673e900: 0x0      0x14d5830
0x7ffdb673e910: 0x7ffdb673e930  0x3
0x7ffdb673e920: 0x7ffdb673ecd0  0x491e8b <_Unwind_RaiseException_Phase2+75>
0x7ffdb673e930: 0x0      0x0
0x7ffdb673e940: 0x0      0x0
0x7ffdb673e950: 0x0      0x0
0x7ffdb673e960: 0xfffffffffffffe8        0x1
0x7ffdb673e970: 0x0      0x0
0x7ffdb673e980: 0x0      0x0
0x7ffdb673e990: 0xfffffffffffffff0       0x1
0x7ffdb673e9a0: 0x0      0x0
0x7ffdb673e9b0: 0x0      0x0
0x7ffdb673e9c0: 0x0      0x0
0x7ffdb673e9d0: 0x0      0x0
0x7ffdb673e9e0: 0x0      0x0
0x7ffdb673e9f0: 0x0      0x0
0x7ffdb673ea00: 0x0      0x0
0x7ffdb673ea10: 0x0      0x0
0x7ffdb673ea20: 0x0      0x0
0x7ffdb673ea30: 0xfffffffffffffff8       0x1
0x7ffdb673ea40: 0x0      0x0
0x7ffdb673ea50: 0x0      0x10
0x7ffdb673ea60: 0x6      0x0
0x7ffdb673ea70: 0x1      0x404453 <CDerived::m_Try()+9>
0x7ffdb673ea80: 0x404e50 <__gxx_personality_v0> 0xfffffffffffffff8
0x7ffdb673ea90: 0x1      0x10
```

--Type <RET> for more, q to quit, c to continue without paging--
```
0x7ffdb673eaa0: 0x11b1b  0x0
0x7ffdb673eab0: 0x14d5830        0x7ffdb673ebe0
0x7ffdb673eac0: 0x7ffdb673ee90  0x7ffdb673ecd0
0x7ffdb673ead0: 0x14d5830        0x7ffdb673f0f0
0x7ffdb673eae0: 0x0     0x49273a <_Unwind_RaiseException+730>
0x7ffdb673eaf0: 0x7ffdb673ee58  0x7ffdb673ee60
0x7ffdb673eb00: 0x0     0x7ffdb673ee68
0x7ffdb673eb10: 0x0     0x0
0x7ffdb673eb20: 0x7ffdb673ee90  0x0
0x7ffdb673eb30: 0x0     0x0
0x7ffdb673eb40: 0x0     0x0
0x7ffdb673eb50: 0x7ffdb673ee70  0x7ffdb673ee78
0x7ffdb673eb60: 0x7ffdb673ee80  0x493f76 <search_object+854>
0x7ffdb673eb70: 0x7ffdb673ee98  0x7ffdb673ebb8
0x7ffdb673eb80: 0x7ffdb673ebc0  0x7ffd0000001b
0x7ffdb673eb90: 0x0     0x7ffd0000000b
0x7ffdb673eba0: 0x7ffdb673f0a8  0x7ffdb673f0b0
0x7ffdb673ebb0: 0x0     0x404116 <start_modeling()>
0x7ffdb673ebc0: 0x10c   0x0
0x7ffdb673ebd0: 0x7ffdb673f0e0  0x599580 <object>
0x7ffdb673ebe0: 0x7ffdb673ecf0  0x7ffdb673f058
0x7ffdb673ebf0: 0x0     0x404f08 <__gxx_personality_v0+184>
0x7ffdb673ec00: 0x4041b9 <start_modeling()+163> 0x14d5830
0x7ffdb673ec10: 0x601404116     0x0
0x7ffdb673ec20: 0x586770        0x7ffdb673ec01
0x7ffdb673ec30: 0x7ffdb673f0f0  0x40449b
0x7ffdb673ec40: 0x586758        0x55ba9d
0x7ffdb673ec50: 0x55ba9d        0xb673efb0
0x7ffdb673ec60: 0x0     0x1b
0x7ffdb673ec70: 0x7ffdb673ecf0  0x490d60 <uw_frame_state_for+800>
0x7ffdb673ec80: 0x0     0x9b00000000
0x7ffdb673ec90: 0x55ba21        0x7ffdb673eca8
0x7ffdb673eca0: 0x7ffdb673ecf0  0x586770
0x7ffdb673ecb0: 0x7ffdb673ecf0  0x7ffdb673efb0
0x7ffdb673ecc0: 0x4     0x14d5830
0x7ffdb673ecd0: 0x7ffdb673ecf0  0x2
0x7ffdb673ece0: 0x7ffdb673eeb8  0x491e8b <_Unwind_RaiseException_Phase2+75>
0x7ffdb673ecf0: 0x0     0x0
0x7ffdb673ed00: 0x0     0x0
0x7ffdb673ed10: 0x0     0x0
0x7ffdb673ed20: 0xffffffffffffffe8       0x1
0x7ffdb673ed30: 0x0     0x0
0x7ffdb673ed40: 0x0     0x0
0x7ffdb673ed50: 0xfffffffffffffff0       0x1
0x7ffdb673ed60: 0x0     0x0
```
--Type <RET> for more, q to quit, c to continue without paging--
```
0x7ffdb673ed70: 0x0     0x0
0x7ffdb673ed80: 0x0     0x0
0x7ffdb673ed90: 0x0     0x0
0x7ffdb673eda0: 0x0     0x0
0x7ffdb673edb0: 0x0     0x0
0x7ffdb673edc0: 0x0     0x0
0x7ffdb673edd0: 0x0     0x0
0x7ffdb673ede0: 0x0     0x0
0x7ffdb673edf0: 0xfffffffffffffff8       0x1
0x7ffdb673ee00: 0x0     0x0
0x7ffdb673ee10: 0x7     0x410
0x7ffdb673ee20: 0x400   0x40
```

```
0x7ffdb673ee30: 0x14c3408        0x3ff
0x7ffdb673ee40: 0x430    0x10
0x7ffdb673ee50: 0x4000000041    0x2
0x7ffdb673ee60: 0x770000005d    0x0
0x7ffdb673ee70: 0x6e0000007c    0x0
0x7ffdb673ee80: 0x7ffdb673f0e0  0x3ff
0x7ffdb673ee90: 0x400    0x3f
0x7ffdb673eea0: 0x53c008        0x15
0x7ffdb673eeb0: 0x599260 <_IO_file_jumps>       0x4b69e4 <malloc+132>
0x7ffdb673eec0: 0x400    0x597600 <_IO_2_1_stdout_>
0x7ffdb673eed0: 0x400    0x518c6a <_IO_file_doallocate+170>
0x7ffdb673eee0: 0x28     0x4
0x7ffdb673eef0: 0x1      0x3e800002190
0x7ffdb673ef00: 0x5      0x8801
0x7ffdb673ef10: 0x0      0x400
0x7ffdb673ef20: 0x0      0x632eb888
0x7ffdb673ef30: 0x4d589c4       0x632eb888
0x7ffdb673ef40: 0x4d589c4       0x632e125f
0x7ffdb673ef50: 0x4d589c4       0x0
0x7ffdb673ef60: 0x0      0x0
0x7ffdb673ef70: 0x0      0xfc8fc87ac7b22400
0x7ffdb673ef80: 0x599260 <_IO_file_jumps>       0x1
0x7ffdb673ef90: 0x53c01c        0x4aff3c <_IO_default_xsputn+108>
0x7ffdb673efa0: 0x597600 <_IO_2_1_stdout_>      0x415e3c <std::ctype<char>::_M_widen_init()
const+300>
0x7ffdb673efb0: 0x706050403020100       0xf0e0d0c0b0a0908
0x7ffdb673efc0: 0x1716151413121110      0x1f1e1d1c1b1a1918
```

Note: We see some references to `CDerived::m_Try()`, including the coincidental `CDerived::m_Try()+61` that doesn't have a valid instruction address inside the disassembly. We also don't see references to CDerived::~CDerived(), though, so perhaps the destructor function was not yet called. We also see `_Unwind_RaiseException` references nearby. They are explained because we see __*cxa_throw* call and __*cxa_rethrow* call in a catch block inside *m_Try* and follow their call paths:

```
(gdb) disassemble 0x404453
Dump of assembler code for function _ZN8CDerived5m_TryEv:
   0x000000000040444a <+0>:     push   %rbp
   0x000000000040444b <+1>:     mov    %rsp,%rbp
   0x000000000040444e <+4>:     push   %rbx
   0x000000000040444f <+5>:     sub    $0x18,%rsp
   0x0000000000404453 <+9>:     mov    %rdi,-0x18(%rbp)
   0x0000000000404457 <+13>:    mov    $0x4,%edi
   0x000000000040445c <+18>:    callq  0x405af0 <__cxa_allocate_exception>
   0x0000000000404461 <+23>:    movl   $0xffffffff,(%rax)
   0x0000000000404467 <+29>:    mov    $0x0,%edx
   0x000000000040446c <+34>:    lea    0x18c665(%rip),%rsi      # 0x590ad8 <typeinfo for int>
   0x0000000000404473 <+41>:    mov    %rax,%rdi
   0x0000000000404476 <+44>:    callq  0x4048d0 <__cxa_throw>
   0x000000000040447b <+49>:    mov    %rax,%rdi
   0x000000000040447e <+52>:    callq  0x405590 <__cxa_begin_catch>
   0x0000000000404483 <+57>:    callq  0x404920 <__cxa_rethrow>
   0x0000000000404488 <+62>:    mov    %rax,%rbx
   0x000000000040448b <+65>:    callq  0x405600 <__cxa_end_catch>
   0x0000000000404490 <+70>:    mov    %rbx,%rax
   0x0000000000404493 <+73>:    mov    %rax,%rdi
   0x0000000000404496 <+76>:    callq  0x492910 <_Unwind_Resume>
End of assembler dump.
```

```
(gdb) disassemble __cxa_throw
Dump of assembler code for function __cxa_throw:
   0x00000000004048d0 <+0>:     push   %r12
   0x00000000004048d2 <+2>:     mov    %rdx,%r12
   0x00000000004048d5 <+5>:     push   %rbp
   0x00000000004048d6 <+6>:     mov    %rsi,%rbp
   0x00000000004048d9 <+9>:     push   %rbx
   0x00000000004048da <+10>:    mov    %rdi,%rbx
   0x00000000004048dd <+13>:    nop
   0x00000000004048de <+14>:    callq  0x405430 <__cxa_get_globals>
   0x00000000004048e3 <+19>:    mov    %r12,%rdx
   0x00000000004048e6 <+22>:    mov    %rbp,%rsi
   0x00000000004048e9 <+25>:    mov    %rbx,%rdi
   0x00000000004048ec <+28>:    addl   $0x1,0x8(%rax)
   0x00000000004048f0 <+32>:    callq  0x404880 <__cxa_init_primary_exception>
   0x00000000004048f5 <+37>:    movl   $0x1,(%rax)
   0x00000000004048fb <+43>:    lea    0x60(%rax),%rbx
   0x00000000004048ff <+47>:    mov    %rbx,%rdi
   0x0000000000404902 <+50>:    callq  0x492460 <_Unwind_RaiseException>
   0x0000000000404907 <+55>:    mov    %rbx,%rdi
   0x000000000040490a <+58>:    callq  0x405590 <__cxa_begin_catch>
   0x000000000040490f <+63>:    callq  0x4049c0 <std::terminate()>
End of assembler dump.

(gdb) disassemble _Unwind_RaiseException
Dump of assembler code for function _Unwind_RaiseException:
   0x0000000000492460 <+0>:     push   %rbp
   0x0000000000492461 <+1>:     mov    %rsp,%rbp
   0x0000000000492464 <+4>:     push   %r15
   0x0000000000492466 <+6>:     push   %r14
   0x0000000000492468 <+8>:     lea    -0x3a0(%rbp),%r14
   0x000000000049246f <+15>:    lea    0x10(%rbp),%rsi
   0x0000000000492473 <+19>:    push   %r13
   0x0000000000492475 <+21>:    mov    %rdi,%r13
   0x0000000000492478 <+24>:    mov    %r14,%rdi
   0x000000000049247b <+27>:    push   %r12
   0x000000000049247d <+29>:    lea    -0x1c0(%rbp),%r12
   0x0000000000492484 <+36>:    push   %rbx
   0x0000000000492485 <+37>:    lea    -0x2b0(%rbp),%rbx
   0x000000000049248c <+44>:    push   %rdx
   0x000000000049248d <+45>:    push   %rax
   0x000000000049248e <+46>:    sub    $0x368,%rsp
   0x0000000000492495 <+53>:    mov    0x8(%rbp),%rdx
   0x0000000000492499 <+57>:    callq  0x491c30 <uw_init_context_1>
   0x000000000049249e <+62>:    movdqa -0x3a0(%rbp),%xmm0
   0x00000000004924a6 <+70>:    movdqa -0x390(%rbp),%xmm1
   0x00000000004924ae <+78>:    movdqa -0x380(%rbp),%xmm2
   0x00000000004924b6 <+86>:    movdqa -0x370(%rbp),%xmm3
   0x00000000004924be <+94>:    movdqa -0x360(%rbp),%xmm4
   0x00000000004924c6 <+102>:   movdqa -0x350(%rbp),%xmm5
   0x00000000004924ce <+110>:   movaps %xmm0,-0x2b0(%rbp)
   0x00000000004924d5 <+117>:   movdqa -0x340(%rbp),%xmm6
   0x00000000004924dd <+125>:   movaps %xmm1,-0x2a0(%rbp)
   0x00000000004924e4 <+132>:   movdqa -0x330(%rbp),%xmm7
   0x00000000004924ec <+140>:   movaps %xmm2,-0x290(%rbp)
   0x00000000004924f3 <+147>:   movdqa -0x320(%rbp),%xmm0
   0x00000000004924fb <+155>:   movdqa -0x310(%rbp),%xmm1
   0x0000000000492503 <+163>:   movaps %xmm3,-0x280(%rbp)
```

```
   0x000000000049250a <+170>:    movdqa  -0x300(%rbp),%xmm2
   0x0000000000492512 <+178>:    movdqa  -0x2f0(%rbp),%xmm3
   0x000000000049251a <+186>:    movaps  %xmm4,-0x270(%rbp)
   0x0000000000492521 <+193>:    movdqa  -0x2e0(%rbp),%xmm4
   0x0000000000492529 <+201>:    movaps  %xmm5,-0x260(%rbp)
   0x0000000000492530 <+208>:    movdqa  -0x2d0(%rbp),%xmm5
   0x0000000000492538 <+216>:    movaps  %xmm6,-0x250(%rbp)
   0x000000000049253f <+223>:    movdqa  -0x2c0(%rbp),%xmm6
   0x0000000000492547 <+231>:    movaps  %xmm7,-0x240(%rbp)
   0x000000000049254e <+238>:    movaps  %xmm0,-0x230(%rbp)
   0x0000000000492555 <+245>:    movaps  %xmm1,-0x220(%rbp)
   0x000000000049255c <+252>:    movaps  %xmm2,-0x210(%rbp)
--Type <RET> for more, q to quit, c to continue without paging--
   0x0000000000492563 <+259>:    movaps  %xmm3,-0x200(%rbp)
   0x000000000049256a <+266>:    movaps  %xmm4,-0x1f0(%rbp)
   0x0000000000492571 <+273>:    movaps  %xmm5,-0x1e0(%rbp)
   0x0000000000492578 <+280>:    movaps  %xmm6,-0x1d0(%rbp)
   0x000000000049257f <+287>:    jmp     0x4925c0 <_Unwind_RaiseException+352>
   0x0000000000492581 <+289>:    nopl    0x0(%rax)
   0x0000000000492588 <+296>:    test    %eax,%eax
   0x000000000049258a <+298>:    jne     0x4925f0 <_Unwind_RaiseException+400>
   0x000000000049258c <+300>:    mov     -0x70(%rbp),%rax
   0x0000000000492590 <+304>:    test    %rax,%rax
   0x0000000000492593 <+307>:    je      0x4925b5 <_Unwind_RaiseException+341>
   0x0000000000492595 <+309>:    mov     %rbx,%r8
   0x0000000000492598 <+312>:    mov     %r13,%rcx
   0x000000000049259b <+315>:    mov     0x0(%r13),%rdx
   0x000000000049259f <+319>:    mov     $0x1,%esi
   0x00000000004925a4 <+324>:    mov     $0x1,%edi
   0x00000000004925a9 <+329>:    callq   *%rax
   0x00000000004925ab <+331>:    cmp     $0x6,%eax
   0x00000000004925ae <+334>:    je      0x492600 <_Unwind_RaiseException+416>
   0x00000000004925b0 <+336>:    cmp     $0x8,%eax
   0x00000000004925b3 <+339>:    jne     0x4925f0 <_Unwind_RaiseException+400>
   0x00000000004925b5 <+341>:    mov     %r12,%rsi
   0x00000000004925b8 <+344>:    mov     %rbx,%rdi
   0x00000000004925bb <+347>:    callq   0x491db0 <uw_update_context>
   0x00000000004925c0 <+352>:    mov     %r12,%rsi
   0x00000000004925c3 <+355>:    mov     %rbx,%rdi
   0x00000000004925c6 <+358>:    callq   0x490a40 <uw_frame_state_for>
   0x00000000004925cb <+363>:    cmp     $0x5,%eax
   0x00000000004925ce <+366>:    jne     0x492588 <_Unwind_RaiseException+296>
   0x00000000004925d0 <+368>:    mov     -0x28(%rbp),%rbx
   0x00000000004925d4 <+372>:    mov     -0x20(%rbp),%r12
   0x00000000004925d8 <+376>:    mov     -0x18(%rbp),%r13
   0x00000000004925dc <+380>:    mov     -0x10(%rbp),%r14
   0x00000000004925e0 <+384>:    mov     -0x8(%rbp),%r15
   0x00000000004925e4 <+388>:    leaveq
   0x00000000004925e5 <+389>:    retq
   0x00000000004925e6 <+390>:    nopw    %cs:0x0(%rax,%rax,1)
   0x00000000004925f0 <+400>:    mov     $0x3,%eax
   0x00000000004925f5 <+405>:    jmp     0x4925d0 <_Unwind_RaiseException+368>
   0x00000000004925f7 <+407>:    nopw    0x0(%rax,%rax,1)
   0x0000000000492600 <+416>:    movdqa  -0x3a0(%rbp),%xmm7
   0x0000000000492608 <+424>:    mov     -0x1f0(%rbp),%rax
   0x000000000049260f <+431>:    movq    $0x0,0x10(%r13)
   0x0000000000492617 <+439>:    mov     %r12,%rdx
   0x000000000049261a <+442>:    movdqa  -0x350(%rbp),%xmm0
--Type <RET> for more, q to quit, c to continue without paging--
```

198

```
   0x0000000000492622 <+450>:    mov     -0x220(%rbp),%rcx
   0x0000000000492629 <+457>:    mov     %rbx,%rsi
   0x000000000049262c <+460>:    mov     %r13,%rdi
   0x000000000049262f <+463>:    movaps  %xmm7,-0x2b0(%rbp)
   0x0000000000492636 <+470>:    movdqa  -0x390(%rbp),%xmm7
   0x000000000049263e <+478>:    shr     $0x3f,%rax
   0x0000000000492642 <+482>:    movdqa  -0x340(%rbp),%xmm1
   0x000000000049264a <+490>:    movaps  %xmm0,-0x260(%rbp)
   0x0000000000492651 <+497>:    movdqa  -0x330(%rbp),%xmm2
   0x0000000000492659 <+505>:    movdqa  -0x320(%rbp),%xmm3
   0x0000000000492661 <+513>:    sub     %rax,%rcx
   0x0000000000492664 <+516>:    movaps  %xmm7,-0x2a0(%rbp)
   0x000000000049266b <+523>:    movdqa  -0x380(%rbp),%xmm7
   0x0000000000492673 <+531>:    movdqa  -0x310(%rbp),%xmm4
   0x000000000049267b <+539>:    movdqa  -0x300(%rbp),%xmm5
   0x0000000000492683 <+547>:    movdqa  -0x2f0(%rbp),%xmm6
   0x000000000049268b <+555>:    mov     %rcx,0x18(%r13)
   0x000000000049268f <+559>:    movaps  %xmm7,-0x290(%rbp)
   0x0000000000492696 <+566>:    movdqa  -0x370(%rbp),%xmm7
   0x000000000049269e <+574>:    movdqa  -0x2d0(%rbp),%xmm0
   0x00000000004926a6 <+582>:    movaps  %xmm1,-0x250(%rbp)
   0x00000000004926ad <+589>:    movaps  %xmm7,-0x280(%rbp)
   0x00000000004926b4 <+596>:    movdqa  -0x360(%rbp),%xmm7
   0x00000000004926bc <+604>:    movaps  %xmm2,-0x240(%rbp)
   0x00000000004926c3 <+611>:    movaps  %xmm7,-0x270(%rbp)
   0x00000000004926ca <+618>:    movdqa  -0x2e0(%rbp),%xmm7
   0x00000000004926d2 <+626>:    movaps  %xmm3,-0x230(%rbp)
   0x00000000004926d9 <+633>:    movaps  %xmm4,-0x220(%rbp)
   0x00000000004926e0 <+640>:    movaps  %xmm5,-0x210(%rbp)
   0x00000000004926e7 <+647>:    movaps  %xmm6,-0x200(%rbp)
   0x00000000004926ee <+654>:    movaps  %xmm7,-0x1f0(%rbp)
   0x00000000004926f5 <+661>:    movaps  %xmm0,-0x1e0(%rbp)
   0x00000000004926fc <+668>:    movdqa  -0x2c0(%rbp),%xmm1
   0x0000000000492704 <+676>:    movaps  %xmm1,-0x1d0(%rbp)
   0x000000000049270b <+683>:    callq   0x491e40 <_Unwind_RaiseException_Phase2>
   0x0000000000492710 <+688>:    cmp     $0x7,%eax
   0x0000000000492713 <+691>:    jne     0x4925d0 <_Unwind_RaiseException+368>
   0x0000000000492719 <+697>:    mov     %rbx,%rsi
   0x000000000049271c <+700>:    mov     %r14,%rdi
   0x000000000049271f <+703>:    callq   0x492020 <uw_install_context_1>
   0x0000000000492724 <+708>:    mov     -0x218(%rbp),%r8
   0x000000000049272b <+715>:    mov     -0x220(%rbp),%rdi
   0x0000000000492732 <+722>:    mov     %r8,%rsi
   0x0000000000492735 <+725>:    callq   0x492450 <_Unwind_DebugHook>
   0x000000000049273a <+730>:    mov     %rax,%rcx
--Type <RET> for more, q to quit, c to continue without paging--
   0x000000000049273d <+733>:    mov     %r8,0x8(%rbp,%rax,1)
   0x0000000000492742 <+738>:    mov     -0x38(%rbp),%rax
   0x0000000000492746 <+742>:    lea     0x8(%rbp,%rcx,1),%rcx
   0x000000000049274b <+747>:    mov     -0x30(%rbp),%rdx
   0x000000000049274f <+751>:    mov     -0x28(%rbp),%rbx
   0x0000000000492753 <+755>:    mov     -0x20(%rbp),%r12
   0x0000000000492757 <+759>:    mov     -0x18(%rbp),%r13
   0x000000000049275b <+763>:    mov     -0x10(%rbp),%r14
   0x000000000049275f <+767>:    mov     -0x8(%rbp),%r15
   0x0000000000492763 <+771>:    mov     0x0(%rbp),%rbp
   0x0000000000492767 <+775>:    mov     %rcx,%rsp
   0x000000000049276a <+778>:    retq
End of assembler dump.
```

```
(gdb) disassemble _Unwind_RaiseException_Phase2
Dump of assembler code for function _Unwind_RaiseException_Phase2:
   0x0000000000491e40 <+0>:     push   %r15
   0x0000000000491e42 <+2>:     mov    %rdx,%r15
   0x0000000000491e45 <+5>:     push   %r14
   0x0000000000491e47 <+7>:     mov    $0x1,%r14d
   0x0000000000491e4d <+13>:    push   %r13
   0x0000000000491e4f <+15>:    push   %r12
   0x0000000000491e51 <+17>:    mov    %rdi,%r12
   0x0000000000491e54 <+20>:    push   %rbp
   0x0000000000491e55 <+21>:    push   %rbx
   0x0000000000491e56 <+22>:    mov    %rsi,%rbx
   0x0000000000491e59 <+25>:    sub    $0x188,%rsp
   0x0000000000491e60 <+32>:    mov    %rsp,%r13
   0x0000000000491e63 <+35>:    jmp    0x491ea8 <_Unwind_RaiseException_Phase2+104>
   0x0000000000491e65 <+37>:    nopl   (%rax)
   0x0000000000491e68 <+40>:    mov    0x150(%rsp),%rax
   0x0000000000491e70 <+48>:    test   %rax,%rax
   0x0000000000491e73 <+51>:    je     0x491e95 <_Unwind_RaiseException_Phase2+85>
   0x0000000000491e75 <+53>:    mov    %ebp,%esi
   0x0000000000491e77 <+55>:    mov    %rbx,%r8
   0x0000000000491e7a <+58>:    mov    %r12,%rcx
   0x0000000000491e7d <+61>:    mov    (%r12),%rdx
   0x0000000000491e81 <+65>:    or     $0x2,%esi
   0x0000000000491e84 <+68>:    mov    $0x1,%edi
   0x0000000000491e89 <+73>:    callq  *%rax
   0x0000000000491e8b <+75>:    cmp    $0x7,%eax
   0x0000000000491e8e <+78>:    je     0x491ef8 <_Unwind_RaiseException_Phase2+184>
   0x0000000000491e90 <+80>:    cmp    $0x8,%eax
   0x0000000000491e93 <+83>:    jne    0x491eda <_Unwind_RaiseException_Phase2+154>
   0x0000000000491e95 <+85>:    test   %ebp,%ebp
   0x0000000000491e97 <+87>:    jne    0x491efd <_Unwind_RaiseException_Phase2+189>
   0x0000000000491e99 <+89>:    mov    %r13,%rsi
   0x0000000000491e9c <+92>:    mov    %rbx,%rdi
   0x0000000000491e9f <+95>:    add    $0x1,%r14
   0x0000000000491ea3 <+99>:    callq  0x491db0 <uw_update_context>
   0x0000000000491ea8 <+104>:   mov    %r13,%rsi
   0x0000000000491eab <+107>:   mov    %rbx,%rdi
   0x0000000000491eae <+110>:   xor    %ebp,%ebp
   0x0000000000491eb0 <+112>:   callq  0x490a40 <uw_frame_state_for>
   0x0000000000491eb5 <+117>:   mov    0xc0(%rbx),%rdx
   0x0000000000491ebc <+124>:   mov    0x90(%rbx),%rcx
   0x0000000000491ec3 <+131>:   shr    $0x3f,%rdx
   0x0000000000491ec7 <+135>:   sub    %rdx,%rcx
   0x0000000000491eca <+138>:   cmp    %rcx,0x18(%r12)
   0x0000000000491ecf <+143>:   sete   %bpl
--Type <RET> for more, q to quit, c to continue without paging--
   0x0000000000491ed3 <+147>:   shl    $0x2,%ebp
   0x0000000000491ed6 <+150>:   test   %eax,%eax
   0x0000000000491ed8 <+152>:   je     0x491e68 <_Unwind_RaiseException_Phase2+40>
   0x0000000000491eda <+154>:   mov    $0x2,%eax
   0x0000000000491edf <+159>:   add    $0x188,%rsp
   0x0000000000491ee6 <+166>:   pop    %rbx
   0x0000000000491ee7 <+167>:   pop    %rbp
   0x0000000000491ee8 <+168>:   pop    %r12
   0x0000000000491eea <+170>:   pop    %r13
   0x0000000000491eec <+172>:   pop    %r14
   0x0000000000491eee <+174>:   pop    %r15
```

```
0x0000000000491ef0 <+176>:    retq
0x0000000000491ef1 <+177>:    nopl    0x0(%rax)
0x0000000000491ef8 <+184>:    mov     %r14,(%r15)
0x0000000000491efb <+187>:    jmp     0x491edf <_Unwind_RaiseException_Phase2+159>
0x0000000000491efd <+189>:    jmpq    0x402f8e <_Unwind_RaiseException_Phase2.cold.11>
End of assembler dump.
```

Note: If we look at *m_Try* disassembly, we see that an exception object is allocated, and its size is 4 (EDI). Then we see **Pointer Dereference**, and it now contains -1 (0xffffffff). After that, we see three **Call Parameters** to the *__cxa_throw* function call. The first one is an address of exception object (RAX -> RDI), the second is a **Static Variable** for int typeinfo at offset RIP+0x18c665 (RSI), and the last one is 0 (EDX).

```
0x0000000000404457 <+13>:    mov     $0x4,%edi
0x000000000040445c <+18>:    callq   0x405af0 <__cxa_allocate_exception>
0x0000000000404461 <+23>:    movl    $0xffffffff,(%rax)
0x0000000000404467 <+29>:    mov     $0x0,%edx
0x000000000040446c <+34>:    lea     0x18c665(%rip),%rsi       # 0x590ad8 <typeinfo for int>
0x0000000000404473 <+41>:    mov     %rax,%rdi
0x0000000000404476 <+44>:    callq   0x4048d0 <__cxa_throw>
```

It corresponds to the following C++ code:

```
void m_Try ()
{
try

      {
             throw -1;
      }
      catch (...)
      {
             throw;
      }
}
```

5.   Let's now look at the *start_modeling* function again, where we previously found the call to the *m_Try* member function:

```
(gdb) disassemble start_modeling
Dump of assembler code for function _Z14start_modelingv:
   0x0000000000404116 <+0>:     push    %rbp
   0x0000000000404117 <+1>:     mov     %rsp,%rbp
   0x000000000040411a <+4>:     push    %rbx
   0x000000000040411b <+5>:     sub     $0x38,%rsp
   0x000000000040411f <+9>:     lea     -0x30(%rbp),%rax
   0x0000000000404123 <+13>:    mov     %rax,%rdi
   0x0000000000404126 <+16>:    callq   0x40449c <CDerived::CDerived()>
   0x000000000040412b <+21>:    movl    $0x1,-0x34(%rbp)
   0x0000000000404132 <+28>:    lea     -0x34(%rbp),%rax
   0x0000000000404136 <+32>:    mov     %rax,-0x40(%rbp)
   0x000000000040413a <+36>:    lea     -0x40(%rbp),%rcx
   0x000000000040413e <+40>:    lea     -0x34(%rbp),%rdx
   0x0000000000404142 <+44>:    lea     -0x30(%rbp),%rax
   0x0000000000404146 <+48>:    mov     $0x5,%esi
   0x000000000040414b <+53>:    mov     %rax,%rdi
```

```
   0x000000000040414e <+56>:    callq  0x40430e <CBase::m_Proc(int, int*, int**)>
   0x0000000000404153 <+61>:    lea    -0x40(%rbp),%rcx
   0x0000000000404157 <+65>:    lea    -0x34(%rbp),%rdx
   0x000000000040415b <+69>:    lea    -0x30(%rbp),%rax
   0x000000000040415f <+73>:    mov    $0xa,%esi
   0x0000000000404164 <+78>:    mov    %rax,%rdi
   0x0000000000404167 <+81>:    callq  0x404388 <CBase::m_vProc(int, int*, int**)>
   0x000000000040416c <+86>:    lea    -0x30(%rbp),%rax
   0x0000000000404170 <+90>:    mov    %rax,-0x18(%rbp)
   0x0000000000404174 <+94>:    mov    -0x18(%rbp),%rax
   0x0000000000404178 <+98>:    lea    -0x40(%rbp),%rcx
   0x000000000040417c <+102>:   lea    -0x34(%rbp),%rdx
   0x0000000000404180 <+106>:   mov    $0xf,%esi
   0x0000000000404185 <+111>:   mov    %rax,%rdi
   0x0000000000404188 <+114>:   callq  0x40430e <CBase::m_Proc(int, int*, int**)>
   0x000000000040418d <+119>:   mov    -0x18(%rbp),%rdi
   0x0000000000404191 <+123>:   mov    -0x18(%rbp),%rax
   0x0000000000404195 <+127>:   mov    (%rax),%rax
   0x0000000000404198 <+130>:   add    $0x8,%rax
   0x000000000040419c <+134>:   mov    (%rax),%rax
   0x000000000040419f <+137>:   lea    -0x40(%rbp),%rcx
   0x00000000004041a3 <+141>:   lea    -0x34(%rbp),%rdx
   0x00000000004041a7 <+145>:   mov    $0x14,%esi
   0x00000000004041ac <+150>:   callq  *%rax
   0x00000000004041ae <+152>:   lea    -0x30(%rbp),%rax
   0x00000000004041b2 <+156>:   mov    %rax,%rdi
   0x00000000004041b5 <+159>:   callq  0x40444a <CDerived::m_Try()>
   0x00000000004041ba <+164>:   lea    -0x30(%rbp),%rax
   0x00000000004041be <+168>:   mov    %rax,%rdi
--Type <RET> for more, q to quit, c to continue without paging--
   0x00000000004041c1 <+171>:   callq  0x4044c6 <CDerived::~CDerived()>
   0x00000000004041c6 <+176>:   jmp    0x40421b <start_modeling()+261>
   0x00000000004041c8 <+178>:   mov    %rax,%rbx
   0x00000000004041cb <+181>:   lea    -0x30(%rbp),%rax
   0x00000000004041cf <+185>:   mov    %rax,%rdi
   0x00000000004041d2 <+188>:   callq  0x4044c6 <CDerived::~CDerived()>
   0x00000000004041d7 <+193>:   mov    %rbx,%rax
   0x00000000004041da <+196>:   jmp    0x4041dc <start_modeling()+198>
   0x00000000004041dc <+198>:   mov    %rax,%rdi
   0x00000000004041df <+201>:   callq  0x405590 <__cxa_begin_catch>
   0x00000000004041e4 <+206>:   mov    $0x100,%ecx
   0x00000000004041e9 <+211>:   lea    0x137e18(%rip),%rdx        # 0x53c008
   0x00000000004041f0 <+218>:   lea    0x137e27(%rip),%rsi        # 0x53c01e
   0x00000000004041f7 <+225>:   mov    $0x0,%edi
   0x00000000004041fc <+230>:   callq  0x40409d <message_box(void*, char const*, char const*,
unsigned int)>
   0x0000000000404201 <+235>:   callq  0x405600 <__cxa_end_catch>
   0x0000000000404206 <+240>:   jmp    0x40421b <start_modeling()+261>
   0x0000000000404208 <+242>:   mov    %rax,%rbx
   0x000000000040420b <+245>:   callq  0x405600 <__cxa_end_catch>
   0x0000000000404210 <+250>:   mov    %rbx,%rax
   0x0000000000404213 <+253>:   mov    %rax,%rdi
   0x0000000000404216 <+256>:   callq  0x492910 <_Unwind_Resume>
   0x000000000040421b <+261>:   add    $0x38,%rsp
   0x000000000040421f <+265>:   pop    %rbx
   0x0000000000404220 <+266>:   pop    %rbp
   0x0000000000404221 <+267>:   retq
End of assembler dump.
```

Note: The code highlighted in yellow shows that the direct member call is the same as in compiled C code, with the first call parameter as an address of the object (RDI). This also includes constructors and destructors for local variables. The only difference is a virtual call through an object pointer. Shown in blue (in green are call parameters). If we track backward the RBP-0x18 memory cell (shown in bold italics), we see it contains and address a local variable (RBP-0x30). This is most likely an object address as it is also used in other member calls:

```
[...]
   0x000000000040411f <+9>:     lea     -0x30(%rbp),%rax
   0x0000000000404123 <+13>:    mov     %rax,%rdi
   0x0000000000404126 <+16>:    callq   0x40449c <CDerived::CDerived()>
[...]
   0x0000000000404142 <+44>:    lea     -0x30(%rbp),%rax
   0x0000000000404146 <+48>:    mov     $0x5,%esi
   0x000000000040414b <+53>:    mov     %rax,%rdi
   0x000000000040414e <+56>:    callq   0x40430e <CBase::m_Proc(int, int*, int**)>
[...]
   0x000000000040416c <+86>:    lea     -0x30(%rbp),%rax
   0x0000000000404170 <+90>:    mov     %rax,-0x18(%rbp)
[...]
```

Here this address is loaded into RAX:

```
   0x0000000000404191 <+123>:   mov     -0x18(%rbp),%rax
```

Then the first memory cell it points to is loaded to RAX too:

```
   0x0000000000404195 <+127>:   mov     (%rax),%rax
```

This is a pointer to a virtual function table. The second function from it is called:

```
   0x0000000000404198 <+130>:   add     $0x8,%rax
   0x000000000040419c <+134>:   mov     (%rax),%rax
   0x00000000004041ac <+150>:   callq   *%rax
```

6.   We can now dump the object layout and corresponding virtual function table (we calculate the RBP value using the method from Exercise R4):

```
(gdb) bt
#0  0x000000000049d2f9 in raise ()
#1  0x0000000000404113 in message_box(void*, char const*, char const*, unsigned int) ()
#2  0x0000000000404201 in start_modeling() ()
#3  0x0000000000404236 in main ()

(gdb) find/g $rsp, $rsp+1000, 0x0000000000404201
0x7ffdb673f118
1 pattern found.

(gdb) x/gx 0x7ffdb673f118-8
0x7ffdb673f160: 0x00007ffdb673f160

(gdb) x/gx 0x00007ffdb673f160-0x18
0x7ffdb673f148: 0x00007ffdb673f130

(gdb) x/10a 0x00007ffdb673f130
0x7ffdb673f130: 0x58d260 <vtable for CBase+16>   0x12345678
```

```
0x7ffdb673f140: 0x14d57b0        0x7ffdb673f130
0x7ffdb673f150: 0x7ffdb673f2a8  0x400548
0x7ffdb673f160: 0x7ffdb673f180  0x404236 <main+20>
0x7ffdb673f170: 0x7ffdb673f2a8  0x100597018
```

(gdb) **x/10a** 0x58d260

```
0x58d260 <vtable for CBase+16>: 0x404388 <CBase::m_vProc(int, int*, int**)>    0x4043b8
<CBase::m_vProc2(int, int*, int**)>
0x58d270 <vtable for CBase+32>: 0x4043ec <CBase::~CBase()>     0x40441e <CBase::~CBase()>
0x58d280 <std::locale::_S_categories>:  0x58d2a0 <__gnu_cxx::category_names>    0x0
0x58d290:       0x0      0x0
0x58d2a0 <__gnu_cxx::category_names>:    0x5419f9            0x53cde4
```

Note: After VPTR that points to VTBL, we see an object member 0x12345678. All this corresponds to this pre-C++11 code:

```
class CBase
{
public:
        int m_nMember;
        char *m_psMember;

        static char s_sMember[];

        CBase()
        {
                m_nMember = 0x12345678;
                m_psMember = new char [strlen(s_sMember)+1];
        }

        bool m_Proc(int nParam, int *pnParam, int **ppnParam)
        {
                if (ppnParam && *ppnParam)
                {
                        **ppnParam = *pnParam;
                }

                if (pnParam)
                {
                        while (nParam--)
                        {
                                sleep(*pnParam);
                        }

                        *pnParam = 0;

                        return true;
                }

                return false;
        }

        virtual bool m_vProc(int nParam, int *pnParam, int **ppnParam)
        {
                return m_Proc(nParam, pnParam, ppnParam);
        }

        virtual bool m_vProc2(int nParam, int *pnParam, int **ppnParam)
        {
                return m_vProc(nParam, pnParam, ppnParam);
        }
```

```cpp
        virtual ~CBase()
        {
                delete m_psMember;
        }
};

char CBase::s_sMember[] = { "Hello Class!" };

class CDerived : public CBase
{
public:
        void m_Try ()
        {
                try
                {
                        throw -1;
                }
                catch (...)
                {
                        throw;
                }
        }
};

CDerived s_Class;

#define MB_STOP 0x100

void message_box (void *window, const char *title, const char *message, unsigned int type)
{
        std::cout << title << ": " << message << std::endl;

        if (type&MB_STOP)
        {
                raise(SIGSTOP);
        }
}

void start_modeling()
{
        try
        {
                CDerived Class;

                int nDelay = 1;
                int *pnDelay = &nDelay;

                Class.m_Proc(5, &nDelay, &pnDelay);
                Class.m_vProc(10, &nDelay, &pnDelay);

                CDerived *pClass = &Class;

                pClass->m_Proc(15, &nDelay, &pnDelay);
                pClass->m_vProc2(20, &nDelay, &pnDelay);

                Class.m_Try();
        }
        catch(...)
        {
                message_box(NULL, "Error", "Exception was caught!", MB_STOP);
        }
}
```

Note: The Virtual Call is illustrated in MCD-R6-x64.xlsx.

7.   The default Clang-generated code is different. Let's look at the core dump differences.

```
~/ADDR-Linux/x64/MemoryDumps$ gdb -c cpp-clang.148 -se cpp-clang
```

```
(gdb) set print asm-demangle on
```

```
(gdb) disassemble start_modeling
Dump of assembler code for function _Z14start_modelingv:
   0x00000000004041e0 <+0>:     push   %rbp
   0x00000000004041e1 <+1>:     mov    %rsp,%rbp
   0x00000000004041e4 <+4>:     sub    $0x70,%rsp
   0x00000000004041e8 <+8>:     lea    -0x18(%rbp),%rdi
   0x00000000004041ec <+12>:    callq  0x404380 <CDerived::CDerived()>
   0x00000000004041f1 <+17>:    jmpq   0x4041f6 <start_modeling()+22>
   0x00000000004041f6 <+22>:    movl   $0x1,-0x28(%rbp)
   0x00000000004041fd <+29>:    lea    -0x28(%rbp),%rax
   0x0000000000404201 <+33>:    mov    %rax,-0x30(%rbp)
   0x0000000000404205 <+37>:    lea    -0x18(%rbp),%rdi
   0x0000000000404209 <+41>:    mov    $0x5,%esi
   0x000000000040420e <+46>:    lea    -0x30(%rbp),%rcx
   0x0000000000404212 <+50>:    mov    %rax,%rdx
   0x0000000000404215 <+53>:    callq  0x4043e0 <CBase::m_Proc(int, int*, int**)>
   0x000000000040421a <+58>:    mov    %al,-0x39(%rbp)
   0x000000000040421d <+61>:    jmpq   0x404222 <start_modeling()+66>
   0x0000000000404222 <+66>:    lea    -0x18(%rbp),%rdi
   0x0000000000404226 <+70>:    mov    $0xa,%esi
   0x000000000040422b <+75>:    lea    -0x28(%rbp),%rdx
   0x000000000040422f <+79>:    lea    -0x30(%rbp),%rcx
   0x0000000000404233 <+83>:    callq  0x404480 <CBase::m_vProc(int, int*, int**)>
   0x0000000000404238 <+88>:    mov    %al,-0x3a(%rbp)
   0x000000000040423b <+91>:    jmpq   0x404240 <start_modeling()+96>
   0x0000000000404240 <+96>:    lea    -0x18(%rbp),%rax
   0x0000000000404244 <+100>:   mov    %rax,-0x38(%rbp)
   0x0000000000404248 <+104>:   mov    -0x38(%rbp),%rdi
   0x000000000040424c <+108>:   mov    $0xf,%esi
   0x0000000000404251 <+113>:   lea    -0x28(%rbp),%rdx
   0x0000000000404255 <+117>:   lea    -0x30(%rbp),%rcx
   0x0000000000404259 <+121>:   callq  0x4043e0 <CBase::m_Proc(int, int*, int**)>
   0x000000000040425e <+126>:   mov    %al,-0x3b(%rbp)
   0x0000000000404261 <+129>:   jmpq   0x404266 <start_modeling()+134>
   0x0000000000404266 <+134>:   mov    -0x38(%rbp),%rax
   0x000000000040426a <+138>:   mov    (%rax),%rcx
   0x000000000040426d <+141>:   mov    0x8(%rcx),%rcx
   0x0000000000404271 <+145>:   mov    $0x14,%esi
   0x0000000000404276 <+150>:   lea    -0x28(%rbp),%rdx
   0x000000000040427a <+154>:   lea    -0x30(%rbp),%rdi
   0x000000000040427e <+158>:   mov    %rdi,-0x48(%rbp)
   0x0000000000404282 <+162>:   mov    %rax,%rdi
   0x0000000000404285 <+165>:   mov    -0x48(%rbp),%rax
   0x0000000000404289 <+169>:   mov    %rcx,-0x50(%rbp)
   0x000000000040428d <+173>:   mov    %rax,%rcx
   0x0000000000404290 <+176>:   mov    -0x50(%rbp),%r8
   0x0000000000404294 <+180>:   callq  *%r8
   0x0000000000404297 <+183>:   mov    %al,-0x51(%rbp)
   0x000000000040429a <+186>:   jmpq   0x40429f <start_modeling()+191>
   0x000000000040429f <+191>:   lea    -0x18(%rbp),%rdi
   0x00000000004042a3 <+195>:   callq  0x4044c0 <CDerived::m_Try()>
   0x00000000004042a8 <+200>:   jmpq   0x4042ad <start_modeling()+205>
   0x00000000004042ad <+205>:   lea    -0x18(%rbp),%rdi
```

```
0x00000000004042b1 <+209>:    callq   0x4043c0 <CDerived::~CDerived()>
0x00000000004042b6 <+214>:    jmpq    0x40430e <start_modeling()+302>
0x00000000004042bb <+219>:    mov     %edx,%ecx
0x00000000004042bd <+221>:    mov     %rax,-0x20(%rbp)
0x00000000004042c1 <+225>:    mov     %ecx,-0x24(%rbp)
0x00000000004042c4 <+228>:    jmpq    0x4042db <start_modeling()+251>
0x00000000004042c9 <+233>:    mov     %edx,%ecx
0x00000000004042cb <+235>:    mov     %rax,-0x20(%rbp)
0x00000000004042cf <+239>:    mov     %ecx,-0x24(%rbp)
0x00000000004042d2 <+242>:    lea     -0x18(%rbp),%rdi
0x00000000004042d6 <+246>:    callq   0x4043c0 <CDerived::~CDerived()>
0x00000000004042db <+251>:    mov     -0x20(%rbp),%rdi
0x00000000004042df <+255>:    callq   0x405730 <__cxa_begin_catch>
0x00000000004042e4 <+260>:    mov     $0x53c004,%ecx
0x00000000004042e9 <+265>:    mov     %ecx,%esi
0x00000000004042eb <+267>:    mov     $0x53c00a,%ecx
0x00000000004042f0 <+272>:    mov     %ecx,%edx
0x00000000004042f2 <+274>:    xor     %ecx,%ecx
0x00000000004042f4 <+276>:    mov     %ecx,%edi
0x00000000004042f6 <+278>:    mov     $0x100,%ecx
0x00000000004042fb <+283>:    mov     %rax,-0x60(%rbp)
0x00000000004042ff <+287>:    callq   0x404150 <message_box(void*, char const*, char const*,
unsigned int)>
0x0000000000404304 <+292>:    jmpq    0x404309 <start_modeling()+297>
0x0000000000404309 <+297>:    callq   0x4057a0 <__cxa_end_catch>
0x000000000040430e <+302>:    add     $0x70,%rsp
0x0000000000404312 <+306>:    pop     %rbp
0x0000000000404313 <+307>:    retq
0x0000000000404314 <+308>:    mov     %edx,%ecx
0x0000000000404316 <+310>:    mov     %rax,-0x20(%rbp)
0x000000000040431a <+314>:    mov     %ecx,-0x24(%rbp)
0x000000000040431d <+317>:    callq   0x4057a0 <__cxa_end_catch>
0x0000000000404322 <+322>:    jmpq    0x404327 <start_modeling()+327>
0x0000000000404327 <+327>:    jmpq    0x40432c <start_modeling()+332>
0x000000000040432c <+332>:    mov     -0x20(%rbp),%rdi
0x0000000000404330 <+336>:    callq   0x492ab0 <_Unwind_Resume>
0x0000000000404335 <+341>:    mov     %edx,%ecx
0x0000000000404337 <+343>:    mov     %rax,%rdi
0x000000000040433a <+346>:    mov     %ecx,-0x64(%rbp)
0x000000000040433d <+349>:    callq   0x404550 <__clang_call_terminate>
End of assembler dump.
```

Note: The compiler code generator uses different registers for the virtual call calculations.

Exercise R6 (A64, GDB)

Goal: Learn how to map code to execution residue and reconstruct past behavior; recognize previously introduced ADDR patterns in the context of compiled C++ code.

ADDR Patterns: Virtual Call.

Memory Cell Diagrams: Virtual Call.

1.   Load a core dump *cpp.85775* and *cpp* executable from A64/MemoryDumps directory:

```
~/ADDR-Linux/A64/MemoryDumps$ gdb -c cpp.85775 -se cpp
GNU gdb (Ubuntu 12.0.90-0ubuntu1) 12.0.90
Copyright (C) 2022 Free Software Foundation, Inc.
License GPLv3+: GNU GPL version 3 or later <http://gnu.org/licenses/gpl.html>
This is free software: you are free to change and redistribute it.
There is NO WARRANTY, to the extent permitted by law.
Type "show copying" and "show warranty" for details.
This GDB was configured as "aarch64-linux-gnu".
Type "show configuration" for configuration details.
For bug reporting instructions, please see:
<https://www.gnu.org/software/gdb/bugs/>.
Find the GDB manual and other documentation resources online at:
    <http://www.gnu.org/software/gdb/documentation/>.

For help, type "help".
Type "apropos word" to search for commands related to "word"...
Reading symbols from cpp...
(No debugging symbols found in cpp)

warning: Can't open file /home/ubuntu/ADDR-Linux/Source/cpp during file-backed mapping note
processing
[New LWP 85775]
Core was generated by `./cpp'.
#0  0x00000000004cb280 in __pthread_kill_implementation.constprop.0 ()
```

2.   We open a log file and set color highlighting off:

```
(gdb) set logging file R6.log
```

```
(gdb) set logging enabled on
Copying output to R6.log.
Copying debug output to R6.log.
```

```
(gdb) set style enabled off
```

3.   We get the following stack trace:

```
(gdb) bt
#0  0x00000000004cb280 in __pthread_kill_implementation.constprop.0 ()
#1  0x00000000004b6d1c in raise ()
#2  0x00000000004023c4 in message_box(void*, char const*, char const*, unsigned int) ()
#3  0x00000000004024d8 in start_modeling() ()
#4  0x0000000000402530 in main ()
```

208

4.	We now check **Call Parameters** for the *message_box* function:

```
(gdb) disassemble 0x000000000004024d8
Dump of assembler code for function _Z14start_modelingv:
   0x00000000004023d0 <+0>:     stp     x29, x30, [sp, #-96]!
   0x00000000004023d4 <+4>:     mov     x29, sp
   0x00000000004023d8 <+8>:     str     x19, [sp, #16]
   0x00000000004023dc <+12>:    adrp    x0, 0x584000
   0x00000000004023e0 <+16>:    ldr     x0, [x0, #1440]
   0x00000000004023e4 <+20>:    ldr     x1, [x0]
   0x00000000004023e8 <+24>:    str     x1, [sp, #88]
   0x00000000004023ec <+28>:    mov     x1, #0x0                      // #0
   0x00000000004023f0 <+32>:    add     x0, sp, #0x40
   0x00000000004023f4 <+36>:    bl      0x402804 <_ZN8CDerivedC2Ev>
   0x00000000004023f8 <+40>:    mov     w0, #0x1                      // #1
   0x00000000004023fc <+44>:    str     w0, [sp, #44]
   0x0000000000402400 <+48>:    add     x0, sp, #0x2c
   0x0000000000402404 <+52>:    str     x0, [sp, #48]
   0x0000000000402408 <+56>:    add     x2, sp, #0x30
   0x000000000040240c <+60>:    add     x1, sp, #0x2c
   0x0000000000402410 <+64>:    add     x0, sp, #0x40
   0x0000000000402414 <+68>:    mov     x3, x2
   0x0000000000402418 <+72>:    mov     x2, x1
   0x000000000040241c <+76>:    mov     w1, #0x5                      // #5
   0x0000000000402420 <+80>:    bl      0x402638 <_ZN5CBase6m_ProcEiPiPS0_>
   0x0000000000402424 <+84>:    add     x2, sp, #0x30
   0x0000000000402428 <+88>:    add     x1, sp, #0x2c
   0x000000000040242c <+92>:    add     x0, sp, #0x40
   0x0000000000402430 <+96>:    mov     x3, x2
   0x0000000000402434 <+100>:   mov     x2, x1
   0x0000000000402438 <+104>:   mov     w1, #0xa                      // #10
   0x000000000040243c <+108>:   bl      0x4026d8 <_ZN5CBase7m_vProcEiPiPS0_>
   0x0000000000402440 <+112>:   add     x0, sp, #0x40
   0x0000000000402444 <+116>:   str     x0, [sp, #56]
   0x0000000000402448 <+120>:   ldr     x0, [sp, #56]
   0x000000000040244c <+124>:   add     x2, sp, #0x30
   0x0000000000402450 <+128>:   add     x1, sp, #0x2c
   0x0000000000402454 <+132>:   mov     x3, x2
   0x0000000000402458 <+136>:   mov     x2, x1
   0x000000000040245c <+140>:   mov     w1, #0xf                      // #15
   0x0000000000402460 <+144>:   bl      0x402638 <_ZN5CBase6m_ProcEiPiPS0_>
   0x0000000000402464 <+148>:   ldr     x0, [sp, #56]
   0x0000000000402468 <+152>:   ldr     x0, [x0]
   0x000000000040246c <+156>:   add     x0, x0, #0x8
   0x0000000000402470 <+160>:   ldr     x4, [x0]
--Type <RET> for more, q to quit, c to continue without paging--
   0x0000000000402474 <+164>:   ldr     x0, [sp, #56]
   0x0000000000402478 <+168>:   add     x2, sp, #0x30
   0x000000000040247c <+172>:   add     x1, sp, #0x2c
   0x0000000000402480 <+176>:   mov     x3, x2
   0x0000000000402484 <+180>:   mov     x2, x1
   0x0000000000402488 <+184>:   mov     w1, #0x14                     // #20
   0x000000000040248c <+188>:   blr     x4
   0x0000000000402490 <+192>:   add     x0, sp, #0x40
   0x0000000000402494 <+196>:   bl      0x4027bc <_ZN8CDerived5m_TryEv>
   0x0000000000402498 <+200>:   add     x0, sp, #0x40
   0x000000000040249c <+204>:   bl      0x402834 <_ZN8CDerivedD2Ev>
   0x00000000004024a0 <+208>:   b       0x4024f0 <_Z14start_modelingv+288>
   0x00000000004024a4 <+212>:   mov     x19, x0
```

```
0x00000000004024a8 <+216>:   add     x0, sp, #0x40
0x00000000004024ac <+220>:   bl      0x402834 <_ZN8CDerivedD2Ev>
0x00000000004024b0 <+224>:   mov     x0, x19
0x00000000004024b4 <+228>:   b       0x4024b8 <_Z14start_modelingv+232>
0x00000000004024b8 <+232>:   bl      0x402fc0 <__cxa_begin_catch>
0x00000000004024bc <+236>:   mov     w3, #0x100                       // #256
0x00000000004024c0 <+240>:   adrp    x0, 0x518000 <free_mem+80>
0x00000000004024c4 <+244>:   add     x2, x0, #0x4e0
0x00000000004024c8 <+248>:   adrp    x0, 0x518000 <free_mem+80>
0x00000000004024cc <+252>:   add     x1, x0, #0x4f8
0x00000000004024d0 <+256>:   mov     x0, #0x0                         // #0
0x00000000004024d4 <+260>:   bl      0x402354 <_Z11message_boxPvPKcS1_j>
0x00000000004024d8 <+264>:   bl      0x403060 <__cxa_end_catch>
0x00000000004024dc <+268>:   b       0x4024f0 <_Z14start_modelingv+288>
0x00000000004024e0 <+272>:   mov     x19, x0
0x00000000004024e4 <+276>:   bl      0x403060 <__cxa_end_catch>
0x00000000004024e8 <+280>:   mov     x0, x19
0x00000000004024ec <+284>:   bl      0x4a3100 <_Unwind_Resume>
0x00000000004024f0 <+288>:   adrp    x0, 0x584000
0x00000000004024f4 <+292>:   ldr     x0, [x0, #1440]
0x00000000004024f8 <+296>:   ldr     x2, [sp, #88]
0x00000000004024fc <+300>:   ldr     x1, [x0]
0x0000000000402500 <+304>:   subs    x2, x2, x1
0x0000000000402504 <+308>:   mov     x1, #0x0                         // #0
0x0000000000402508 <+312>:   b.eq    0x402510 <_Z14start_modelingv+320>  // b.none
0x000000000040250c <+316>:   bl      0x4e71c0 <__stack_chk_fail_local>
0x0000000000402510 <+320>:   ldr     x19, [sp, #16]
0x0000000000402514 <+324>:   ldp     x29, x30, [sp], #96
0x0000000000402518 <+328>:   ret
--Type <RET> for more, q to quit, c to continue without paging--
End of assembler dump.
```

Note: We set C++ name de-mangling on and disassemble again:

```
(gdb) set print asm-demangle on
```

```
(gdb) disassemble 0x00000000004024d8
Dump of assembler code for function start_modeling():
   0x00000000004023d0 <+0>:    stp     x29, x30, [sp, #-96]!
   0x00000000004023d4 <+4>:    mov     x29, sp
   0x00000000004023d8 <+8>:    str     x19, [sp, #16]
   0x00000000004023dc <+12>:   adrp    x0, 0x584000
   0x00000000004023e0 <+16>:   ldr     x0, [x0, #1440]
   0x00000000004023e4 <+20>:   ldr     x1, [x0]
   0x00000000004023e8 <+24>:   str     x1, [sp, #88]
   0x00000000004023ec <+28>:   mov     x1, #0x0                         // #0
   0x00000000004023f0 <+32>:   add     x0, sp, #0x40
   0x00000000004023f4 <+36>:   bl      0x402804 <CDerived::CDerived()>
   0x00000000004023f8 <+40>:   mov     w0, #0x1                         // #1
   0x00000000004023fc <+44>:   str     w0, [sp, #44]
   0x0000000000402400 <+48>:   add     x0, sp, #0x2c
   0x0000000000402404 <+52>:   str     x0, [sp, #48]
   0x0000000000402408 <+56>:   add     x2, sp, #0x30
   0x000000000040240c <+60>:   add     x1, sp, #0x2c
   0x0000000000402410 <+64>:   add     x0, sp, #0x40
   0x0000000000402414 <+68>:   mov     x3, x2
   0x0000000000402418 <+72>:   mov     x2, x1
   0x000000000040241c <+76>:   mov     w1, #0x5                         // #5
```

```
   0x0000000000402420 <+80>:    bl      0x402638 <CBase::m_Proc(int, int*, int**)>
   0x0000000000402424 <+84>:    add     x2, sp, #0x30
   0x0000000000402428 <+88>:    add     x1, sp, #0x2c
   0x000000000040242c <+92>:    add     x0, sp, #0x40
   0x0000000000402430 <+96>:    mov     x3, x2
   0x0000000000402434 <+100>:   mov     x2, x1
   0x0000000000402438 <+104>:   mov     w1, #0xa                       // #10
   0x000000000040243c <+108>:   bl      0x4026d8 <CBase::m_vProc(int, int*, int**)>
   0x0000000000402440 <+112>:   add     x0, sp, #0x40
   0x0000000000402444 <+116>:   str     x0, [sp, #56]
   0x0000000000402448 <+120>:   ldr     x0, [sp, #56]
   0x000000000040244c <+124>:   add     x2, sp, #0x30
   0x0000000000402450 <+128>:   add     x1, sp, #0x2c
   0x0000000000402454 <+132>:   mov     x3, x2
   0x0000000000402458 <+136>:   mov     x2, x1
   0x000000000040245c <+140>:   mov     w1, #0xf                       // #15
   0x0000000000402460 <+144>:   bl      0x402638 <CBase::m_Proc(int, int*, int**)>
   0x0000000000402464 <+148>:   ldr     x0, [sp, #56]
   0x0000000000402468 <+152>:   ldr     x0, [x0]
   0x000000000040246c <+156>:   add     x0, x0, #0x8
   0x0000000000402470 <+160>:   ldr     x4, [x0]
--Type <RET> for more, q to quit, c to continue without paging--
   0x0000000000402474 <+164>:   ldr     x0, [sp, #56]
   0x0000000000402478 <+168>:   add     x2, sp, #0x30
   0x000000000040247c <+172>:   add     x1, sp, #0x2c
   0x0000000000402480 <+176>:   mov     x3, x2
   0x0000000000402484 <+180>:   mov     x2, x1
   0x0000000000402488 <+184>:   mov     w1, #0x14                      // #20
   0x000000000040248c <+188>:   blr     x4
   0x0000000000402490 <+192>:   add     x0, sp, #0x40
   0x0000000000402494 <+196>:   bl      0x4027bc <CDerived::m_Try()>
   0x0000000000402498 <+200>:   add     x0, sp, #0x40
   0x000000000040249c <+204>:   bl      0x402834 <CDerived::~CDerived()>
   0x00000000004024a0 <+208>:   b       0x4024f0 <start_modeling()+288>
   0x00000000004024a4 <+212>:   mov     x19, x0
   0x00000000004024a8 <+216>:   add     x0, sp, #0x40
   0x00000000004024ac <+220>:   bl      0x402834 <CDerived::~CDerived()>
   0x00000000004024b0 <+224>:   mov     x0, x19
   0x00000000004024b4 <+228>:   b       0x4024b8 <start_modeling()+232>
   0x00000000004024b8 <+232>:   bl      0x402fc0 <__cxa_begin_catch>
   0x00000000004024bc <+236>:   mov     w3, #0x100                     // #256
   0x00000000004024c0 <+240>:   adrp    x0, 0x518000 <free_mem+80>
   0x00000000004024c4 <+244>:   add     x2, x0, #0x4e0
   0x00000000004024c8 <+248>:   adrp    x0, 0x518000 <free_mem+80>
   0x00000000004024cc <+252>:   add     x1, x0, #0x4f8
   0x00000000004024d0 <+256>:   mov     x0, #0x0                       // #0
   0x00000000004024d4 <+260>:   bl      0x402354 <message_box(void*, char const*, char const*,
unsigned int)>
   0x00000000004024d8 <+264>:   bl      0x403060 <__cxa_end_catch>
   0x00000000004024dc <+268>:   b       0x4024f0 <start_modeling()+288>
   0x00000000004024e0 <+272>:   mov     x19, x0
   0x00000000004024e4 <+276>:   bl      0x403060 <__cxa_end_catch>
   0x00000000004024e8 <+280>:   mov     x0, x19
   0x00000000004024ec <+284>:   bl      0x4a3100 <_Unwind_Resume>
   0x00000000004024f0 <+288>:   adrp    x0, 0x584000
   0x00000000004024f4 <+292>:   ldr     x0, [x0, #1440]
   0x00000000004024f8 <+296>:   ldr     x2, [sp, #88]
   0x00000000004024fc <+300>:   ldr     x1, [x0]
   0x0000000000402500 <+304>:   subs    x2, x2, x1
```

```
0x0000000000402504 <+308>:   mov    x1, #0x0                          // #0
0x0000000000402508 <+312>:   b.eq   0x402510 <start_modeling()+320>  // b.none
0x000000000040250c <+316>:   bl     0x4e71c0 <__stack_chk_fail_local>
0x0000000000402510 <+320>:   ldr    x19, [sp, #16]
0x0000000000402514 <+324>:   ldp    x29, x30, [sp], #96
0x0000000000402518 <+328>:   ret
--Type <RET> for more, q to quit, c to continue without paging--
End of assembler dump.
```

Note: This function has 4 call parameters:

```
void message_box (void *window, const char *title, const char *message, unsigned int type);
```

We see that *window* is NULL (X0), *type* is 0x100 (W3), *title* and *message* are **Static Variables** whose addresses are loaded to X1 and X2:

```
(gdb) x/s 0x518000+0x4f8
0x5184f8:       "Error"
```

```
(gdb) x/s 0x518000+0x4e0
0x5184e0:       "Exception was caught!"
```

Note: We see that we are actually in the catch block. Let's look at the previous **Last Calls**:

```
0x0000000000402490 <+192>:   add    x0, sp, #0x40
0x0000000000402494 <+196>:   bl     0x4027bc <CDerived::m_Try()>
0x0000000000402498 <+200>:   add    x0, sp, #0x40
0x000000000040249c <+204>:   bl     0x402834 <CDerived::~CDerived()>
0x00000000004024a0 <+208>:   b      0x4024f0 <start_modeling()+288>
0x00000000004024a4 <+212>:   mov    x19, x0
0x00000000004024a8 <+216>:   add    x0, sp, #0x40
0x00000000004024ac <+220>:   bl     0x402834 <CDerived::~CDerived()>
0x00000000004024b0 <+224>:   mov    x0, x19
0x00000000004024b4 <+228>:   b      0x4024b8 <start_modeling()+232>
0x00000000004024b8 <+232>:   bl     0x402fc0 <__cxa_begin_catch>
```

Note: The class object is a **Local Variable**, and its address SP+0x40 is loaded into X0. We don't see any other **Call Parameters** so that the member function may have a *void* parameter list. So let's look at execution residue, past survived addresses in the raw stack region just before the current SP address, and try to find those last calls:

```
(gdb) x/1024a $sp-0x2000
0xffffdec6c880: 0xffffdec6e108   0xffffdec6c788
0xffffdec6c890: 0x0      0x0
0xffffdec6c8a0: 0x0      0x0
0xffffdec6c8b0: 0x0      0x0
0xffffdec6c8c0: 0x0      0x0
0xffffdec6c8d0: 0x0      0x0
0xffffdec6c8e0: 0x0      0x0
0xffffdec6c8f0: 0x0      0x0
0xffffdec6c900: 0x0      0x0
0xffffdec6c910: 0x0      0x0
0xffffdec6c920: 0x0      0x0
0xffffdec6c930: 0x0      0x0
0xffffdec6c940: 0x0      0x0
0xffffdec6c950: 0x0      0x0
0xffffdec6c960: 0x0      0x0
```

```
0xffffdec6c970: 0x0      0x0
0xffffdec6c980: 0x0      0x0
0xffffdec6c990: 0x0      0x0
0xffffdec6c9a0: 0x0      0x0
0xffffdec6c9b0: 0x0      0x0
0xffffdec6c9c0: 0x0      0x0
0xffffdec6c9d0: 0xffffdec6e180  0xffffdec6e188
0xffffdec6c9e0: 0xffffdec6e190  0xffffdec6e198
0xffffdec6c9f0: 0xffffdec6e1a0  0xffffdec6e1a8
0xffffdec6ca00: 0xffffdec6caa0  0x4a5268 <_Unwind_Find_FDE+216>
0xffffdec6ca10: 0x587248 <object>        0x4027f3 <CDerived::m_Try()+55>
0xffffdec6ca20: 0xffffdec6d6c0  0xffffdec6d9e8
0xffffdec6ca30: 0x3      0x583000 <tunable_list+512>
0xffffdec6ca40: 0x589000 <(anonymous namespace)::ctype_w+240>   0x0
0xffffdec6ca50: 0x400280 <_init>         0x585030
0xffffdec6ca60: 0xffffdec6ca90  0x4038cc <__gxx_personality_v0+236>
0xffffdec6ca70: 0xffffdec6d6c0  0x0
0xffffdec6ca80: 0x23e29220      0x2
0xffffdec6ca90: 0xffffdec6cb80  0x4a2a7c <_Unwind_RaiseException_Phase2+124>
0xffffdec6caa0: 0xffffdec6d6c0  0x0
0xffffdec6cab0: 0x23e29220      0xffffdec6cbc0
0xffffdec6cac0: 0x3      0xffffdec6da80
0xffffdec6cad0: 0x18     0x0
0xffffdec6cae0: 0x400280 <_init>         0x585030
0xffffdec6caf0: 0x400280 <_init>         0x563ad8
0xffffdec6cb00: 0x0      0xffffdec6cb48
0xffffdec6cb10: 0x0      0x0
--Type <RET> for more, q to quit, c to continue without paging--
0xffffdec6cb20: 0xdec6cb80       0x0
0xffffdec6cb30: 0x34     0x4
0xffffdec6cb40: 0x38     0x4027bc <CDerived::m_Try()>
0xffffdec6cb50: 0x4027bc <CDerived::m_Try()>     0x0
0xffffdec6cb60: 0x563af0         0x563ae9
0xffffdec6cb70: 0xffffdec6019b  0x7bac1c2ec8be0b00
0xffffdec6cb80: 0xffffdec6d240  0x4a2fd8 <_Unwind_RaiseException+324>
0xffffdec6cb90: 0xffffdec6d6c0  0x23e29220
0xffffdec6cba0: 0xffffdec6d300  0xffffdec6da80
0xffffdec6cbb0: 0x9      0x579200
0xffffdec6cbc0: 0x0      0x0
0xffffdec6cbd0: 0x0      0x0
0xffffdec6cbe0: 0x0      0x0
0xffffdec6cbf0: 0x0      0x0
0xffffdec6cc00: 0x0      0x0
0xffffdec6cc10: 0x0      0x0
0xffffdec6cc20: 0x0      0x0
0xffffdec6cc30: 0x0      0x0
0xffffdec6cc40: 0x0      0x0
0xffffdec6cc50: 0x0      0x0
0xffffdec6cc60: 0x0      0x0
0xffffdec6cc70: 0x0      0x0
0xffffdec6cc80: 0x0      0x0
0xffffdec6cc90: 0x0      0x0
0xffffdec6cca0: 0x0      0x0
0xffffdec6ccb0: 0x0      0x0
0xffffdec6ccc0: 0x0      0x0
0xffffdec6ccd0: 0x0      0x0
0xffffdec6cce0: 0x0      0x0
0xffffdec6ccf0: 0xffffffffffffffe0       0x1
0xffffdec6cd00: 0x0      0x0
```

```
0xffffdec6cd10: 0x0          0x0
0xffffdec6cd20: 0x0          0x0
0xffffdec6cd30: 0x0          0x0
0xffffdec6cd40: 0x0          0x0
0xffffdec6cd50: 0x0          0x0
0xffffdec6cd60: 0x0          0x0
0xffffdec6cd70: 0x0          0x0
0xffffdec6cd80: 0x0          0x0
0xffffdec6cd90: 0xffffffffffffffd0      0x1
0xffffdec6cda0: 0xffffffffffffffd8      0x1
0xffffdec6cdb0: 0x0          0x0
--Type <RET> for more, q to quit, c to continue without paging--
0xffffdec6cdc0: 0x0          0x0
0xffffdec6cdd0: 0x0          0x0
0xffffdec6cde0: 0x0          0x0
0xffffdec6cdf0: 0x0          0x0
0xffffdec6ce00: 0x0          0x0
0xffffdec6ce10: 0x0          0x0
0xffffdec6ce20: 0x0          0x0
0xffffdec6ce30: 0x0          0x0
0xffffdec6ce40: 0x0          0x0
0xffffdec6ce50: 0x0          0x0
0xffffdec6ce60: 0x0          0x0
0xffffdec6ce70: 0x0          0x0
0xffffdec6ce80: 0x0          0x0
0xffffdec6ce90: 0x0          0x0
0xffffdec6cea0: 0x0          0x0
0xffffdec6ceb0: 0x0          0x0
0xffffdec6cec0: 0x0          0x0
0xffffdec6ced0: 0x0          0x0
0xffffdec6cee0: 0x0          0x0
0xffffdec6cef0: 0x0          0x0
0xffffdec6cf00: 0x0          0x0
0xffffdec6cf10: 0x0          0x0
0xffffdec6cf20: 0x0          0x0
0xffffdec6cf30: 0x0          0x0
0xffffdec6cf40: 0x0          0x0
0xffffdec6cf50: 0x0          0x0
0xffffdec6cf60: 0x0          0x0
0xffffdec6cf70: 0x0          0x0
0xffffdec6cf80: 0x0          0x0
0xffffdec6cf90: 0x0          0x0
0xffffdec6cfa0: 0x0          0x0
0xffffdec6cfb0: 0x0          0x0
0xffffdec6cfc0: 0x0          0x0
0xffffdec6cfd0: 0x0          0x0
0xffffdec6cfe0: 0x0          0x0
0xffffdec6cff0: 0x0          0x0
0xffffdec6d000: 0x0          0x0
0xffffdec6d010: 0x0          0x0
0xffffdec6d020: 0x0          0x0
0xffffdec6d030: 0x0          0x0
0xffffdec6d040: 0x0          0x0
0xffffdec6d050: 0x0          0x0
--Type <RET> for more, q to quit, c to continue without paging--
0xffffdec6d060: 0x0          0x0
0xffffdec6d070: 0x0          0x0
0xffffdec6d080: 0x0          0x0
0xffffdec6d090: 0x0          0x0
```

```
0xffffdec6d0a0: 0x0        0x0
0xffffdec6d0b0: 0x0        0x0
0xffffdec6d0c0: 0x0        0x0
0xffffdec6d0d0: 0x0        0x0
0xffffdec6d0e0: 0x0        0x0
0xffffdec6d0f0: 0x0        0x0
0xffffdec6d100: 0x0        0x0
0xffffdec6d110: 0x0        0x0
0xffffdec6d120: 0x0        0x0
0xffffdec6d130: 0x0        0x0
0xffffdec6d140: 0x0        0x0
0xffffdec6d150: 0x0        0x0
0xffffdec6d160: 0x0        0x0
0xffffdec6d170: 0x0        0x0
0xffffdec6d180: 0x0        0x0
0xffffdec6d190: 0x0        0x0
0xffffdec6d1a0: 0x0        0x0
0xffffdec6d1b0: 0x0        0x0
0xffffdec6d1c0: 0x0        0x0
0xffffdec6d1d0: 0x0        0x0
0xffffdec6d1e0: 0x0        0x30
0xffffdec6d1f0: 0xffffdec6d240   0x4a2ff0 <_Unwind_RaiseException+348>
0xffffdec6d200: 0xffffdec6d6c0   0x23e29220
0xffffdec6d210: 0xffffdec6d300   0xffffdec6da80
0xffffdec6d220: 0x9        0x579200
0xffffdec6d230: 0x11b1b    0xffffdec6e970
0xffffdec6d240: 0xffffdec6e970   0x4027f4 <CDerived::m_Try()+56>
0xffffdec6d250: 0x23e29220     0x0
0xffffdec6d260: 0x57cfe0 <typeinfo for int>      0x474e5543432b2b00
0xffffdec6d270: 0x1        0xffffdec6ebd8
0xffffdec6d280: 0x9        0xffffdec6ebe8
0xffffdec6d290: 0x9        0x579200
0xffffdec6d2a0: 0x18       0x0
0xffffdec6d2b0: 0x400280 <_init>        0x585030
0xffffdec6d2c0: 0x0        0x0
0xffffdec6d2d0: 0x0        0x0
0xffffdec6d2e0: 0x0        0x0
0xffffdec6d2f0: 0x0        0x0
--Type <RET> for more, q to quit, c to continue without paging--
0xffffdec6d300: 0xffffdec6d250   0xffffdec6d258
0xffffdec6d310: 0xffffdec6d260   0xffffdec6d268
0xffffdec6d320: 0x0        0x0
0xffffdec6d330: 0x0        0x0
0xffffdec6d340: 0x0        0x0
0xffffdec6d350: 0x0        0x0
0xffffdec6d360: 0x0        0x0
0xffffdec6d370: 0x0        0x0
0xffffdec6d380: 0x0        0x0
0xffffdec6d390: 0x0        0xffffdec6d270
0xffffdec6d3a0: 0xffffdec6d278   0xffffdec6d280
0xffffdec6d3b0: 0xffffdec6d288   0xffffdec6d290
0xffffdec6d3c0: 0xffffdec6d298   0xffffdec6d2a0
0xffffdec6d3d0: 0xffffdec6d2a8   0xffffdec6d2b0
0xffffdec6d3e0: 0xffffdec6d2b8   0xffffdec6d240
0xffffdec6d3f0: 0xffffdec6d248   0x0
0xffffdec6d400: 0x0        0x0
0xffffdec6d410: 0x0        0x0
0xffffdec6d420: 0x0        0x0
0xffffdec6d430: 0x0        0x0
```

```
0xffffdec6d440: 0x0       0x0
0xffffdec6d450: 0x0       0x0
0xffffdec6d460: 0x0       0x0
0xffffdec6d470: 0x0       0x0
0xffffdec6d480: 0x0       0x0
0xffffdec6d490: 0x0       0x0
0xffffdec6d4a0: 0x0       0x0
0xffffdec6d4b0: 0x0       0x0
0xffffdec6d4c0: 0x0       0x0
0xffffdec6d4d0: 0x0       0x0
0xffffdec6d4e0: 0x0       0x0
0xffffdec6d4f0: 0x0       0x0
0xffffdec6d500: 0x0       0x0
0xffffdec6d510: 0x0       0x0
0xffffdec6d520: 0x0       0x0
0xffffdec6d530: 0x0       0x0
0xffffdec6d540: 0xffffdec6d2c0  0xffffdec6d2c8
0xffffdec6d550: 0xffffdec6d2d0  0xffffdec6d2d8
0xffffdec6d560: 0xffffdec6d2e0  0xffffdec6d2e8
0xffffdec6d570: 0xffffdec6d2f0  0xffffdec6d2f8
0xffffdec6d580: 0x0       0x0
0xffffdec6d590: 0x0       0x0
--Type <RET> for more, q to quit, c to continue without paging--
0xffffdec6d5a0: 0x0       0x0
0xffffdec6d5b0: 0x0       0x0
0xffffdec6d5c0: 0x0       0x0
0xffffdec6d5d0: 0x0       0x0
0xffffdec6d5e0: 0xffffdec6da30  0x4a1978 <uw_update_context+24>
0xffffdec6d5f0: 0xffffdec6daa0  0xffffdec6e5b0
0xffffdec6d600: 0x23e29220     0xffffdec6daa0
0xffffdec6d610: 0x2       0xffffdec6e1e8
0xffffdec6d620: 0x18      0x0
0xffffdec6d630: 0x400280 <_init>        0x585030
0xffffdec6d640: 0x589d60 <dwarf_reg_size_table> 0xffffdec6daa0
0xffffdec6d650: 0xffffdec6e5b0  0x4000000000000000
0xffffdec6d660: 0x589d60 <dwarf_reg_size_table> 0xffffdec6e970
0xffffdec6d670: 0xffffdec6e130  0xffffdec6e138
0xffffdec6d680: 0xffffdec6e140  0xffffdec6e148
0xffffdec6d690: 0x0       0x0
0xffffdec6d6a0: 0x0       0x0
0xffffdec6d6b0: 0x0       0x0
0xffffdec6d6c0: 0x0       0x0
0xffffdec6d6d0: 0x0       0x0
0xffffdec6d6e0: 0x0       0x0
0xffffdec6d6f0: 0x0       0x0
0xffffdec6d700: 0x0       0xffffdec6e150
0xffffdec6d710: 0xffffdec6e158  0xffffdec6e160
0xffffdec6d720: 0xffffdec6e168  0xffffdec6e170
0xffffdec6d730: 0xffffdec6e178  0xffffdec6e180
0xffffdec6d740: 0xffffdec6e188  0xffffdec6e190
0xffffdec6d750: 0xffffdec6e198  0xffffdec6e120
0xffffdec6d760: 0xffffdec6e128  0xffffdec6d668
0xffffdec6d770: 0x0       0x0
0xffffdec6d780: 0x0       0x0
0xffffdec6d790: 0x0       0x0
0xffffdec6d7a0: 0x0       0x0
0xffffdec6d7b0: 0x0       0x0
0xffffdec6d7c0: 0x0       0x0
0xffffdec6d7d0: 0x0       0x0
```

```
0xffffdec6d7e0: 0x0       0x0
0xffffdec6d7f0: 0x0       0x0
0xffffdec6d800: 0x0       0x0
0xffffdec6d810: 0x0       0x0
0xffffdec6d820: 0x0       0x0
0xffffdec6d830: 0x0       0x0
--Type <RET> for more, q to quit, c to continue without paging--
0xffffdec6d840: 0x0       0x0
0xffffdec6d850: 0x0       0x0
0xffffdec6d860: 0x0       0x0
0xffffdec6d870: 0x0       0x0
0xffffdec6d880: 0x0       0x0
0xffffdec6d890: 0x0       0x0
0xffffdec6d8a0: 0x0       0x0
0xffffdec6d8b0: 0xffffdec6e1a0  0xffffdec6e1a8
0xffffdec6d8c0: 0xffffdec6e1b0  0xffffdec6e1b8
0xffffdec6d8d0: 0xffffdec6e1c0  0xffffdec6e1c8
0xffffdec6d8e0: 0xffffdec6d980  0x4a5268 <_Unwind_Find_FDE+216>
0xffffdec6d8f0: 0x587248 <object>        0x402497 <start_modeling()+199>
0xffffdec6d900: 0xffffdec6e5b0  0xffffdec6e8d8
0xffffdec6d910: 0x2       0x583000 <tunable_list+512>
0xffffdec6d920: 0x589000 <(anonymous namespace)::ctype_w+240>    0x0
0xffffdec6d930: 0x400280 <_init>        0x585030
0xffffdec6d940: 0x0       0xb
0xffffdec6d950: 0x0       0x0
0xffffdec6d960: 0x0       0x4023d0 <start_modeling()>
0xffffdec6d970: 0xffffdec6da60  0x4a2a7c <_Unwind_RaiseException_Phase2+124>
0xffffdec6d980: 0xffffdec6e5b0  0x4
0xffffdec6d990: 0x23e29220      0xffffdec6daa0
0xffffdec6d9a0: 0x2       0xffffdec6e1e8
0xffffdec6d9b0: 0x18      0x0
0xffffdec6d9c0: 0x400280 <_init>        0x585030
0xffffdec6d9d0: 0x400280 <_init>        0x563af0
0xffffdec6d9e0: 0x0       0x0
0xffffdec6d9f0: 0x1       0x0
0xffffdec6da00: 0xdec6da60       0x0
0xffffdec6da10: 0xffffdec6e5b0  0x0
0xffffdec6da20: 0x23e29220      0xffffdec6daa0
0xffffdec6da30: 0x2       0xffffdec6e1e8
0xffffdec6da40: 0x18      0x0
0xffffdec6da50: 0xffffdec6019b  0x7bac1c2ec8be0b00
0xffffdec6da60: 0xffffdec6e120  0x4a3180 <_Unwind_Resume+128>
0xffffdec6da70: 0x23e29220      0xffffdec6e1f0
0xffffdec6da80: 0xffffdec6e5b0  0xffffdec6ebe8
0xffffdec6da90: 0x9       0x579200
0xffffdec6daa0: 0x0       0x0
0xffffdec6dab0: 0x0       0x0
0xffffdec6dac0: 0x0       0x0
0xffffdec6dad0: 0x0       0x0
--Type <RET> for more, q to quit, c to continue without paging--
0xffffdec6dae0: 0x0       0x0
0xffffdec6daf0: 0x0       0x0
0xffffdec6db00: 0x0       0x0
0xffffdec6db10: 0x0       0x0
0xffffdec6db20: 0x0       0x0
0xffffdec6db30: 0x0       0x0
0xffffdec6db40: 0x0       0x0
0xffffdec6db50: 0x0       0x0
0xffffdec6db60: 0x0       0x0
```

```
0xffffdec6db70:  0x0        0x0
0xffffdec6db80:  0x0        0x0
0xffffdec6db90:  0x0        0x0
0xffffdec6dba0:  0x0        0x0
0xffffdec6dbb0:  0x0        0x0
0xffffdec6dbc0:  0x0        0x0
0xffffdec6dbd0:  0xfffffffffffffffb0    0x1
0xffffdec6dbe0:  0x0        0x0
0xffffdec6dbf0:  0x0        0x0
0xffffdec6dc00:  0x0        0x0
0xffffdec6dc10:  0x0        0x0
0xffffdec6dc20:  0x0        0x0
0xffffdec6dc30:  0x0        0x0
0xffffdec6dc40:  0x0        0x0
0xffffdec6dc50:  0x0        0x0
0xffffdec6dc60:  0x0        0x0
0xffffdec6dc70:  0xfffffffffffffffa0    0x1
0xffffdec6dc80:  0xfffffffffffffffa8    0x1
0xffffdec6dc90:  0x0        0x0
0xffffdec6dca0:  0x0        0x0
0xffffdec6dcb0:  0x0        0x0
0xffffdec6dcc0:  0x0        0x0
0xffffdec6dcd0:  0x0        0x0
0xffffdec6dce0:  0x0        0x0
0xffffdec6dcf0:  0x0        0x0
0xffffdec6dd00:  0x0        0x0
0xffffdec6dd10:  0x0        0x0
0xffffdec6dd20:  0x0        0x0
0xffffdec6dd30:  0x0        0x0
0xffffdec6dd40:  0x0        0x0
0xffffdec6dd50:  0x0        0x0
0xffffdec6dd60:  0x0        0x0
0xffffdec6dd70:  0x0        0x0
--Type <RET> for more, q to quit, c to continue without paging--
0xffffdec6dd80:  0x0        0x0
0xffffdec6dd90:  0x0        0x0
0xffffdec6dda0:  0x0        0x0
0xffffdec6ddb0:  0x0        0x0
0xffffdec6ddc0:  0x0        0x0
0xffffdec6ddd0:  0x0        0x0
0xffffdec6dde0:  0x0        0x0
0xffffdec6ddf0:  0x0        0x0
0xffffdec6de00:  0x0        0x0
0xffffdec6de10:  0x0        0x0
0xffffdec6de20:  0x0        0x0
0xffffdec6de30:  0x0        0x0
0xffffdec6de40:  0x0        0x0
0xffffdec6de50:  0x0        0x0
0xffffdec6de60:  0x0        0x0
0xffffdec6de70:  0x0        0x0
0xffffdec6de80:  0x0        0x0
0xffffdec6de90:  0x0        0x0
0xffffdec6dea0:  0x0        0x0
0xffffdec6deb0:  0x0        0x0
0xffffdec6dec0:  0x0        0x0
0xffffdec6ded0:  0x0        0x0
0xffffdec6dee0:  0x0        0x0
0xffffdec6def0:  0x0        0x0
0xffffdec6df00:  0x0        0x0
```

218

```
0xffffdec6df10: 0x0      0x0
0xffffdec6df20: 0x0      0x0
0xffffdec6df30: 0x0      0x0
0xffffdec6df40: 0x0      0x0
0xffffdec6df50: 0x0      0x0
0xffffdec6df60: 0x0      0x0
0xffffdec6df70: 0x0      0x0
0xffffdec6df80: 0x0      0x0
0xffffdec6df90: 0x0      0x0
0xffffdec6dfa0: 0x0      0x0
0xffffdec6dfb0: 0x0      0x0
0xffffdec6dfc0: 0x0      0x0
0xffffdec6dfd0: 0x0      0x0
0xffffdec6dfe0: 0x0      0x0
0xffffdec6dff0: 0x0      0x0
0xffffdec6e000: 0x0      0x0
0xffffdec6e010: 0x0      0x0
--Type <RET> for more, q to quit, c to continue without paging--
0xffffdec6e020: 0x0      0x0
0xffffdec6e030: 0x0      0x0
0xffffdec6e040: 0x0      0x0
0xffffdec6e050: 0x0      0x0
0xffffdec6e060: 0x0      0x0
0xffffdec6e070: 0x0      0x0
0xffffdec6e080: 0x0      0x0
0xffffdec6e090: 0x0      0x0
0xffffdec6e0a0: 0x0      0x0
0xffffdec6e0b0: 0x0      0x0
0xffffdec6e0c0: 0x0      0x60
0xffffdec6e0d0: 0xffffdec6e120   0x4a3194 <_Unwind_Resume+148>
0xffffdec6e0e0: 0x23e29220       0xffffdec6e1f0
0xffffdec6e0f0: 0xffffdec6e5b0   0xffffdec6ebe8
0xffffdec6e100: 0x9      0x579200
0xffffdec6e110: 0x11b1b 0xffffdec6e9a0
0xffffdec6e120: 0xffffdec6e9a0   0x4024a4 <start_modeling()+212>
0xffffdec6e130: 0x23e29220       0x1
0xffffdec6e140: 0x0      0x0
0xffffdec6e150: 0x1      0xffffdec6ebd8
0xffffdec6e160: 0x9      0xffffdec6ebe8
0xffffdec6e170: 0x9      0x579200
0xffffdec6e180: 0x18     0x0
0xffffdec6e190: 0x400280 <_init>         0x585030
0xffffdec6e1a0: 0x0      0x0
0xffffdec6e1b0: 0x0      0x0
0xffffdec6e1c0: 0x0      0x0
0xffffdec6e1d0: 0x0      0x0
0xffffdec6e1e0: 0x0      0x2
0xffffdec6e1f0: 0xffffdec6e130   0xffffdec6e138
0xffffdec6e200: 0xffffdec6e140   0xffffdec6e148
0xffffdec6e210: 0x0      0x0
0xffffdec6e220: 0x0      0x0
0xffffdec6e230: 0x0      0x0
0xffffdec6e240: 0x0      0x0
0xffffdec6e250: 0x0      0x0
0xffffdec6e260: 0x0      0x0
0xffffdec6e270: 0x0      0x0
0xffffdec6e280: 0x0      0xffffdec6e150
0xffffdec6e290: 0xffffdec6e158   0xffffdec6e160
0xffffdec6e2a0: 0xffffdec6e168   0xffffdec6e170
```

219

```
0xffffdec6e2b0: 0xffffdec6e178   0xffffdec6e180
--Type <RET> for more, q to quit, c to continue without paging--
0xffffdec6e2c0: 0xffffdec6e188   0xffffdec6e190
0xffffdec6e2d0: 0xffffdec6e198   0xffffdec6e120
0xffffdec6e2e0: 0xffffdec6e128   0x0
0xffffdec6e2f0: 0x0         0x0
0xffffdec6e300: 0x0         0x0
0xffffdec6e310: 0x0         0x0
0xffffdec6e320: 0x0         0x0
0xffffdec6e330: 0x0         0x0
0xffffdec6e340: 0x0         0x0
0xffffdec6e350: 0x0         0x0
0xffffdec6e360: 0x0         0x0
0xffffdec6e370: 0x0         0x0
0xffffdec6e380: 0x0         0x0
0xffffdec6e390: 0x0         0x0
0xffffdec6e3a0: 0x0         0x0
0xffffdec6e3b0: 0x0         0x0
0xffffdec6e3c0: 0x0         0x0
0xffffdec6e3d0: 0x0         0x0
0xffffdec6e3e0: 0x0         0x0
0xffffdec6e3f0: 0x0         0x0
0xffffdec6e400: 0x0         0x0
0xffffdec6e410: 0x0         0x0
0xffffdec6e420: 0x0         0x0
0xffffdec6e430: 0xffffdec6e1a0   0xffffdec6e1a8
0xffffdec6e440: 0xffffdec6e1b0   0xffffdec6e1b8
0xffffdec6e450: 0xffffdec6e1c0   0xffffdec6e1c8
0xffffdec6e460: 0xffffdec6e1d0   0xffffdec6e1d8
0xffffdec6e470: 0x0         0x0
0xffffdec6e480: 0x0         0x0
0xffffdec6e490: 0x0         0x0
0xffffdec6e4a0: 0x0         0x0
0xffffdec6e4b0: 0x0         0x0
0xffffdec6e4c0: 0x0         0x0
0xffffdec6e4d0: 0x0         0x0
0xffffdec6e4e0: 0x0         0x0
0xffffdec6e4f0: 0x0         0x0
0xffffdec6e500: 0xffffdec6e970   0x402804 <CDerived::CDerived()>
0xffffdec6e510: 0x0         0x0
0xffffdec6e520: 0x0         0x4a3100 <_Unwind_Resume>
0xffffdec6e530: 0x4000000000000000       0x0
0xffffdec6e540: 0x0         0x0
0xffffdec6e550: 0x0         0x0
--Type <RET> for more, q to quit, c to continue without paging--
0xffffdec6e560: 0x0         0x0
0xffffdec6e570: 0x0         0x0
0xffffdec6e580: 0x0         0x0
0xffffdec6e590: 0x0         0x0
0xffffdec6e5a0: 0x0         0x0
0xffffdec6e5b0: 0xffffdec6e130   0xffffdec6e138
0xffffdec6e5c0: 0xffffdec6e140   0xffffdec6e148
0xffffdec6e5d0: 0x0         0x0
0xffffdec6e5e0: 0x0         0x0
0xffffdec6e5f0: 0x0         0x0
0xffffdec6e600: 0x0         0x0
0xffffdec6e610: 0x0         0x0
0xffffdec6e620: 0xffffdec6e6e0   0x4d19f0 <malloc+448>
0xffffdec6e630: 0x585b60 <main_arena>    0x400
```

```
0xffffdec6e640: 0x23e167c0        0x23e16868
0xffffdec6e650: 0x5184e0          0x1
0xffffdec6e660: 0x23e16000        0x0
0xffffdec6e670: 0x0       0x585030
0xffffdec6e680: 0xffffdec6e188  0xffff00000040
0xffffdec6e690: 0x585b60 <main_arena>   0x10
0xffffdec6e6a0: 0xffff00000040  0x2
0xffffdec6e6b0: 0x0       0x0
0xffffdec6e6c0: 0x770000007c      0x5d0000006e
0xffffdec6e6d0: 0x0       0x0
0xffffdec6e6e0: 0xffffdec6e710  0x4f4e78 <_IO_file_doallocate+168>
0xffffdec6e6f0: 0x583000 <tunable_list+512>      0x585710 <_IO_2_1_stdout_>
0xffffdec6e700: 0x400    0x585710 <_IO_2_1_stdout_>
0xffffdec6e710: 0xffffdec6e7e0  0x4c90ac <_IO_doallocbuf+104>
0xffffdec6e720: 0x585710 <_IO_2_1_stdout_>       0x586da0 <_IO_file_jumps>
0xffffdec6e730: 0x15     0x585710 <_IO_2_1_stdout_>
0xffffdec6e740: 0x0       0x0
0xffffdec6e750: 0x0       0x1a
0xffffdec6e760: 0x4       0x100002190
0xffffdec6e770: 0x5000003e9      0x8801
0xffffdec6e780: 0x0       0x0
0xffffdec6e790: 0x400    0x0
0xffffdec6e7a0: 0x632eb928       0x384c1382
0xffffdec6e7b0: 0x632eb928       0x384c1382
0xffffdec6e7c0: 0xffffdec6e7f0  0x4c922c <_IO_default_xsputn+140>
0xffffdec6e7d0: 0x5184f5          0x586da0 <_IO_file_jumps>
0xffffdec6e7e0: 0xffffdec6e810  0x4c82f8 <_IO_new_file_overflow+360>
0xffffdec6e7f0: 0xffffdec6e840  0x4c77b8 <_IO_new_file_xsputn+392>
--Type <RET> for more, q to quit, c to continue without paging--
0xffffdec6e800: 0x15     0x0
0xffffdec6e810: 0xffffdec6e840  0x4c709c <_IO_new_file_write+60>
0xffffdec6e820: 0x1d     0x23e31750
0xffffdec6e830: 0x585710 <_IO_2_1_stdout_>       0x1d
0xffffdec6e840: 0xffffdec6e870  0x4c6204 <new_do_write+100>
0xffffdec6e850: 0x585710 <_IO_2_1_stdout_>       0x738
0xffffdec6e860: 0x586da0 <_IO_file_jumps>        0x2a0
0xffffdec6e870: 0xffffdec6e8b0  0x4c7b40 <_IO_new_do_write+32>
```

Note: We see some references to CDerived::m_Try(), including the coincidental CDerived::m_Try()+55 that doesn't have a valid instruction address inside the disassembly. We also don't see references to CDerived::~CDerived(), though, so perhaps the destructor function was not yet called. We also see _Unwind_RaiseException references nearby. They are explained because we see __cxa_throw call and __cxa_rethrow call in a catch block inside m_Try and follow their call paths:

```
(gdb) disassemble 0x4027bc
Dump of assembler code for function CDerived::m_Try():
   0x00000000004027bc <+0>:     stp     x29, x30, [sp, #-48]!
   0x00000000004027c0 <+4>:     mov     x29, sp
   0x00000000004027c4 <+8>:     str     x19, [sp, #16]
   0x00000000004027c8 <+12>:    str     x0, [sp, #40]
   0x00000000004027cc <+16>:    mov     x0, #0x4                    // #4
   0x00000000004027d0 <+20>:    bl      0x402e80 <__cxa_allocate_exception>
   0x00000000004027d4 <+24>:    mov     w1, #0xffffffff             // #-1
   0x00000000004027d8 <+28>:    str     w1, [x0]
   0x00000000004027dc <+32>:    mov     x2, #0x0                    // #0
   0x00000000004027e0 <+36>:    adrp    x1, 0x583000 <tunable_list+512>
   0x00000000004027e4 <+40>:    ldr     x1, [x1, #3192]
```
221

```
0x00000000004027e8 <+44>:    bl      0x403fd0 <__cxa_throw>
0x00000000004027ec <+48>:    bl      0x402fc0 <__cxa_begin_catch>
0x00000000004027f0 <+52>:    bl      0x404040 <__cxa_rethrow>
0x00000000004027f4 <+56>:    mov     x19, x0
0x00000000004027f8 <+60>:    bl      0x403060 <__cxa_end_catch>
0x00000000004027fc <+64>:    mov     x0, x19
0x0000000000402800 <+68>:    bl      0x4a3100 <_Unwind_Resume>
End of assembler dump.
```

(gdb) **disassemble** __cxa_throw
```
Dump of assembler code for function __cxa_throw:
0x0000000000403fd0 <+0>:     stp     x29, x30, [sp, #-48]!
0x0000000000403fd4 <+4>:     mov     x29, sp
0x0000000000403fd8 <+8>:     stp     x19, x20, [sp, #16]
0x0000000000403fdc <+12>:    mov     x19, x0
0x0000000000403fe0 <+16>:    mov     x20, x1
0x0000000000403fe4 <+20>:    str     x21, [sp, #32]
0x0000000000403fe8 <+24>:    mov     x21, x2
0x0000000000403fec <+28>:    nop
0x0000000000403ff0 <+32>:    bl      0x4032e0 <__cxa_get_globals>
0x0000000000403ff4 <+36>:    mov     x3, x0
0x0000000000403ff8 <+40>:    mov     x2, x21
0x0000000000403ffc <+44>:    mov     x1, x20
0x0000000000404000 <+48>:    mov     x0, x19
0x0000000000404004 <+52>:    ldr     w4, [x3, #8]
0x0000000000404008 <+56>:    add     w4, w4, #0x1
0x000000000040400c <+60>:    str     w4, [x3, #8]
0x0000000000404010 <+64>:    bl      0x403f70 <__cxa_init_primary_exception>
0x0000000000404014 <+68>:    mov     x19, x0
0x0000000000404018 <+72>:    mov     w0, #0x1                        // #1
0x000000000040401c <+76>:    str     w0, [x19], #96
0x0000000000404020 <+80>:    mov     x0, x19
0x0000000000404024 <+84>:    bl      0x4a2e94 <_Unwind_RaiseException>
0x0000000000404028 <+88>:    mov     x0, x19
0x000000000040402c <+92>:    bl      0x402fc0 <__cxa_begin_catch>
0x0000000000404030 <+96>:    bl      0x403e90 <std::terminate()>
End of assembler dump.
```

(gdb) **disassemble** _Unwind_RaiseException
```
Dump of assembler code for function _Unwind_RaiseException:
0x00000000004a2e94 <+0>:     sub     sp, sp, #0xec0
0x00000000004a2e98 <+4>:     stp     x29, x30, [sp]
0x00000000004a2e9c <+8>:     mov     x29, sp
0x00000000004a2ea0 <+12>:    xpaclri
0x00000000004a2ea4 <+16>:    stp     x21, x22, [sp, #64]
0x00000000004a2ea8 <+20>:    add     x21, sp, #0xc0
0x00000000004a2eac <+24>:    add     x22, sp, #0x840
0x00000000004a2eb0 <+28>:    stp     x0, x1, [sp, #16]
0x00000000004a2eb4 <+32>:    add     x1, sp, #0xec0
0x00000000004a2eb8 <+36>:    stp     x2, x3, [sp, #32]
0x00000000004a2ebc <+40>:    mov     x2, x30
0x00000000004a2ec0 <+44>:    stp     x19, x20, [sp, #48]
0x00000000004a2ec4 <+48>:    mov     x20, x0
0x00000000004a2ec8 <+52>:    add     x19, sp, #0x480
0x00000000004a2ecc <+56>:    mov     x0, x21
0x00000000004a2ed0 <+60>:    stp     x23, x24, [sp, #80]
0x00000000004a2ed4 <+64>:    stp     x25, x26, [sp, #96]
0x00000000004a2ed8 <+68>:    stp     x27, x28, [sp, #112]
0x00000000004a2edc <+72>:    stp     d8, d9, [sp, #128]
```

```
0x00000000004a2ee0 <+76>:    stp    d10, d11, [sp, #144]
0x00000000004a2ee4 <+80>:    stp    d12, d13, [sp, #160]
0x00000000004a2ee8 <+84>:    stp    d14, d15, [sp, #176]
0x00000000004a2eec <+88>:    bl     0x4a27b4 <uw_init_context_1>
0x00000000004a2ef0 <+92>:    mov    x1, x21
0x00000000004a2ef4 <+96>:    mov    x0, x19
0x00000000004a2ef8 <+100>:   mov    x2, #0x3c0                        // #960
0x00000000004a2efc <+104>:   bl     0x4002f0
0x00000000004a2f00 <+108>:   b      0x4a2f34 <_Unwind_RaiseException+160>
0x00000000004a2f04 <+112>:   cbnz   w2, 0x4a2fa0 <_Unwind_RaiseException+268>
0x00000000004a2f08 <+116>:   ldr    x5, [sp, #3728]
0x00000000004a2f0c <+120>:   cbz    x5, 0x4a2f28 <_Unwind_RaiseException+148>
0x00000000004a2f10 <+124>:   ldr    x2, [x20]
0x00000000004a2f14 <+128>:   blr    x5
0x00000000004a2f18 <+132>:   cmp    w0, #0x6
0x00000000004a2f1c <+136>:   b.eq   0x4a2fa8 <_Unwind_RaiseException+276>  // b.none
0x00000000004a2f20 <+140>:   cmp    w0, #0x8
0x00000000004a2f24 <+144>:   b.ne   0x4a2fa0 <_Unwind_RaiseException+268>  // b.any
0x00000000004a2f28 <+148>:   mov    x1, x22
0x00000000004a2f2c <+152>:   mov    x0, x19
0x00000000004a2f30 <+156>:   bl     0x4a1960 <uw_update_context>
0x00000000004a2f34 <+160>:   mov    x1, x22
--Type <RET> for more, q to quit, c to continue without paging--
0x00000000004a2f38 <+164>:   mov    x0, x19
0x00000000004a2f3c <+168>:   bl     0x4a22b0 <uw_frame_state_for>
0x00000000004a2f40 <+172>:   mov    w2, w0
0x00000000004a2f44 <+176>:   mov    w1, #0x1                          // #1
0x00000000004a2f48 <+180>:   mov    x4, x19
0x00000000004a2f4c <+184>:   mov    x3, x20
0x00000000004a2f50 <+188>:   mov    w0, w1
0x00000000004a2f54 <+192>:   cmp    w2, #0x5
0x00000000004a2f58 <+196>:   b.ne   0x4a2f04 <_Unwind_RaiseException+112>  // b.any
0x00000000004a2f5c <+200>:   mov    x4, #0x0                          // #0
0x00000000004a2f60 <+204>:   mov    w0, w2
0x00000000004a2f64 <+208>:   ldp    x29, x30, [sp]
0x00000000004a2f68 <+212>:   ldp    x0, x1, [sp, #16]
0x00000000004a2f6c <+216>:   ldp    x2, x3, [sp, #32]
0x00000000004a2f70 <+220>:   ldp    x19, x20, [sp, #48]
0x00000000004a2f74 <+224>:   ldp    x21, x22, [sp, #64]
0x00000000004a2f78 <+228>:   ldp    x23, x24, [sp, #80]
0x00000000004a2f7c <+232>:   ldp    x25, x26, [sp, #96]
0x00000000004a2f80 <+236>:   ldp    x27, x28, [sp, #112]
0x00000000004a2f84 <+240>:   ldp    d8, d9, [sp, #128]
0x00000000004a2f88 <+244>:   ldp    d10, d11, [sp, #144]
0x00000000004a2f8c <+248>:   ldp    d12, d13, [sp, #160]
0x00000000004a2f90 <+252>:   ldp    d14, d15, [sp, #176]
0x00000000004a2f94 <+256>:   add    sp, sp, #0xec0
0x00000000004a2f98 <+260>:   add    sp, sp, x4
0x00000000004a2f9c <+264>:   ret
0x00000000004a2fa0 <+268>:   mov    w2, #0x3                          // #3
0x00000000004a2fa4 <+272>:   b      0x4a2f5c <_Unwind_RaiseException+200>
0x00000000004a2fa8 <+276>:   ldr    x4, [sp, #1936]
0x00000000004a2fac <+280>:   mov    x1, x21
0x00000000004a2fb0 <+284>:   ldr    x3, [sp, #1984]
0x00000000004a2fb4 <+288>:   mov    x2, #0x3c0                        // #960
0x00000000004a2fb8 <+292>:   mov    x0, x19
0x00000000004a2fbc <+296>:   sub    x3, x4, x3, lsr #63
0x00000000004a2fc0 <+300>:   stp    xzr, x3, [x20, #16]
0x00000000004a2fc4 <+304>:   bl     0x4002f0
```

```
    0x00000000004a2fc8 <+308>:     mov      x2, x22
    0x00000000004a2fcc <+312>:     mov      x1, x19
    0x00000000004a2fd0 <+316>:     mov      x0, x20
    0x00000000004a2fd4 <+320>:     bl       0x4a2a00 <_Unwind_RaiseException_Phase2>
    0x00000000004a2fd8 <+324>:     mov      w2, w0
    0x00000000004a2fdc <+328>:     cmp      w0, #0x7
--Type <RET> for more, q to quit, c to continue without paging--
    0x00000000004a2fe0 <+332>:     b.ne     0x4a2f5c <_Unwind_RaiseException+200>  // b.any
    0x00000000004a2fe4 <+336>:     mov      x1, x19
    0x00000000004a2fe8 <+340>:     mov      x0, x21
    0x00000000004a2fec <+344>:     bl       0x4a0ba0 <uw_install_context_1>
    0x00000000004a2ff0 <+348>:     mov      x4, x0
    0x00000000004a2ff4 <+352>:     ldr      x0, [sp, #1936]
    0x00000000004a2ff8 <+356>:     ldr      x1, [sp, #1944]
    0x00000000004a2ffc <+360>:     bl       0x4a2e90 <_Unwind_DebugHook>
    0x00000000004a3000 <+364>:     str      x1, [x29, #8]
    0x00000000004a3004 <+368>:     b        0x4a2f60 <_Unwind_RaiseException+204>
End of assembler dump.

(gdb) disassemble _Unwind_RaiseException_Phase2
Dump of assembler code for function _Unwind_RaiseException_Phase2:
    0x00000000004a2a00 <+0>:       sub      sp, sp, #0x6c0
    0x00000000004a2a04 <+4>:       stp      x29, x30, [sp]
    0x00000000004a2a08 <+8>:       mov      x29, sp
    0x00000000004a2a0c <+12>:      stp      x19, x20, [sp, #16]
    0x00000000004a2a10 <+16>:      mov      x19, x1
    0x00000000004a2a14 <+20>:      stp      x21, x22, [sp, #32]
    0x00000000004a2a18 <+24>:      mov      x21, x0
    0x00000000004a2a1c <+28>:      add      x22, sp, #0x40
    0x00000000004a2a20 <+32>:      stp      x23, x24, [sp, #48]
    0x00000000004a2a24 <+36>:      mov      x24, x2
    0x00000000004a2a28 <+40>:      mov      x23, #0x1                       // #1
    0x00000000004a2a2c <+44>:      nop
    0x00000000004a2a30 <+48>:      mov      x1, x22
    0x00000000004a2a34 <+52>:      mov      x0, x19
    0x00000000004a2a38 <+56>:      bl       0x4a22b0 <uw_frame_state_for>
    0x00000000004a2a3c <+60>:      ldr      x3, [x19, #784]
    0x00000000004a2a40 <+64>:      ldr      x1, [x19, #832]
    0x00000000004a2a44 <+68>:      ldr      x2, [x21, #24]
    0x00000000004a2a48 <+72>:      sub      x1, x3, x1, lsr #63
    0x00000000004a2a4c <+76>:      cmp      x1, x2
    0x00000000004a2a50 <+80>:      cset     w20, eq  // eq = none
    0x00000000004a2a54 <+84>:      lsl      w20, w20, #2
    0x00000000004a2a58 <+88>:      cbnz     w0, 0x4a2aa4 <_Unwind_RaiseException_Phase2+164>
    0x00000000004a2a5c <+92>:      ldr      x5, [sp, #1680]
    0x00000000004a2a60 <+96>:      cbz      x5, 0x4a2a8c <_Unwind_RaiseException_Phase2+140>
    0x00000000004a2a64 <+100>:     ldr      x2, [x21]
    0x00000000004a2a68 <+104>:     mov      x4, x19
    0x00000000004a2a6c <+108>:     mov      x3, x21
    0x00000000004a2a70 <+112>:     orr      w1, w20, #0x2
    0x00000000004a2a74 <+116>:     mov      w0, #0x1                        // #1
    0x00000000004a2a78 <+120>:     blr      x5
    0x00000000004a2a7c <+124>:     cmp      w0, #0x7
    0x00000000004a2a80 <+128>:     b.eq     0x4a2ac0 <_Unwind_RaiseException_Phase2+192>  // b.none
    0x00000000004a2a84 <+132>:     cmp      w0, #0x8
    0x00000000004a2a88 <+136>:     b.ne     0x4a2aa4 <_Unwind_RaiseException_Phase2+164>  // b.any
    0x00000000004a2a8c <+140>:     cbnz     w20, 0x4a2adc <_Unwind_RaiseException_Phase2+220>
    0x00000000004a2a90 <+144>:     add      x23, x23, #0x1
    0x00000000004a2a94 <+148>:     mov      x1, x22
```

224

```
   0x00000000004a2a98 <+152>:    mov    x0, x19
   0x00000000004a2a9c <+156>:    bl     0x4a1960 <uw_update_context>
   0x00000000004a2aa0 <+160>:    b      0x4a2a30 <_Unwind_RaiseException_Phase2+48>
--Type <RET> for more, q to quit, c to continue without paging--
   0x00000000004a2aa4 <+164>:    mov    w0, #0x2                           // #2
   0x00000000004a2aa8 <+168>:    ldp    x29, x30, [sp]
   0x00000000004a2aac <+172>:    ldp    x19, x20, [sp, #16]
   0x00000000004a2ab0 <+176>:    ldp    x21, x22, [sp, #32]
   0x00000000004a2ab4 <+180>:    ldp    x23, x24, [sp, #48]
   0x00000000004a2ab8 <+184>:    add    sp, sp, #0x6c0
   0x00000000004a2abc <+188>:    ret
   0x00000000004a2ac0 <+192>:    str    x23, [x24]
   0x00000000004a2ac4 <+196>:    ldp    x29, x30, [sp]
   0x00000000004a2ac8 <+200>:    ldp    x19, x20, [sp, #16]
   0x00000000004a2acc <+204>:    ldp    x21, x22, [sp, #32]
   0x00000000004a2ad0 <+208>:    ldp    x23, x24, [sp, #48]
   0x00000000004a2ad4 <+212>:    add    sp, sp, #0x6c0
   0x00000000004a2ad8 <+216>:    ret
   0x00000000004a2adc <+220>:    bl     0x400b18 <abort>
End of assembler dump.
```

Note: If we look at *m_Try* disassembly, we see that an exception object is allocated (address is in X0 **Call Result** and, implicitly, **Call Parameter** to __*cxa_throw*), and its size is 4 (X0 as **Call Parameter**). Then we see X0 **Pointer Dereference**, and it now contains -1 (0xffffffff). After that, we see three **Call Parameters** to the __*cxa_throw* function call. The first one is an address of exception object (X0), the second is a **Static Variable** at offset 0x583000+3192 (X1), and the last one is 0 (X2).

```
   0x00000000004027cc <+16>:    mov    x0, #0x4                           // #4
   0x00000000004027d0 <+20>:    bl     0x402e80 <__cxa_allocate_exception>
   0x00000000004027d4 <+24>:    mov    w1, #0xffffffff                    // #-1
   0x00000000004027d8 <+28>:    str    w1, [x0]
   0x00000000004027dc <+32>:    mov    x2, #0x0                           // #0
   0x00000000004027e0 <+36>:    adrp   x1, 0x583000 <tunable_list+512>
   0x00000000004027e4 <+40>:    ldr    x1, [x1, #3192]
   0x00000000004027e8 <+44>:    bl     0x403fd0 <__cxa_throw>
```

It corresponds to the following C++ code:

```
void m_Try ()
{
try
        {
                throw -1;
        }
        catch (...)
        {
                throw;
        }
}
```

5.   Let's now look at the *start_modeling* function again, where we previously found the call to the *m_Try* member function:

```
(gdb) disassemble start_modeling
Dump of assembler code for function start_modeling():
   0x00000000004023d0 <+0>:     stp     x29, x30, [sp, #-96]!
   0x00000000004023d4 <+4>:     mov     x29, sp
   0x00000000004023d8 <+8>:     str     x19, [sp, #16]
   0x00000000004023dc <+12>:    adrp    x0, 0x584000
   0x00000000004023e0 <+16>:    ldr     x0, [x0, #1440]
   0x00000000004023e4 <+20>:    ldr     x1, [x0]
   0x00000000004023e8 <+24>:    str     x1, [sp, #88]
   0x00000000004023ec <+28>:    mov     x1, #0x0                        // #0
   0x00000000004023f0 <+32>:    add     x0, sp, #0x40
   0x00000000004023f4 <+36>:    bl      0x402804 <CDerived::CDerived()>
   0x00000000004023f8 <+40>:    mov     w0, #0x1                        // #1
   0x00000000004023fc <+44>:    str     w0, [sp, #44]
   0x0000000000402400 <+48>:    add     x0, sp, #0x2c
   0x0000000000402404 <+52>:    str     x0, [sp, #48]
   0x0000000000402408 <+56>:    add     x2, sp, #0x30
   0x000000000040240c <+60>:    add     x1, sp, #0x2c
   0x0000000000402410 <+64>:    add     x0, sp, #0x40
   0x0000000000402414 <+68>:    mov     x3, x2
   0x0000000000402418 <+72>:    mov     x2, x1
   0x000000000040241c <+76>:    mov     w1, #0x5                        // #5
   0x0000000000402420 <+80>:    bl      0x402638 <CBase::m_Proc(int, int*, int**)>
   0x0000000000402424 <+84>:    add     x2, sp, #0x30
   0x0000000000402428 <+88>:    add     x1, sp, #0x2c
   0x000000000040242c <+92>:    add     x0, sp, #0x40
   0x0000000000402430 <+96>:    mov     x3, x2
   0x0000000000402434 <+100>:   mov     x2, x1
   0x0000000000402438 <+104>:   mov     w1, #0xa                        // #10
   0x000000000040243c <+108>:   bl      0x4026d8 <CBase::m_vProc(int, int*, int**)>
   0x0000000000402440 <+112>:   add     x0, sp, #0x40
   0x0000000000402444 <+116>:   str     x0, [sp, #56]
   0x0000000000402448 <+120>:   ldr     x0, [sp, #56]
   0x000000000040244c <+124>:   add     x2, sp, #0x30
   0x0000000000402450 <+128>:   add     x1, sp, #0x2c
   0x0000000000402454 <+132>:   mov     x3, x2
   0x0000000000402458 <+136>:   mov     x2, x1
   0x000000000040245c <+140>:   mov     w1, #0xf                        // #15
   0x0000000000402460 <+144>:   bl      0x402638 <CBase::m_Proc(int, int*, int**)>
   0x0000000000402464 <+148>:   ldr     x0, [sp, #56]
   0x0000000000402468 <+152>:   ldr     x0, [x0]
   0x000000000040246c <+156>:   add     x0, x0, #0x8
   0x0000000000402470 <+160>:   ldr     x4, [x0]
--Type <RET> for more, q to quit, c to continue without paging--
   0x0000000000402474 <+164>:   ldr     x0, [sp, #56]
   0x0000000000402478 <+168>:   add     x2, sp, #0x30
   0x000000000040247c <+172>:   add     x1, sp, #0x2c
   0x0000000000402480 <+176>:   mov     x3, x2
   0x0000000000402484 <+180>:   mov     x2, x1
   0x0000000000402488 <+184>:   mov     w1, #0x14                       // #20
   0x000000000040248c <+188>:   blr     x4
   0x0000000000402490 <+192>:   add     x0, sp, #0x40
   0x0000000000402494 <+196>:   bl      0x4027bc <CDerived::m_Try()>
   0x0000000000402498 <+200>:   add     x0, sp, #0x40
   0x000000000040249c <+204>:   bl      0x402834 <CDerived::~CDerived()>
   0x00000000004024a0 <+208>:   b       0x4024f0 <start_modeling()+288>
   0x00000000004024a4 <+212>:   mov     x19, x0
   0x00000000004024a8 <+216>:   add     x0, sp, #0x40
   0x00000000004024ac <+220>:   bl      0x402834 <CDerived::~CDerived()>
```

```
0x00000000004024b0 <+224>:    mov     x0, x19
0x00000000004024b4 <+228>:    b       0x4024b8 <start_modeling()+232>
0x00000000004024b8 <+232>:    bl      0x402fc0 <__cxa_begin_catch>
0x00000000004024bc <+236>:    mov     w3, #0x100                        // #256
0x00000000004024c0 <+240>:    adrp    x0, 0x518000 <free_mem+80>
0x00000000004024c4 <+244>:    add     x2, x0, #0x4e0
0x00000000004024c8 <+248>:    adrp    x0, 0x518000 <free_mem+80>
0x00000000004024cc <+252>:    add     x1, x0, #0x4f8
0x00000000004024d0 <+256>:    mov     x0, #0x0                          // #0
0x00000000004024d4 <+260>:    bl      0x402354 <message_box(void*, char const*, char const*,
unsigned int)>
0x00000000004024d8 <+264>:    bl      0x403060 <__cxa_end_catch>
0x00000000004024dc <+268>:    b       0x4024f0 <start_modeling()+288>
0x00000000004024e0 <+272>:    mov     x19, x0
0x00000000004024e4 <+276>:    bl      0x403060 <__cxa_end_catch>
0x00000000004024e8 <+280>:    mov     x0, x19
0x00000000004024ec <+284>:    bl      0x4a3100 <_Unwind_Resume>
0x00000000004024f0 <+288>:    adrp    x0, 0x584000
0x00000000004024f4 <+292>:    ldr     x0, [x0, #1440]
0x00000000004024f8 <+296>:    ldr     x2, [sp, #88]
0x00000000004024fc <+300>:    ldr     x1, [x0]
0x0000000000402500 <+304>:    subs    x2, x2, x1
0x0000000000402504 <+308>:    mov     x1, #0x0                          // #0
0x0000000000402508 <+312>:    b.eq    0x402510 <start_modeling()+320>   // b.none
0x000000000040250c <+316>:    bl      0x4e71c0 <__stack_chk_fail_local>
0x0000000000402510 <+320>:    ldr     x19, [sp, #16]
0x0000000000402514 <+324>:    ldp     x29, x30, [sp], #96
0x0000000000402518 <+328>:    ret
--Type <RET> for more, q to quit, c to continue without paging--
End of assembler dump.
```

Note: The code highlighted in yellow shows that the direct member call is the same as in compiled C code, with the first call parameter as an address of the object (X0). This also includes constructors and destructors for local variables. The only difference is a virtual call through an object pointer. Shown in blue (in green are call parameters). If we track backward the SP+56 memory cell (shown in bold italics), we see it contains and address a local variable (SP+0x40). This is most likely an object address as it is also used in other member calls:

```
[...]
0x00000000004023f0 <+32>:     add     x0, sp, #0x40
0x00000000004023f4 <+36>:     bl      0x402804 <CDerived::CDerived()>
[...]
0x0000000000402410 <+64>:     add     x0, sp, #0x40
0x0000000000402414 <+68>:     mov     x3, x2
0x0000000000402418 <+72>:     mov     x2, x1
0x000000000040241c <+76>:     mov     w1, #0x5                          // #5
0x0000000000402420 <+80>:     bl      0x402638 <CBase::m_Proc(int, int*, int**)>
[...]
0x0000000000402440 <+112>:    add     x0, sp, #0x40
0x0000000000402444 <+116>:    str     x0, [sp, #56]
[...]
```

Here this address is loaded into X0:

```
0x0000000000402464 <+148>:    ldr     x0, [sp, #56]
```

227

Then the first memory cell it points to is loaded to X0 too:

```
0x0000000000402468 <+152>:    ldr    x0, [x0]
```

This is a pointer to a virtual function table. The second function from it is called:

```
0x000000000040246c <+156>:    add    x0, x0, #0x8
0x0000000000402470 <+160>:    ldr    x4, [x0]
0x000000000040248c <+188>:    blr    x4
```

6.   We can now dump the object layout and corresponding virtual function table (we calculate the SP value using the method from Exercise R4):

```
(gdb) bt
#0  0x00000000004cb280 in __pthread_kill_implementation.constprop.0 ()
#1  0x00000000004b6d1c in raise ()
#2  0x00000000004023c4 in message_box(void*, char const*, char const*, unsigned int) ()
#3  0x00000000004024d8 in start_modeling() ()
#4  0x0000000000402530 in main ()

(gdb) find/g $sp, $sp+1000, 0x00000000004024d8
0xffffdec6e978
1 pattern found.

(gdb) x/gx 0xffffdec6e978-8
0xffffdec6e970: 0x0000ffffdec6e9a0

(gdb) x/gx 0x0000ffffdec6e9a0+56
0xffffdec6e9d8: 0x0000ffffdec6e9e0

(gdb) x/10a 0x0000ffffdec6e9e0
0xffffdec6e9e0: 0x579290 <vtable for CBase+16>   0x12345678
0xffffdec6e9f0: 0x23e291a0       0x7bac1c2ec8be0b00
0xffffdec6ea00: 0xffffdec6ea20   0x4a5464 <__libc_start_call_main+84>
0xffffdec6ea10: 0xffffdec6ebd8   0x100000002
0xffffdec6ea20: 0xffffdec6eb30   0x4a57e4 <__libc_start_main_impl+836>

(gdb) x/10a 0x579290
0x579290 <vtable for CBase+16>: 0x4026d8 <CBase::m_vProc(int, int*, int**)>     0x402710
<CBase::m_vProc2(int, int*, int**)>
0x5792a0 <vtable for CBase+32>: 0x402754 <CBase::~CBase()>       0x402794 <CBase::~CBase()>
0x5792b0 <vtable for std::__facet_shims::(anonymous namespace)::messages_shim<char>>:   0x0
0x57e0f8 <typeinfo for std::__facet_shims::(anonymous namespace)::messages_shim<char>>
0x5792c0 <vtable for std::__facet_shims::(anonymous namespace)::messages_shim<char>+16>:
0x411200 <std::__facet_shims::(anonymous namespace)::messages_shim<char>::~messages_shim()>
0x4114b0 <std::__facet_shims::(anonymous namespace)::messages_shim<char>::~messages_shim()>
0x5792d0 <vtable for std::__facet_shims::(anonymous namespace)::messages_shim<char>+32>:
0x410430 <std::__facet_shims::(anonymous namespace)::messages_shim<char>::do_open(std::string
const&, std::locale const&) const>      0x410c30 <std::__facet_shims::(anonymous
namespace)::messages_shim<char>::do_get(int, int, int, std::string const&) const>
```

Note: After VPTR that points to VTBL, we see an object member 0x12345678. All this corresponds to this pre-C++11 code:

```
class CBase
{
public:
        int m_nMember;
        char *m_psMember;

        static char s_sMember[];

        CBase()
        {
                m_nMember = 0x12345678;
                m_psMember = new char [strlen(s_sMember)+1];
        }

        bool m_Proc(int nParam, int *pnParam, int **ppnParam)
        {
                if (ppnParam && *ppnParam)
                {
                        **ppnParam = *pnParam;
                }

                if (pnParam)
                {
                        while (nParam--)
                        {
                                sleep(*pnParam);
                        }

                        *pnParam = 0;

                        return true;
                }

                return false;
        }

        virtual bool m_vProc(int nParam, int *pnParam, int **ppnParam)
        {
                return m_Proc(nParam, pnParam, ppnParam);
        }

        virtual bool m_vProc2(int nParam, int *pnParam, int **ppnParam)
        {
                return m_vProc(nParam, pnParam, ppnParam);
        }

        virtual ~CBase()
        {
                delete m_psMember;
        }
};

char CBase::s_sMember[] = { "Hello Class!" };

class CDerived : public CBase
{
public:
        void m_Try ()
        {
                try
                {
                        throw -1;
                }
```

```
                        catch (...)
                        {
                                throw;
                        }
                }
};

CDerived s_Class;

#define MB_STOP 0x100

void message_box (void *window, const char *title, const char *message, unsigned int type)
{
        std::cout << title << ": " << message << std::endl;

        if (type&MB_STOP)
        {
                raise(SIGSTOP);
        }
}

void start_modeling()
{
        try
        {
                CDerived Class;

                int nDelay = 1;
                int *pnDelay = &nDelay;

                Class.m_Proc(5, &nDelay, &pnDelay);
                Class.m_vProc(10, &nDelay, &pnDelay);

                CDerived *pClass = &Class;

                pClass->m_Proc(15, &nDelay, &pnDelay);
                pClass->m_vProc2(20, &nDelay, &pnDelay);

                Class.m_Try();
        }
        catch(...)
        {
                message_box(NULL, "Error", "Exception was caught!", MB_STOP);
        }
}
```

Note: The Virtual Call is illustrated in MCD-R6-ARM64.xlsx (offsets are hexadecimal).

7.   The default Clang-generated code is different. Let's look at the core dump differences.

```
~/ADDR-Linux/A64/MemoryDumps$ gdb -c cpp-clang.919010 -se cpp-clang

(gdb) set print asm-demangle on

(gdb) disassemble start_modeling
Dump of assembler code for function start_modeling():
   0x0000000000401444 <+0>:     sub     sp, sp, #0x50
   0x0000000000401448 <+4>:     stp     x29, x30, [sp, #64]
   0x000000000040144c <+8>:     add     x29, sp, #0x40
   0x0000000000401450 <+12>:    sub     x0, x29, #0x18
   0x0000000000401454 <+16>:    bl      0x4015b0 <CDerived::CDerived()>
   0x0000000000401458 <+20>:    b       0x40145c <start_modeling()+24>
```

230

```
0x000000000040145c <+24>:    add    x2, sp, #0x18
0x0000000000401460 <+28>:    mov    w8, #0x1                        // #1
0x0000000000401464 <+32>:    str    w8, [sp, #24]
0x0000000000401468 <+36>:    add    x3, sp, #0x10
0x000000000040146c <+40>:    mov    x8, x2
0x0000000000401470 <+44>:    str    x8, [sp, #16]
0x0000000000401474 <+48>:    sub    x0, x29, #0x18
0x0000000000401478 <+52>:    mov    w1, #0x5                        // #5
0x000000000040147c <+56>:    bl     0x401618 <CBase::m_Proc(int, int*, int**)>
0x0000000000401480 <+60>:    b      0x401484 <start_modeling()+64>
0x0000000000401484 <+64>:    sub    x0, x29, #0x18
0x0000000000401488 <+68>:    mov    w1, #0xa                        // #10
0x000000000040148c <+72>:    add    x2, sp, #0x18
0x0000000000401490 <+76>:    add    x3, sp, #0x10
0x0000000000401494 <+80>:    bl     0x4016e0 <CBase::m_vProc(int, int*, int**)>
0x0000000000401498 <+84>:    b      0x40149c <start_modeling()+88>
0x000000000040149c <+88>:    sub    x8, x29, #0x18
0x00000000004014a0 <+92>:    str    x8, [sp, #8]
0x00000000004014a4 <+96>:    ldr    x0, [sp, #8]
0x00000000004014a8 <+100>:   mov    w1, #0xf                        // #15
0x00000000004014ac <+104>:   add    x2, sp, #0x18
0x00000000004014b0 <+108>:   add    x3, sp, #0x10
0x00000000004014b4 <+112>:   bl     0x401618 <CBase::m_Proc(int, int*, int**)>
0x00000000004014b8 <+116>:   b      0x4014bc <start_modeling()+120>
0x00000000004014bc <+120>:   ldr    x0, [sp, #8]
0x00000000004014c0 <+124>:   ldr    x8, [x0]
0x00000000004014c4 <+128>:   ldr    x8, [x8, #8]
0x00000000004014c8 <+132>:   mov    w1, #0x14                       // #20
0x00000000004014cc <+136>:   add    x2, sp, #0x18
0x00000000004014d0 <+140>:   add    x3, sp, #0x10
0x00000000004014d4 <+144>:   blr    x8
0x00000000004014d8 <+148>:   b      0x4014dc <start_modeling()+152>
0x00000000004014dc <+152>:   sub    x0, x29, #0x18
0x00000000004014e0 <+156>:   bl     0x401720 <CDerived::m_Try()>
0x00000000004014e4 <+160>:   b      0x4014e8 <start_modeling()+164>
0x00000000004014e8 <+164>:   sub    x0, x29, #0x18
0x00000000004014ec <+168>:   bl     0x4015f4 <CDerived::~CDerived()>
0x00000000004014f0 <+172>:   b      0x40154c <start_modeling()+264>
--Type <RET> for more, q to quit, c to continue without paging--
0x00000000004014f4 <+176>:   mov    w8, w1
0x00000000004014f8 <+180>:   str    x0, [sp, #32]
0x00000000004014fc <+184>:   str    w8, [sp, #28]
0x0000000000401500 <+188>:   b      0x40151c <start_modeling()+216>
0x0000000000401504 <+192>:   mov    w8, w1
0x0000000000401508 <+196>:   str    x0, [sp, #32]
0x000000000040150c <+200>:   str    w8, [sp, #28]
0x0000000000401510 <+204>:   sub    x0, x29, #0x18
0x0000000000401514 <+208>:   bl     0x4015f4 <CDerived::~CDerived()>
0x0000000000401518 <+212>:   b      0x40151c <start_modeling()+216>
0x000000000040151c <+216>:   ldr    x0, [sp, #32]
0x0000000000401520 <+220>:   bl     0x402040 <__cxa_begin_catch>
0x0000000000401524 <+224>:   mov    x0, xzr
0x0000000000401528 <+228>:   adrp   x1, 0x515000 <_nl_archive_subfreeres+224>
0x000000000040152c <+232>:   add    x1, x1, #0x55b
0x0000000000401530 <+236>:   adrp   x2, 0x515000 <_nl_archive_subfreeres+224>
0x0000000000401534 <+240>:   add    x2, x2, #0x561
0x0000000000401538 <+244>:   mov    w3, #0x100                      // #256
0x000000000040153c <+248>:   bl     0x4013d4 <message_box(void*, char const*, char const*,
unsigned int)>
```

```
0x0000000000401540 <+252>:    b       0x401544 <start_modeling()+256>
0x0000000000401544 <+256>:    bl      0x4020e0 <__cxa_end_catch>
0x0000000000401548 <+260>:    b       0x40154c <start_modeling()+264>
0x000000000040154c <+264>:    ldp     x29, x30, [sp, #64]
0x0000000000401550 <+268>:    add     sp, sp, #0x50
0x0000000000401554 <+272>:    ret
0x0000000000401558 <+276>:    mov     w8, w1
0x000000000040155c <+280>:    str     x0, [sp, #32]
0x0000000000401560 <+284>:    str     w8, [sp, #28]
0x0000000000401564 <+288>:    bl      0x4020e0 <__cxa_end_catch>
0x0000000000401568 <+292>:    b       0x40156c <start_modeling()+296>
0x000000000040156c <+296>:    b       0x401570 <start_modeling()+300>
0x0000000000401570 <+300>:    ldr     x0, [sp, #32]
0x0000000000401574 <+304>:    bl      0x4a0170 <_Unwind_Resume>
0x0000000000401578 <+308>:    bl      0x401798 <__clang_call_terminate>
End of assembler dump.
```

Note: The compiler code generator uses different registers and offsets for the virtual call calculations.

ADDR: Virtual Call

- A call (or branch and link) through virtual function table structure field
- Usually involves a double Pointer Dereference

Additional ADDR Patterns

ADDR: Potential Functionality

- A list of function symbols, for example, a list of imported functions, a list of callbacks, a structure or table with function pointers

ADDR: Structure Field

- An offset to the structure memory address

ADDR: Separator Frames

- Frames that divide a stack trace into separate analysis units

Live Debugging Techniques

- **ADDR Patterns:** Component Dependencies, API Trace, Fiber Bundle (trace analysis pattern)

- Some dependencies can be learnt from crash dump stack traces

- Debugging.TV / YouTube

- Live debugging training: Accelerated Linux Debugging[4]

Fiber Bundle (reprinted in this book)**:**
https://www.dumpanalysis.org/blog/index.php/2012/09/26/trace-analysis-patterns-part-52/

Debugging TV / YouTube:
www.debugging.tv / https://www.youtube.com/DebuggingTV

Accelerated Windows Debugging[4]:
https://www.patterndiagnostics.com/accelerated-windows-debugging-book

Memory Analysis Patterns

Regular Data
Injected Symbols
Execution Residue
Rough Stack Trace
Annotated Disassembly
Historical Information

Reprinted in this book:

Execution Residue
https://www.dumpanalysis.org/blog/index.php/2015/12/19/crash-dump-analysis-patterns-part-60-linux/

Resources

- DumpAnalysis.org / SoftwareDiagnostics.Institute
- PatternDiagnostics.com
- Debugging.TV / YouTube.com/DebuggingTV / YouTube.com/PatternDiagnostics
- A64 Instruction Set Architecture
- A64 Base Instructions
- GDB Pocket Reference
- Accelerated Linux Core Dump Analysis, Third Edition
- Debugging, Disassembly & Reversing in Linux for x64 Architecture
- Foundations of Linux Debugging, Disassembling, and Reversing
- Foundations of ARM64 Linux Debugging, Disassembling, and Reversing
- Memory Dump Analysis Anthology (Diagnomicon) articles in volumes 1, 7, 9A cover GDB

If you don't have experience with assembly language, then the Apress books *Foundations of Linux Debugging, Disassembling, and Reversing* and *Foundations of ARM64 Linux Debugging, Disassembling, and Reversing* teach you assembly language from scratch in the context of GDB. There's also an Educative interactive course: *Debugging, Disassembly & Reversing in Linux for x64 Architecture*.

Software Diagnostics Institute:
https://www.dumpanalysis.org/

Software Diagnostics Library:
https://www.dumpanalysis.org/blog/

Debugging.TV / YouTube Channel:
http://www.debugging.tv/
https://www.youtube.com/DebuggingTV

Pattern Diagnostics YouTube Channel:
https://www.youtube.com/PatternDiagnostics

Foundations of Linux Debugging, Disassembling, Reversing, Second Edition:
https://www.patterndiagnostics.com/practical-foundations-linux-debugging-disassembling-reversing

Foundations of ARM64 Linux Debugging, Disassembling, Reversing, Second Edition:
https://www.patterndiagnostics.com/practical-foundations-arm64-linux-debugging-disassembling-reversing

Memory Dump Analysis Anthology (Diagnomicon):
https://www.dumpanalysis.org/advanced-software-debugging-reference

Accelerated Linux Core Dump Analysis, Third Edition:
https://www.patterndiagnostics.com/accelerated-linux-core-dump-analysis-book

Debugging, Disassembly & Reversing in Linux for x64 Architecture:
https://www.educative.io/courses/debugging-disassembly-reversing-in-linux-x64-architecture

A64 Instruction Set Architecture:
https://developer.arm.com/documentation/102374/latest/

A64 Base Instructions:
https://developer.arm.com/documentation/ddi0596/2021-12/Base-Instructions?lang=en

Memory Cell Diagrams

A. Main Registers

RAX			

RAX		EAX	

RAX		EAX	AX

RAX		EAX	AH | AL

RSI			

RSI		ESI	

RSI		ESI	SI

RSI		ESI	| SIL

R8			

R8		R8D	

R8		R8D	R8W

R8		R8D	|R8L

B. Universal Pointer

We use a similar color for the value it points to

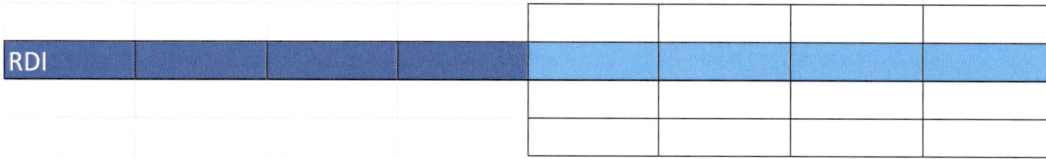

RDI							

C. Pointing to a double word

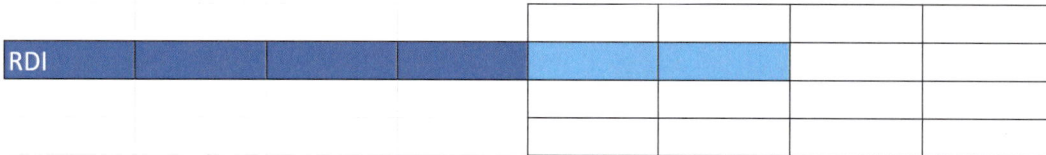

RDI						

D. Stack Frame

RSP				
8				
10				
18				
20				
28				
30				
38				
40				
48				
50				
58				
60				
68				
70				
78				
80				

A. Main Registers

B. Universal Pointer

We use a similar color for the value it points to

C. Pointing to a word

D. Stack Frame

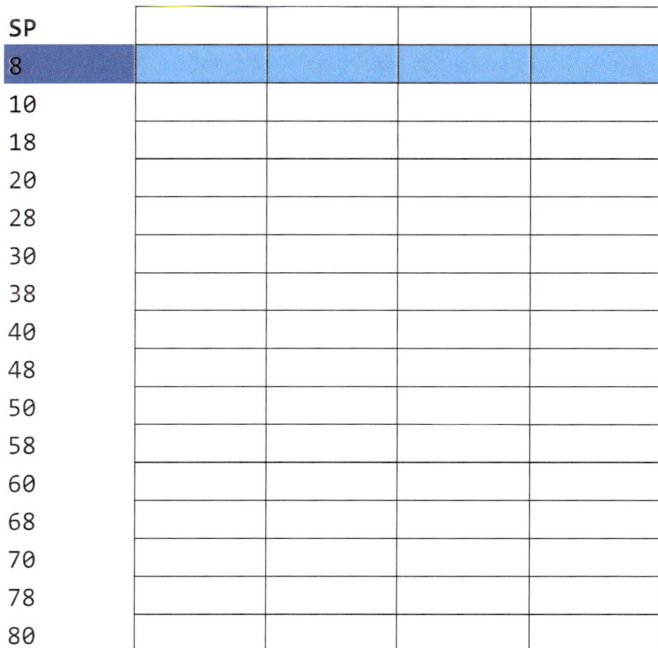

A. Local Variables and Pointers

Block 1

-40				
-38				
-30				
-28				
-20				
-18			ABCD	0
-10				
-8				
RBP				
8				
10				

```
movl    $0xabcd,-0x1c(%rbp)
```

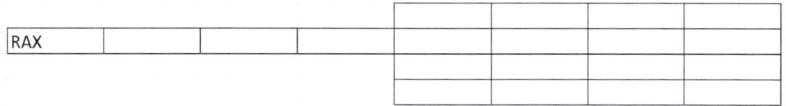

RAX							

Block 2

-40				
-38				
-30				
-28				
-20				
-18			ABCD	0
-10				
-8				
RBP				
8				
10				

```
mov     -0x8(%rbp),%rax
```

RAX							

Block 3

-40				
-38				
-30				
-28				
-20				
-18			ABCD	0
-10				
-8				
RBP				
8				
10				

```
movl    $0xdcba,(%rax)
```

RAX					DCBA	0	

B. Local Variables and Pointers (Correct results)

-40				
-38				
-30				
-28				
-20				
-18				
-10				
-8				
RBP				
8				
10				

```
lea    -0x1c(%rbp),%rax
```

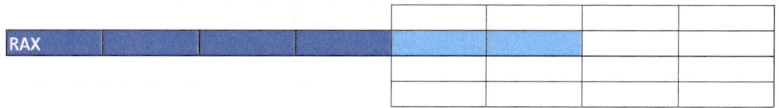

RAX

-40				
-38				
-30				
-28				
-20				
-18				
-10				
-8				
RBP				
8				
10				

```
mov    %rax,-0x8(%rbp)
```

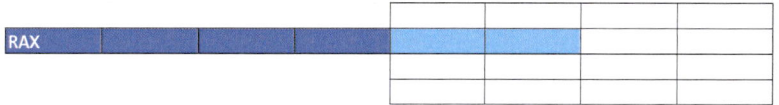

RAX

… RAX was reused in the mean time …

-40				
-38				
-30				
-28				
-20				
-18			ABCD	0
-10				
-8				
RBP				
8				
10				

```
movl   $0xabcd,-0x1c(%rbp)
```

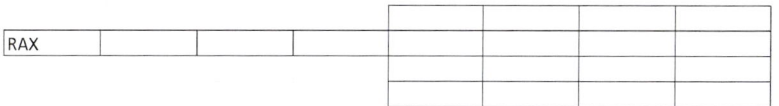

RAX

-40				
-38				
-30				
-28				
-20				
-18			ABCD	0
-10				
-8				
RBP				
8				
10				

```
mov    -0x8(%rbp),%rax
```

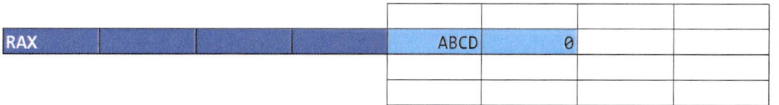

RAX   ABCD   0

-40				
-38				
-30				
-28				
-20				
-18			DCBA	0
-10				
-8				
RBP				
8				
10				

```
movl   $0xdcba,(%rax)
```

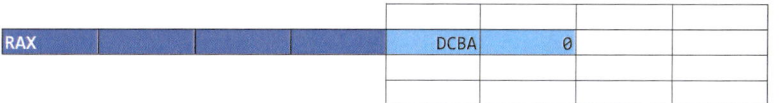

RAX   DCBA   0

C. Static Variables and Pointers

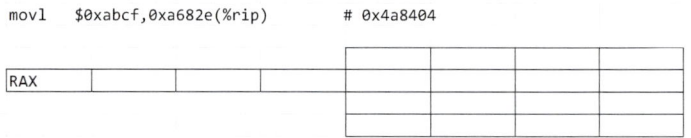

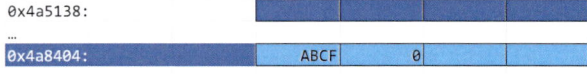

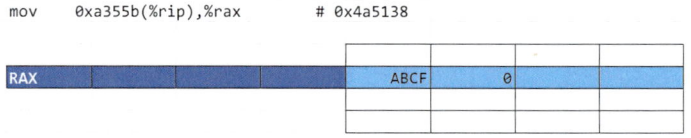

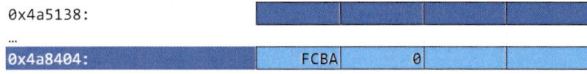

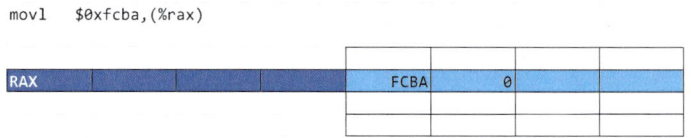

0x4a5138:

0x4a8404:   ABCF   0

```
movl    $0xabcf,0xa682e(%rip)        # 0x4a8404
```

RAX							

0x4a5138:

0x4a8404:   ABCF   0

```
mov     0xa355b(%rip),%rax          # 0x4a5138
```

RAX			ABCF	0	

0x4a5138:

0x4a8404:   FCBA   0

```
movl    $0xfcba,(%rax)
```

RAX			FCBA	0	

248

A. Local Variables and Pointers

SP
8
10
18
20
28
30
38
40
48
50

```
mov    w0, #0xabcd
```

X0		0	ABCD

SP
8
10 | | | ABCD | 0
18
20
28
30
38
40
48
50

```
str    w0, [sp, #20]
```

X0		0	ABCD

SP
8
10 | | | ABCD | 0
18 (green)
20
28
30
38
40
48
50

```
ldr    x0, [sp, #24]
```

X0			

SP
8
10 | | | ABCD | 0
18 (green)
20
28
30
38
40
48
50

```
mov    w1, #0xdcba
```

X0			

x1		0	DCBA

SP
8
10 | | | ABCD | 0
18 (green)
20
28
30
38
40
48
50

```
str    w1, [x0]
```

X0			DCBA	0	

x1		0	DCBA

B. Local Variables and Pointers (Correct results)

```
add    x0, sp, #0x14
```

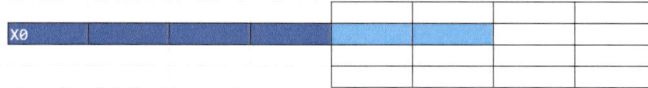

```
str    x0, [sp, #24]
```

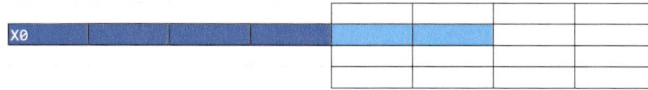

… X0 was reused in the mean time …

```
mov    w0, #0xabcd
```

| X0 | | | 0 | ABCD |

```
str    w0, [sp, #20]
```

| X0 | | | 0 | ABCD |

```
ldr    x0, [sp, #24]
```

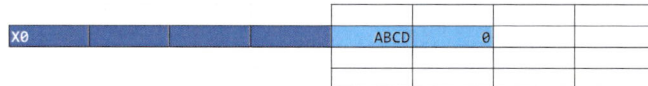

```
mov    w1, #0xdcba
```

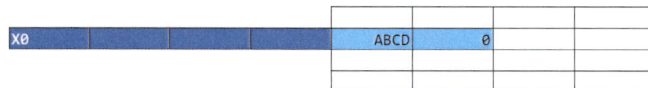

| X1 | | | 0 | DCBA |

```
str    w1, [x0]
```

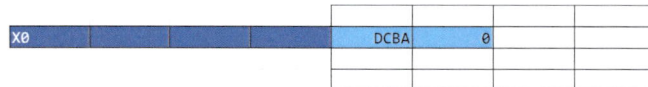

| X1 | | | 0 | DCBA |

C. Static Variables and Pointers

0x491dd0:

0x4940d0:

```
adrp    x0, 0x491000 <tunable_list+1336>
ldr     x0, [x0, #3536]
```

X0							

0x491dd0:

0x4940d0:   ABCF   0

```
mov     w1, #0xabcf
str     w1, [x0]
```

X0				ABCF	0		

X1		0	ABCF

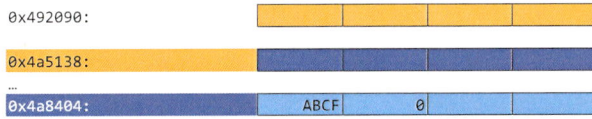

0x492090:

0x4a5138:

0x4a8404:   ABCF   0

```
adrp    x0, 0x491000 <tunable_list+1336>
ldr     x0, [x0, #3784]
```

X0							

X1		0	ABCF

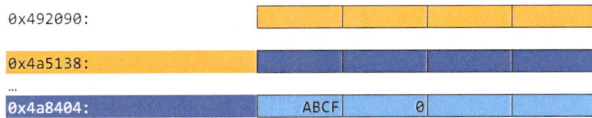

0x492090:

0x4a5138:

0x4a8404:   ABCF   0

```
ldr     x0, [x0]
```

X0				ABCF	0		

X1		0	ABCF

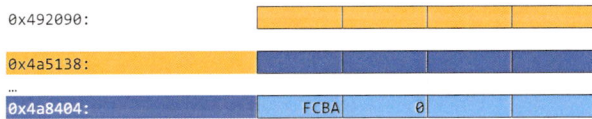

0x492090:

0x4a5138:

0x4a8404:   FCBA   0

```
mov     w1, #0xfcba
str     w1, [x0]
```

X0				FCBA	0		

X1		0	FCBA

A. Function Prologue

-48				
-40				
-38				
-30				
-28				
-20				
-18				
-10				
-8				
RSP				
8	1c09	40	0	0
10				

push   %rbp

0x0000000000401c09 return address of the caller

-48				
-40				
-38				
-30				
-28				
-20				
-18				
-10				
-8				
RSP				
10	1c09	40	0	0
18				

mov   %rsp,%rbp

-48				
RSP				
-38				
-30				
-28				
-20				
-18				
-10				
-8				
RBP				
10	1c09	40	0	0
18				

sub $0x40,%rsp

B. Function Epilogue

leaveq

-50			
-48			
-40			
-38			
-30			
-28			
-20			
-18			
-10			
-8			
RSP	1c09	40	0	0
10			

RBP			
RSP			

RIP		40	1bef

retq

-58			
-50			
-48			
-40			
-38			
-30			
-28			
-20			
-18			
-10			
-8	1c09	40	0	0
RSP			

RBP			
RSP			

RIP		40	1c09

0000000000401c09:	b8	0	c900	53c3

253

A. Function Prologue

-8				
SP	1010	de8e	ffff	0
8	7e8	40	0	0
10				
18				
20				
28				
30				
38				
40				
48				
50				
58				
60				
68				
70				
78				
80				
10				
10				

```
stp     x29, x30, [sp, #-80]!
```

X29

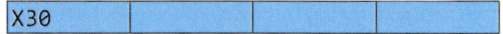
X30

X0

X1

```
# 0x00000000004007e8 return address of the caller
# 0x0000ffffde8e1010 X29 (FP) of the caller
```

-8				
SP	1010	de8e	ffff	0
8	7e8	40	0	0
10				
18				
20				
28				
30				
38				
40				
48				
50				
58				
60				
68				
70				
78				
80				
88				
90				

```
mov     x29, sp
```

X29

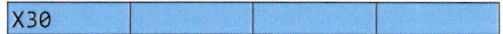
X30

X0

X1

First diagram

-8				
SP	1010	de8e	ffff	0
8	7e8	40	0	0
10				
18				
20				
28				
30				
38				
40				
48				
50				
58				
60				
68				
70				
78				
80				
88				
90				

```
adrp    x0, 0x491000 <tunable_list+1336>
ldr     x0, [x0, #3040]
ldr     x1, [x0]
```

X29			

X30			

X0			

X1			

0x491be0:		9d8	49	0	0

0x4909d8:		5f00	9331	c847	a57a

Second diagram

-8				
SP	1010	de8e	ffff	0
8	7e8	40	0	0
10				
18				
20				
28				
30				
38				
40				
48	5f00	9331	c847	a57a
50				
58				
60				
68				
70				
78				
80				
88				
90				

```
str     x1, [sp, #72]
mov     x1, #0x0
```

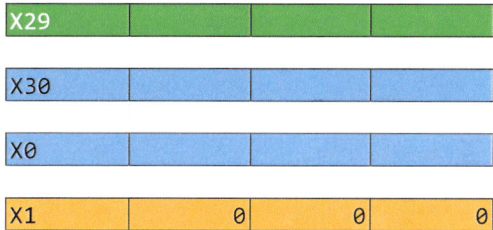

X29			

X30			

X0			

X1	0	0	0

0x491be0:		9d8	49	0	0

0x4909d8:		5f00	9331	c847	a57a

B. Function Epilogue

-8				
SP	1010	de8e	ffff	0
8	7e8	40	0	0
10				
18				
20				
28				
30				
38				
40				
48	5f00	9331	c847	a57a
50				
58				
60				
68				
70				
78				
80				
88				
90				

```
adrp    x0, 0x491000 <tunable_list+1336>
ldr     x0, [x0, #3040]
ldr     x2, [sp, #72]
ldr     x1, [x0]
```

X29			
X30			
X0			
X1			
X2			

0x491be0:		9d8	49	0	0

0x4909d8:		5f00	9331	c847	a57a

-8				
SP	1010	de8e	ffff	0
8	7e8	40	0	0
10				
18				
20				
28				
30				
38				
40				
48	5f00	9331	c847	a57a
50				
58				
60				
68				
70				
78				
80				
88				
90				

```
subs    x2, x2, x1
mov     x1, #0x0
```

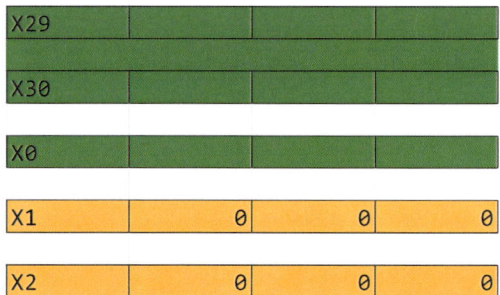

X29			
X30			
X0			
X1		0	0	0
X2		0	0	0

0x491be0:		9d8	49	0	0

0x4909d8:		5f00	9331	c847	a57a

ldp   x29, x30, [sp], #80

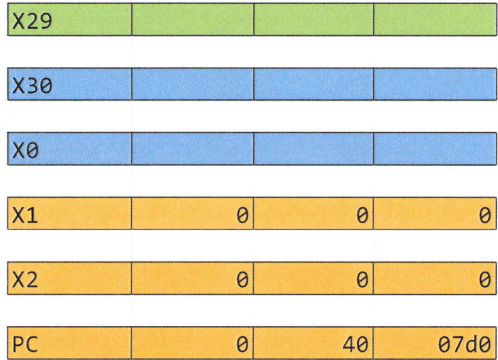

-58				
-50	1010	de8e	ffff	0
-48	7e8	40	0	0
-40				
-38				
-30				
-28				
-20				
-18				
-10				
-8	5f00	9331	c847	a57a
SP				
8				
10				
18				
20				
28				
30				
38				
40				

X29				
X30				
X0				
X1		0	0	0
X2		0	0	0
PC		0	40	07d0

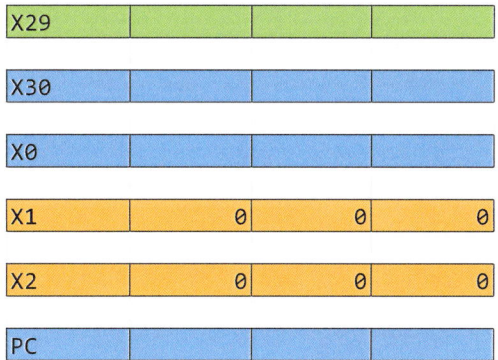

0x491be0:	9d8	49	0	0
0x4909d8:	5f00	9331	c847	a57a

ret

-58				
-50	1010	de8e	ffff	0
-48	7e8	40	0	0
-40				
-38				
-30				
-28				
-20				
-18				
-10				
-8	5f00	9331	c847	a57a
SP				
8				
10				
18				
20				
28				
30				
38				
40				

X29				
X30				
X0				
X1		0	0	0
X2		0	0	0
PC				

0x491be0:	9d8	49	0	0
0x4909d8:	5f00	9331	c847	a57a
0x4007e8:	0	5280	7bfd	a8c2

MCD-R5-x64

A. Exception instruction

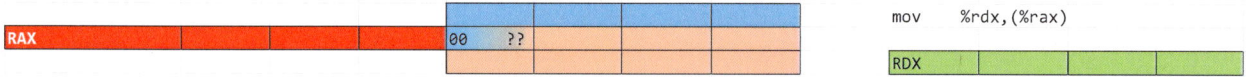

RAX `00` `??`

```
mov    %rdx,(%rax)
```

RDX

B. Complex fragment

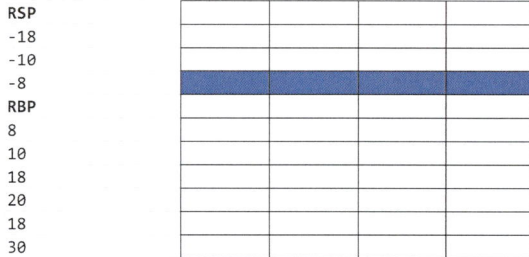

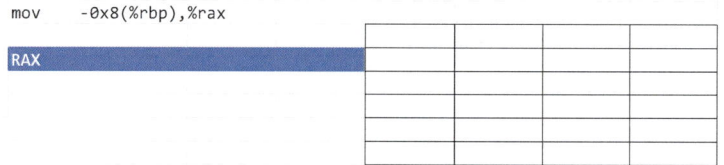

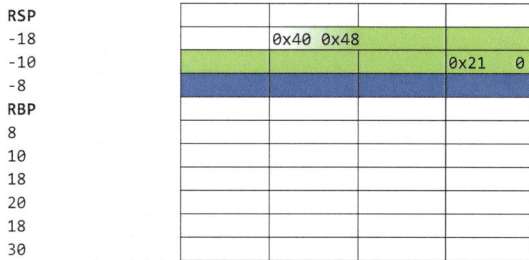

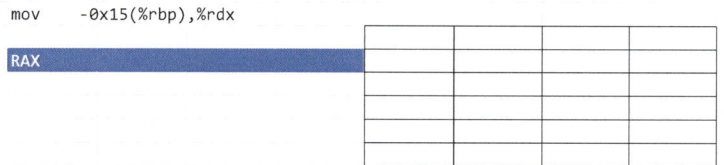

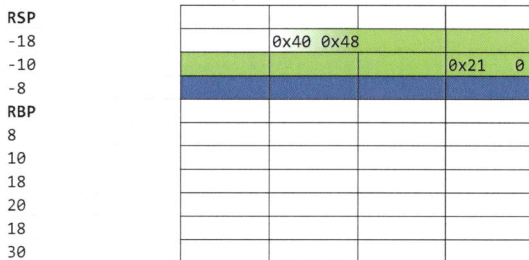

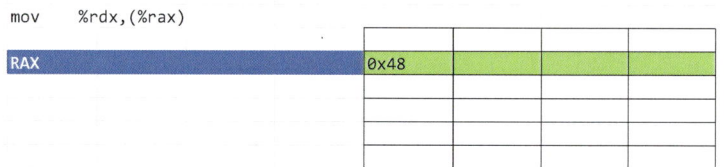

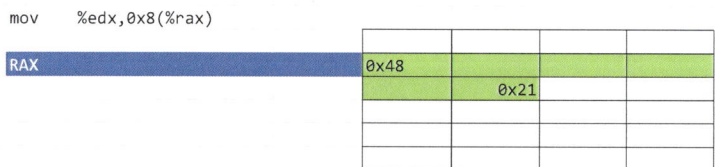

RSP
-18
-10
-8
RBP
8
10
18
20
18
30

```
mov    -0x8(%rbp),%rax
```

RAX

RSP
-18 `0x40 0x48`
-10 `0x21  0`
-8
RBP
8
10
18
20
18
30

```
mov    -0x15(%rbp),%rdx
```

RAX

RDX `0x48`

RSP
-18 `0x40 0x48`
-10 `0x21  0`
-8
RBP
8
10
18
20
18
30

```
mov    %rdx,(%rax)
```

RAX | `0x48`

RDX `0x48`

RSP
-18 `0x40 0x48`
-10 `0x21  0`
-8
RBP
8
10
18
20
18
30

```
mov    -0xd(%rbp),%edx
```

RAX | `0x48`

RDX `0x21`

RSP
-18 `0x40 0x48`
-10 `0x21  0`
-8
RBP
8
10
18
20
18
30

```
mov    %edx,0x8(%rax)
```

RAX | `0x48`
`0x21`

RDX `0x21`

Left column stack diagrams (repeated), each with rows labeled:

RSP				
-18		0x40 0x48		
-10			0x21	0
-8				
RBP				
8				
10				
18				
20				
18				
30				

Right column instructions and registers:

`movzbl -0x9(%rbp),%edx`

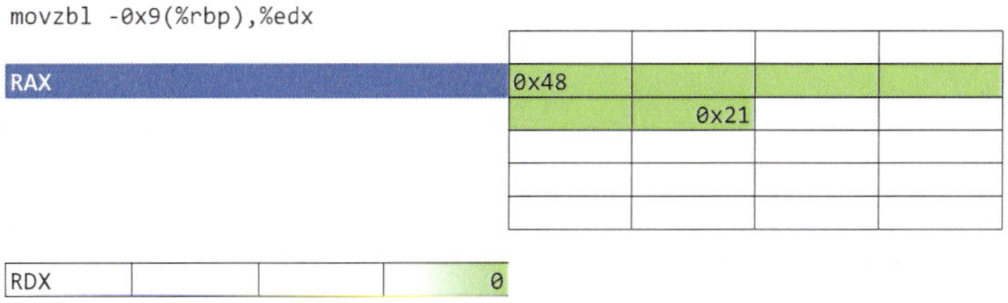

RAX		0x48		
			0x21	

RDX				0

`mov     %dl,0xc(%rax)`

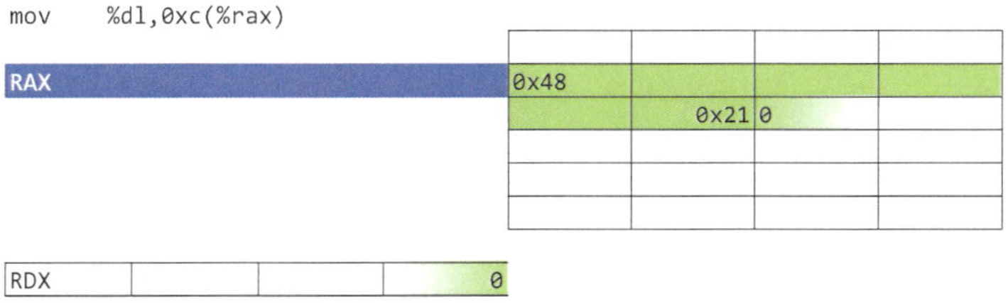

RAX		0x48		
			0x21	0

RDX				0

`addq    $0xd,-0x8(%rbp)`

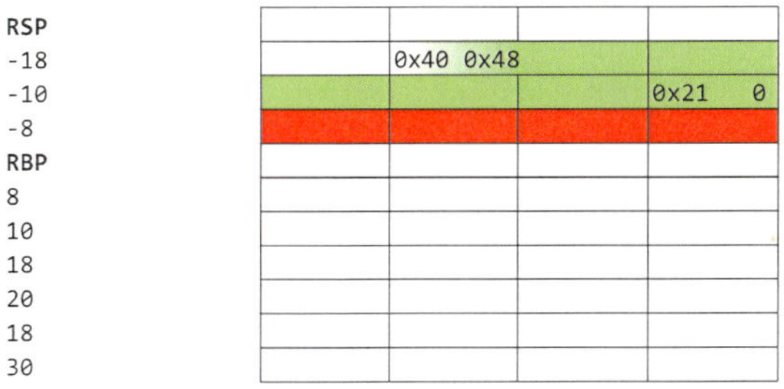

		0x48		
			0x21	0

RDX				0

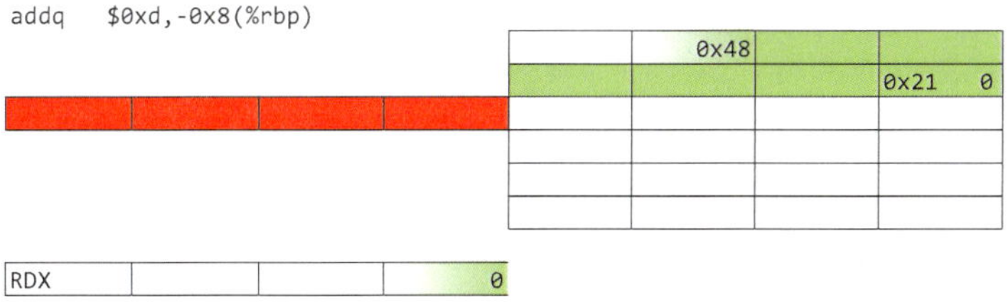

; jmp   0x401bc4 <start_modeling+119>

`mov     -0x8(%rbp),%rax`

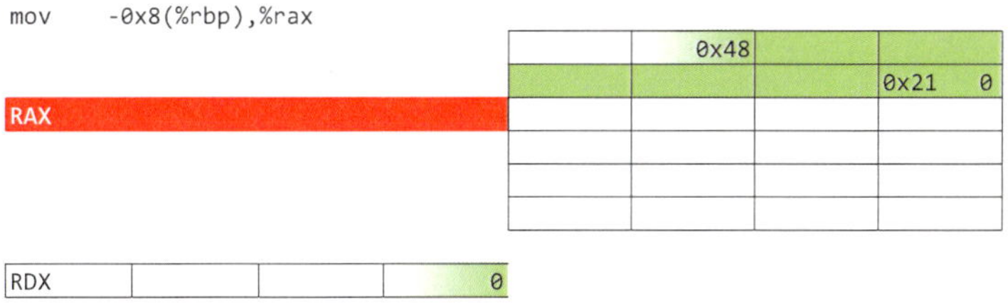

		0x48		
RAX			0x21	0

RDX				0

`mov     -0x15(%rbp),%rdx`

		0x48		
RAX			0x21	0

RDX				0x48

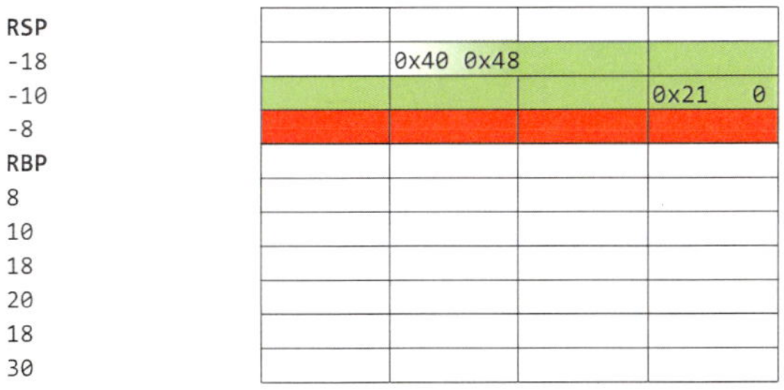

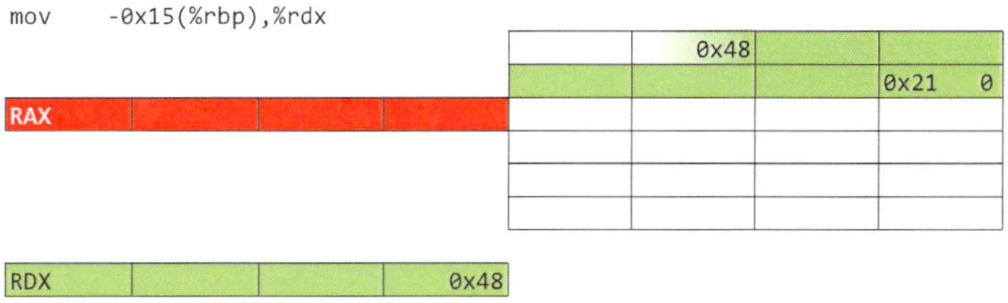

`mov     %rdx,(%rax)`

		0x48		
RAX		0x48	0x21	0

RDX				0x48

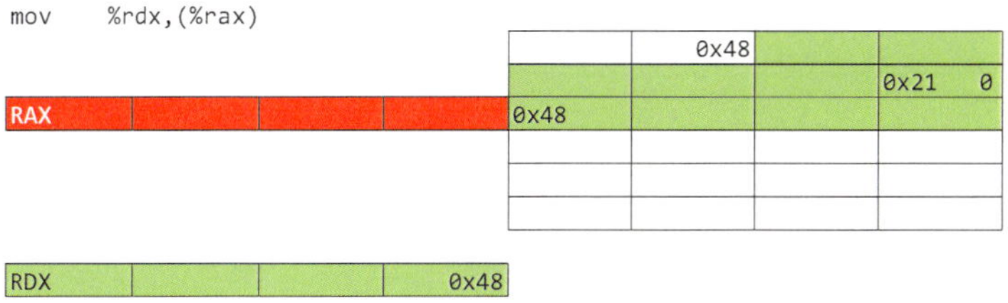

A. Exception instruction

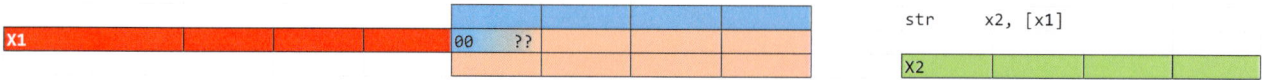

```
str    x2, [x1]
```

B. Complex fragment

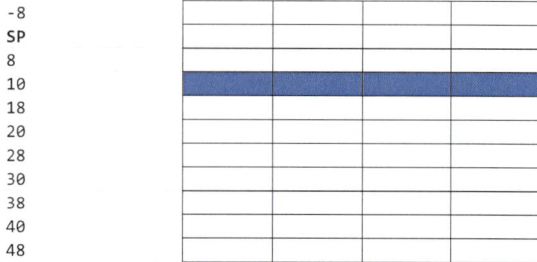

```
ldr    x0, [sp, #16]
mov    x1, x0
```

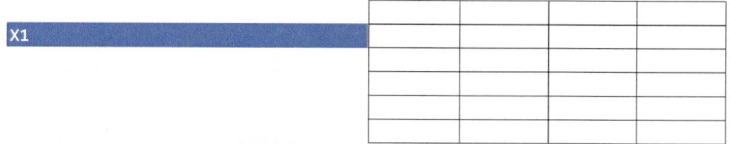

```
add    x0, sp, #0x18
```

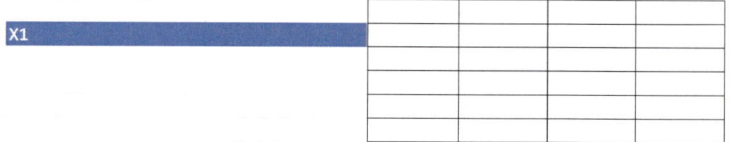

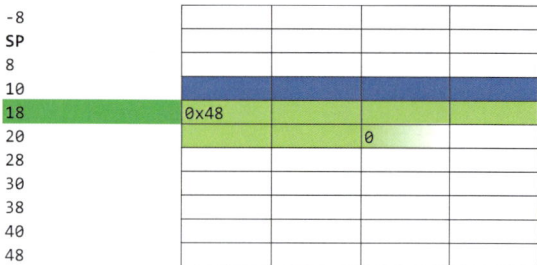

```
ldr    x2, [x0]
```

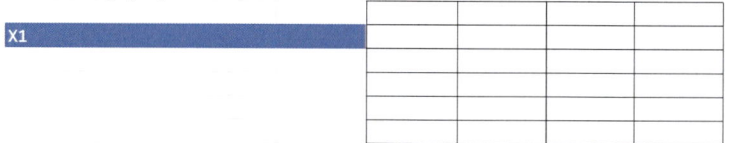

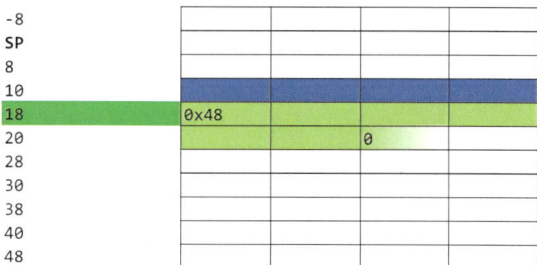

```
str    x2, [x1]
```

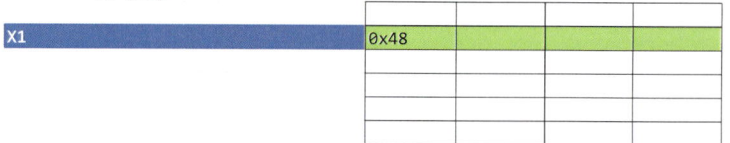

```
ldur   x0, [x0, #5]
```

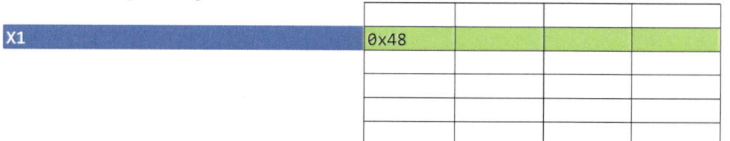

stur   x0, [x1, #5]

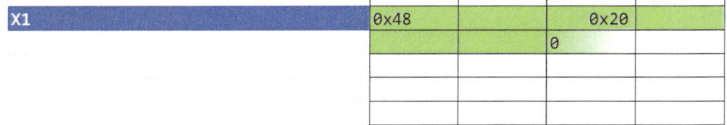

X0 | | | | 0x20 |

X2 | | | | 0x48 |

ldr   x0, [sp, #16]

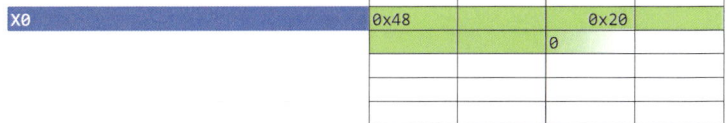

X2 | | | | 0x48 |

add   x0, x0, #0xd

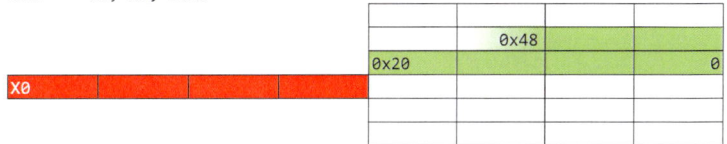

X2 | | | | 0x48 |

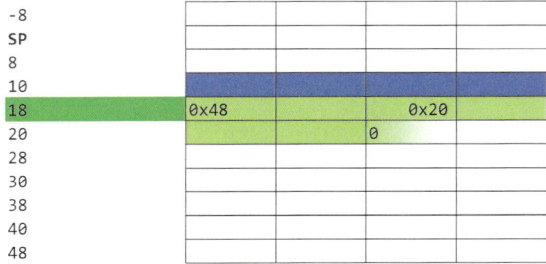

str   x0, [sp, #16]

X2 | | | | 0x48 |

b   0x40074c <start_modeling+120>

ldr   x0, [sp, #16]
mov   x1, x0

X0 | | | | |

X2 | | | | 0x48 |

261

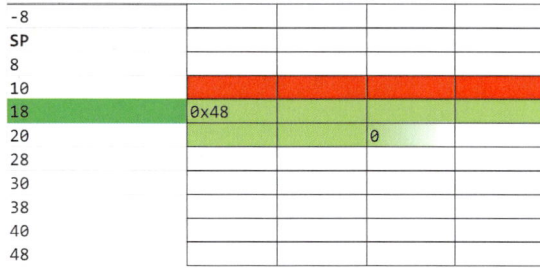

add   x0, sp, #0x18

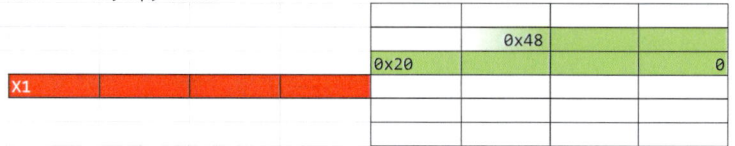

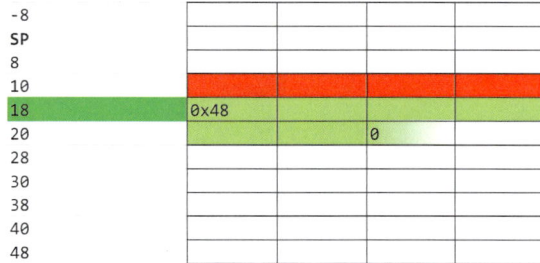

ldr   x2, [x0]

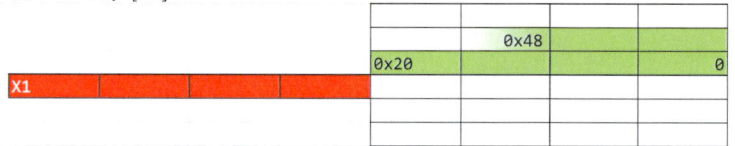

str   x2, [x1]

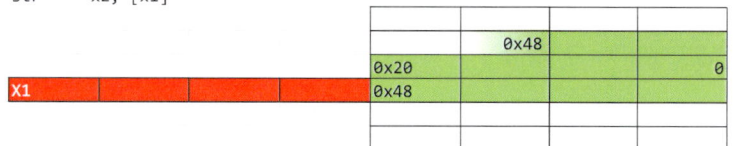

Virtual Call

`lea     -0x30(%rbp),%rax`

-40			
-38			
-30	vtable for CBase+16		
-28	5678	1234	0	0
-20			
-18			
-10			
-8			
RBP			
8			
10			

->

CBase::m_vProc		
CBase::m_vProc2		
CBase::~CBase()		

RAX				vtable for CBase+16		
				5678	1234	0	0

`mov     %rax,-0x18(%rbp)`

-40			
-38			
-30	vtable for CBase+16		
-28	5678	1234	0	0
-20			
-18			
-10			
-8			
RBP			
8			
10			

->

CBase::m_vProc		
CBase::m_vProc2		
CBase::~CBase()		

RAX				vtable for CBase+16		
				5678	1234	0	0

...

-40			
-38			
-30	vtable for CBase+16		
-28	5678	1234	0	0
-20			
-18			
-10			
-8			
RBP			
8			
10			

->

CBase::m_vProc		
CBase::m_vProc2		
CBase::~CBase()		

RAX						

`mov     -0x18(%rbp),%rax`

-40			
-38			
-30	vtable for CBase+16		
-28	5678	1234	0	0
-20			
-18			
-10			
-8			
RBP			
8			
10			

->

CBase::m_vProc		
CBase::m_vProc2		
CBase::~CBase()		

RAX				vtable for CBase+16		
				5678	1234	0	0

```
                                              mov    (%rax),%rax
```

-40				
-38				
-30	vtable for CBase+16			
-28	5678	1234	0	0
-20				
-18				
-10				
-8				
RBP				
8				
10				

->

CBase::m_vProc		
CBase::m_vProc2		
CBase::~CBase()		

	CBase::m_vProc		
RAX	CBase::m_vProc2		
	CBase::~CBase()		

```
                                              add    $0x8,%rax
```

-40				
-38				
-30	vtable for CBase+16			
-28	5678	1234	0	0
-20				
-18				
-10				
-8				
RBP				
8				
10				

->

CBase::m_vProc		
CBase::m_vProc2		
CBase::~CBase()		

	CBase::m_vProc		
RAX	CBase::m_vProc2		
	CBase::~CBase()		

```
                                              mov    (%rax),%rax
```

-40				
-38				
-30	vtable for CBase+16			
-28	5678	1234	0	0
-20				
-18				
-10				
-8				
RBP				
8				
10				

->

CBase::m_vProc		
CBase::m_vProc2		
CBase::~CBase()		

RIP		

RAX	CBase::m_vProc2

```
                                              callq  *%rax
```

-40				
-38				
-30	vtable for CBase+16			
-28	5678	1234	0	0
-20				
-18				
-10				
-8				
RBP				
8				
10				

->

CBase::m_vProc		
CBase::m_vProc2		
CBase::~CBase()		

RIP	CBase::m_vProc2

RAX	CBase::m_vProc2

```
add     x0, sp, #0x40
```

vtable for CBase+16			
5678	1234	0	0

X0				vtable for CBase+16		
				5678	1234	0	0

->

CBase::m_vProc		
CBase::m_vProc2		
CBase::~CBase()		

```
str     x0, [sp, #56]
```

vtable for CBase+16			
5678	1234	0	0

X0				vtable for CBase+16		
				5678	1234	0	0

->

CBase::m_vProc		
CBase::m_vProc2		
CBase::~CBase()		

vtable for CBase+16			
5678	1234	0	0

X0			

->

CBase::m_vProc		
CBase::m_vProc2		
CBase::~CBase()		

```
ldr     x0, [sp, #56]
```

vtable for CBase+16			
5678	1234	0	0

X0				vtable for CBase+16		
				5678	1234	0	0

->

CBase::m_vProc		
CBase::m_vProc2		
CBase::~CBase()		

```
ldr    x0, [x0]
```

-8			
SP			
8			
10			
18			
20			
28			
30			
38			
40	vtable for CBase+16		
48	5678	1234	0	0

X0				CBase::m_vProc		
				CBase::m_vProc2		
				CBase::~CBase()		

->

CBase::m_vProc		
CBase::m_vProc2		
CBase::~CBase()		

```
add    x0, x0, #0x8
```

-8			
SP			
8			
10			
18			
20			
28			
30			
38			
40	vtable for CBase+16		
48	5678	1234	0	0

				CBase::m_vProc		
X0				CBase::m_vProc2		
				CBase::~CBase()		

X4			

->

CBase::m_vProc		
CBase::m_vProc2		
CBase::~CBase()		

```
ldr    x4, [x0]
```

-8			
SP			
8			
10			
18			
20			
28			
30			
38			
40	vtable for CBase+16		
48	5678	1234	0	0

X4		CBase::m_vProc2

PC			

->

CBase::m_vProc		
CBase::m_vProc2		
CBase::~CBase()		

```
blr    x4
```

-8			
SP			
8			
10			
18			
20			
28			
30			
38			
40	vtable for CBase+16		
48	5678	1234	0	0

X4		CBase::m_vProc2

PC		CBase::m_vProc2

->

CBase::m_vProc		
CBase::m_vProc2		
CBase::~CBase()		

Source Code

notepad.c

```c
//
// Modeling application for ADDR-Linux training course
//
// gcc notepad.c -static -g -o notepad
// cp notepad notepad.debug
// objcopy --strip-debug notepad
//
// clang notepad.c -static -g -o notepad-clang
// cp notepad-clang notepad-clang.debug
// objcopy --strip-debug notepad-clang
//

#include <stdint.h>
#include <unistd.h>
#include <stddef.h>

typedef uint64_t hwnd_t;

typedef struct
{
    int32_t x;
    int32_t y;
} POINT;

typedef struct
{
  hwnd_t    hwnd;
  uint64_t  message;
  uint64_t  param1;
  uint64_t  param2;
  uint32_t  time;
  POINT     pt;
  uint32_t  private;
} msg_t, *p_msg_t;

const uint64_t TIMER_ID = 1;
static int g_last_ui_error; // for simulation purposes
static int (*g_hook_proc)(hwnd_t hwnd); // for simulation purposes
static void (*window_proc)(p_msg_t pmessage); // for simulation purposes

uint64_t time_proc()
{
    return TIMER_ID;
}
```

```c
void set_last_ui_error(int result)
{
    g_last_ui_error = result;
}


int call_ui_hooks(hwnd_t hwnd)
{
    if (g_hook_proc)
    {
        return g_hook_proc(hwnd);
    }
}


int internal_get_message(p_msg_t pmessage, hwnd_t hwnd)
{
    if (pmessage)
    {
        pmessage->hwnd = 0;
        pmessage->message = 0x113;
        pmessage->param1 = TIMER_ID;
        pmessage->param2 = (uint64_t)&time_proc;
        pmessage->time = 0x4578350;
        pmessage->pt.x = 156;
        pmessage->pt.y = 327;
        pmessage->private = 0;
    }

    sleep((unsigned int)-1);

    return 0;
}


int get_message(p_msg_t pmessage, hwnd_t hwnd, uint64_t filter_min, uint64_t filter_max)
{
    int result = -1;

    if (pmessage)
    {
        result = internal_get_message(pmessage, hwnd);
    }

    if (result)
    {
        set_last_ui_error(result);
    }
    else
    {
        result = call_ui_hooks(hwnd);
```

```
    }

    return !result;
}

void dispatch_message(p_msg_t pmessage)
{
    if (window_proc)
    {
        window_proc(pmessage);
    }
}

int main(int argc, char *argv[])
{
    msg_t msg;

    // Main message loop:
    while (get_message(&msg, 0, 0, 0))
    {
        dispatch_message(&msg);
    }

    return 0;
}
```

extra-symbols.c

```c
//
// Modeling application for Injected Symbols memory analysis pattern
//
// gcc extra-symbols.c -static -g -o extra-symbols
// objcopy --only-keep-debug extra-symbols extra-symbols
//

#include <stdint.h>

typedef uint64_t hwnd_t;

typedef struct
{
    int32_t x;
    int32_t y;
} POINT;

typedef struct
{
  hwnd_t    hwnd;
  uint64_t  message;
  uint64_t  param1;
  uint64_t  param2;
  uint32_t  time;
  POINT     pt;
  uint32_t  private;
} msg_t, *p_msg_t;

int main(int argc, char *argv[])
{
    msg_t msg;

    return 0;
}
```

```c
//
// Modeling application for ADDR-Linux training course
//
// gcc data-types.c separate.c -static -g -o data-types
// cp data-types data_types.debug
// objcopy --strip-debug data-types
//
// clang data-types.c separate.c -static -g -o data-types-clang
// cp data-types-clang data_types-clang.debug
// objcopy --strip-debug data-types-clang
//

#include <stdint.h>
#include <stdbool.h>
#include <unistd.h>
#include <signal.h>

extern _Bool g_bData;

extern uint32_t g_dwData;
extern uint32_t *g_pdwData;

extern char g_cData;
extern char *g_pcData;

extern const char *g_pcstrData;
extern char g_acData[];

static _Bool s_bData;

static uint32_t s_dwData;
static uint32_t *s_pdwData = &s_dwData;

static char s_cData;
static char *s_pcData = &s_cData;

static const char *s_pcstrData = "Hello ADDR! (Static)";
static char s_acData[] = "Hello ADDR! (Static)";

void debug_break()
{
    raise(SIGSTOP);
}
```

```c
void start_modeling()
{
    _Bool bData;

    uint32_t dwData;
    uint32_t *pdwData = &dwData;

    char cData;
    char *pcData = &cData;

    const char *pcstrData = "Hello ADDR! (Local)";
    char acData[] = "Hello ADDR! (Local)";

    dwData = 0xABCD;
    *pdwData = 0xDCBA;

    s_dwData = 0xABCE;
    *s_pdwData = 0xECBA;

    g_dwData = 0xABCF;
    *g_pdwData = 0xFCBA;

    debug_break();
}

int main(int argc, char *argv[])
{
    start_modeling();
    return 0;
}
```

```c
#include <stdint.h>
#include <stdbool.h>

_Bool g_bData;

uint32_t g_dwData;
uint32_t *g_pdwData = &g_dwData;

char g_cData;
char *g_pcData = &g_cData;

const char *g_pcstrData = "Hello ADDR! (Global)";

char g_acData[] = "Hello ADDR! (Global)";
```

```c
//
// Modeling application for ADDR-Linux training course
//
// gcc cpu.c -static -g -o cpu
// cp cpu cpu.debug
// objcopy --strip-debug cpu
//
// clang cpu.c -static -g -o cpu-clang
// cp cpu-clang cpu-clang.debug
// objcopy --strip-debug cpu-clang
//

#include <stdint.h>
#include <unistd.h>
#include <stdbool.h>
#include <string.h>
#include <sys/mman.h>

void start_modeling()
{
    char *paddr = (char *)mmap(NULL, 0x1000, PROT_WRITE, MAP_PRIVATE|MAP_ANONYMOUS, 0, 0);
    mmap(paddr+0x1000, 0x1000, PROT_READ, MAP_PRIVATE|MAP_ANONYMOUS|MAP_FIXED, 0, 0);

    const char str[] = "Hello World!";

    while (true)
    {
        memcpy((char *)paddr, str, sizeof(str));
        paddr += sizeof(str);
    }
}

int main(int argc, char *argv[])
{
    start_modeling();
    return 0;
}
```

cpp.cpp

```cpp
//
// Modeling application for ADDR-Linux training course
//
// g++ cpp.cpp -static -g -o cpp
// cp cpp cpp.debug
// objcopy --strip-debug cpp
//
// clang++ cpp.cpp -static -g -o cpp-clang
// cp cpp-clang cpp-clang.debug
// objcopy --strip-debug cpp-clang
//

#include <unistd.h>
#include <cstring>
#include <iostream>
#include <signal.h>

class CBase
{
public:
    int m_nMember;
    char *m_psMember;

    static char s_sMember[];

    CBase()
    {
        m_nMember = 0x12345678;
        m_psMember = new char [strlen(s_sMember)+1];
    }

    bool m_Proc(int nParam, int *pnParam, int **ppnParam)
    {
        if (ppnParam && *ppnParam)
        {
            **ppnParam = *pnParam;
        }

        if (pnParam)
        {
            while (nParam--)
            {
                sleep(*pnParam);
            }
```

```cpp
                *pnParam = 0;

                return true;
            }

            return false;
        }

        virtual bool m_vProc(int nParam, int *pnParam, int **ppnParam)
        {
            return m_Proc(nParam, pnParam, ppnParam);
        }

        virtual bool m_vProc2(int nParam, int *pnParam, int **ppnParam)
        {
            return m_vProc(nParam, pnParam, ppnParam);
        }

        virtual ~CBase()
        {
            delete m_psMember;
        }
};

char CBase::s_sMember[] = { "Hello Class!" };

class CDerived : public CBase
{
public:
    void m_Try ()
    {
        try
        {
            throw -1;
        }
        catch (...)
        {
            throw;
        }
    }
};

CDerived s_Class;

#define MB_STOP 0x100
```

```cpp
void message_box (void *window, const char *title, const char *message, unsigned int type)
{
    std::cout << title << ": " << message << std::endl;

    if (type&MB_STOP)
    {
        raise(SIGSTOP);
    }
}

void start_modeling()
{
    try
    {
        CDerived Class;

        int nDelay = 1;
        int *pnDelay = &nDelay;

        Class.m_Proc(5, &nDelay, &pnDelay);
        Class.m_vProc(10, &nDelay, &pnDelay);

        CDerived *pClass = &Class;

        pClass->m_Proc(15, &nDelay, &pnDelay);
        pClass->m_vProc2(20, &nDelay, &pnDelay);

        Class.m_Try();
    }
    catch(...)
    {
        message_box(NULL, "Error", "Exception was caught!", MB_STOP);
    }
}

int main(int argc, char *argv[])
{
    start_modeling();
    return 0;
}
```

Execution Residue

Reprinted with corrections from Memory Dump Analysis Anthology, Volume 9a, pages 118 – 120.

This is a Linux variant of the **Execution Residue** pattern previously described for Mac OS X (Volume 7, page 220) and Windows (Volume 2, page 239) platforms. It is symbolic information left in a stack region, including ASCII and UNICODE fragments or pointers to them, for example, return addresses from past function calls:

```
(gdb) bt
#0  0x00000000004431f1 in nanosleep ()
#1  0x00000000004430c0 in sleep ()
#2  0x0000000000400771 in procNE() ()
#3  0x00000000004007aa in bar_two() ()
#4  0x00000000004007b5 in foo_two() ()
#5  0x00000000004007c8 in thread_two(void*) ()
#6  0x00000000004140f0 in start_thread (arg=<optimized out>)
at pthread_create.c:304
#7  0x0000000000445879 in clone ()
#8  0x0000000000000000 in ?? ()

(gdb) x/512a $rsp-2000
0x7f4cacc42360: 0x0 0x0
0x7f4cacc42370: 0x0 0x0
0x7f4cacc42380: 0x0 0x0
0x7f4cacc42390: 0x0 0x0
[...]
0x7f4cacc42830: 0x0 0x0
0x7f4cacc42840: 0x0 0x0
0x7f4cacc42850: 0x0 0x0
0x7f4cacc42860: 0x7f4cacc42870 0x4005af <_Z6work_8v+9>
0x7f4cacc42870: 0x7f4cacc42880 0x4005ba <_Z6work_7v+9>
0x7f4cacc42880: 0x7f4cacc42890 0x4005c5 <_Z6work_6v+9>
0x7f4cacc42890: 0x7f4cacc428a0 0x4005d0 <_Z6work_5v+9>
0x7f4cacc428a0: 0x7f4cacc428b0 0x4005db <_Z6work_4v+9>
0x7f4cacc428b0: 0x7f4cacc428c0 0x4005e6 <_Z6work_3v+9>
0x7f4cacc428c0: 0x7f4cacc428d0 0x4005f1 <_Z6work_2v+9>
0x7f4cacc428d0: 0x7f4cacc428e0 0x4005fc <_Z6work_1v+9>
0x7f4cacc428e0: 0x7f4cacc42cf0 0x40060e <_Z4workv+16>
0x7f4cacc428f0: 0x0 0x0
0x7f4cacc42900: 0x0 0x0
0x7f4cacc42910: 0x0 0x0
[...]
0x7f4cacc42af0: 0x0 0x0
0x7f4cacc42b00: 0x0 0x0
0x7f4cacc42b10: 0x0 0x0
0x7f4cacc42b20: 0x0 0x4431e6 <nanosleep+38>
0x7f4cacc42b30: 0x0 0x4430c0 <sleep+224>
0x7f4cacc42b40: 0x0 0x0
0x7f4cacc42b50: 0x0 0x0
0x7f4cacc42b60: 0x0 0x0
0x7f4cacc42b70: 0x0 0x0
[...]
0x7f4cacc42cb0: 0x0 0x0
```

```
0x7f4cacc42cc0: 0x0 0x0
0x7f4cacc42cd0: 0x0 0x0
0x7f4cacc42ce0: 0xfffffed2 0x3ad3affa
0x7f4cacc42cf0: 0x7f4cacc42d00 0x0
0x7f4cacc42d00: 0x7f4cacc42d20 0x49c740 <default_attr>
0x7f4cacc42d10: 0x7f4cacc439c0 0x400771 <_Z6procNEv+19>
0x7f4cacc42d20: 0x7f4cacc42d30 0x4007aa <_Z7bar_twov+9>
0x7f4cacc42d30: 0x7f4cacc42d40 0x4007b5 <_Z7foo_twov+9>
0x7f4cacc42d40: 0x7f4cacc42d60 0x4007c8 <_Z10thread_twoPv+17>
0x7f4cacc42d50: 0x0 0x0
0x7f4cacc42d60: 0x0 0x4140f0 <start_thread+208>
0x7f4cacc42d70: 0x0 0x7f4cacc43700
0x7f4cacc42d80: 0x0 0x0
0x7f4cacc42d90: 0x0 0x0
[...]
```

However, supposed return addresses need to be checked for **Coincidental Symbolic Information** pattern.

Fiber Bundle

Reprinted with corrections from Memory Dump Analysis Anthology, Volume 7, pages 294 – 295.

The modern software trace recording, visualization, and analysis tools such as Process Monitor, Xperf, WPR, and WPA provide stack traces associated with trace messages. Considering stack traces as software traces, we have, in a more general case, traces (fibers) bundled together on (attached to) a base software trace. For example, a trace message that mentions an IRP can have its I/O stack attached together with the thread stack trace with function calls leading to a function that emitted the trace message. Another example is an association of different types of traces with trace messages, such as managed and unmanaged ones. This general trace analysis pattern needed a name, so we opted for **Fiber Bundle** as an analogy with a fiber bundle[7] from mathematics. Here's a graphical representation of stack traces recorded for each trace message where one message has also an associated I/O stack trace:

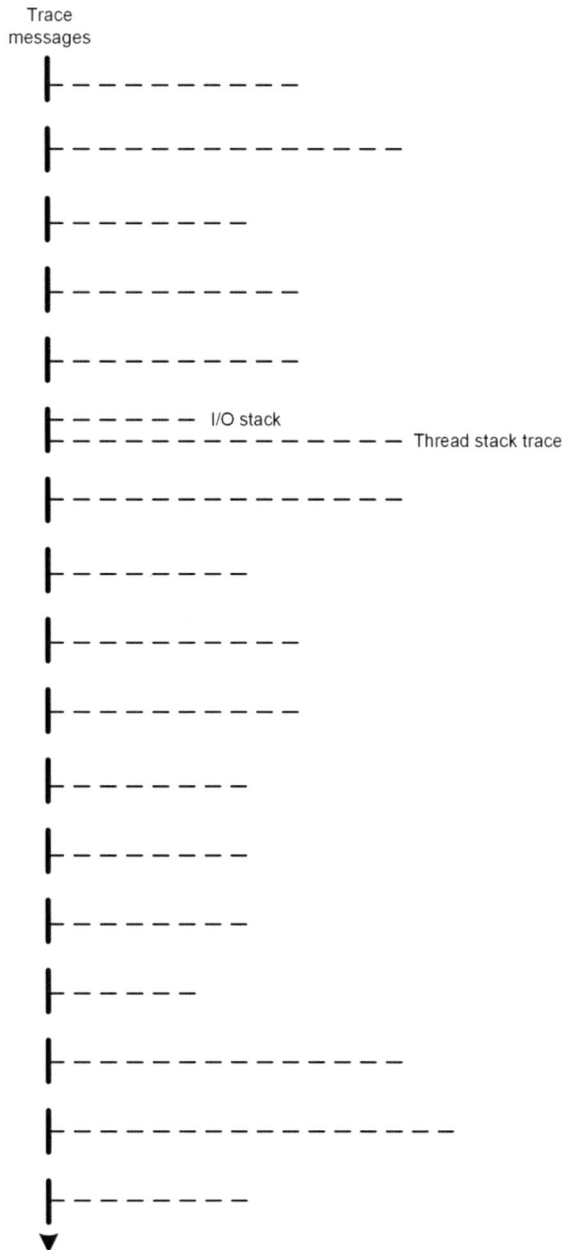

---

[7] http://en.wikipedia.org/wiki/Fiber_bundle

www.ingramcontent.com/pod-product-compliance
Lightning Source LLC
Chambersburg PA
CBRC091939210326
41598CB00012B/865